Howl
on trial

Howl
on trial

The Battle for Free Expression

EDITED BY

BILL MORGAN AND

NANCY J. PETERS

CITY LIGHTS BOOKS SAN FRANCISCO

Cover design: Stefan Gutermuth
Typography: Harvest Graphics
Press section design: Yolanda Montijo

Library of Congress Cataloging-in-Publication Data

Howl on trial : the battle for free expression / edited by Bill Morgan and
Nancy J. Peters.
    p.   cm.
  ISBN-13: 978-0-87286-479-5
  ISBN-10: 0-87286-479-0
  1. Ginsberg, Allen, 1926-1997. Howl. 2. Ginsberg, Allen, 1926-1997—
Censorship. 3. Censorship—United States—History. 4. Trials (Obscenity)—
California—San Francisco. I. Morgan, Bill, 1949- II. Peters, Nancy J. (Nancy
Joyce) III. Title.

  PS3513.I74H634 2006
  811'.54—dc22

CITY LIGHTS BOOKS are edited by Lawrence Ferlinghetti and Nancy J. Peters
and published at the City Lights Bookstore, 261 Columbus Avenue, San Francisco,
CA 94133. www.citylights.com

"The paper burns, but the words fly away."

—Akiba ben Joseph

ACKNOWLEDGMENTS

Fifty years after the trial it seems impossible to believe that anyone could have ever doubted the literary merit of *Howl and Other Poems*. The courage required to take on the government censors cannot be forgotten. Judge Clayton M. Horn, ACLU attorneys Albert M. Bendich and Lawrence Speiser, attorney J.W. Ehrlich, and defendants Lawrence Ferlinghetti and Shigeyoshi Murao have our everlasting gratitude for supporting freedom of speech so unselfishly. Additional heartfelt thanks go to Bendich and Ferlinghetti for contributing their memories to this current book.

The Allen Ginsberg Trust has been instrumental in the creation of this volume as well. Thanks to Bob Rosenthal, Andrew Wylie and Peter Hale of the Trust for their cooperation and for permission to use Ginsberg's words and photographs.

The devotion of the City Lights staff to the work of Allen Ginsberg has been remarkable over the past fifty years and this current book is no exception. Nancy J. Peters, Bob Sharrard, Elaine Katzenberger, Stacey Lewis, and Chanté Mouton have each contributed to what is truly a group effort. Special thanks go to Chanté Mouton for her thorough research into trial records and press coverage of events.

Thanks also go to Brian Chambers at San Francisco State University. Laura Perkins and other staff at the *San Francisco Chronicle* generously gave time and effort to uncover records and arranged for use of staff photographs and news articles. The paper's support during the trial was critical to the case for free speech. David Perlman, who covered the trial for the *Chronicle*, kindly gave permission to reprint his "How Captain Hanrahan Made *Howl* a Best-Seller," published in the *San Francisco Reporter*. John G. Fuller's delightful column on the pending trial appeared in *Saturday Review*. KPFA Pacifica supplied other useful documentation. The support and assistance of Judy Matz and Garret Caples were invaluable.

Various libraries have also been useful sources of information for this book. We are especially grateful to San Francisco State University Library, San Francisco Public Library's San Francisco History Center, and to Princeton University Library's Seeley G. Mudd Manuscript Library, where ACLU records of the period are kept. Tony Bliss of the Bancroft Library at the University of California, Berkeley, is the guardian of the City Lights Archives there and has given assistance in countless ways.

CONTENTS

Lawrence Ferlinghetti at City Lights Bookstore, holding a cover proof of *Howl and Other Poems*, 1956. Courtesy, San Francisco History Center, San Francisco Public Library.

Introduction
"HOWL" AT THE FRONTIERS
by Lawrence Ferlinghetti

The "Howl" that was heard around the world wasn't seized in San Francisco in 1956 just because it was judged obscene by cops, but because it attacked the bare roots of our dominant culture, the very Moloch heart of our consumer society.

At the end of World War II, I came home feeling disconnected from American life, like multitudes of Americans uprooted by military service. And we didn't stay home long. With new larger perspectives of the world, many of us soon took off for parts unknown. And the "white arms of roads" beckoned Westward. I didn't know the actual demographics of it, but I had the sense that the continent had tilted up, with the whole population sliding to the west.

It was a time of born-again optimism, but there were also new elements in the smelting pot of postwar America. There was a sense of great restlessness, a sense of wanting more of life than that offered by local Chambers of Commerce or suburban American Legions, a vision of some new wide open, more creative society than had been possible in pre-war America. And—as an idolizer of James Joyce's Stephen Dedalus—I even envisioned myself articulating "the uncreated conscience of my race."

It took until the mid-1950s for this postwar ferment and the visions of new generations to coalesce in a new cultural synthesis. And it happened in San Francisco, then still the last frontier in so many ways, with its "island mentality" that could be defined as a pioneer attitude of being "out there" on your own, without reliance on government. After all, San Francisco had been founded, not by bourgeoisie, but by prospectors, sailors, railroad workers, gold diggers, ladies of good fortune, roustabouts and carney hustlers.

When I arrived overland by train in January 1951, it didn't take me long to discover that in Italian, bohemian North Beach, I had fallen into a burning bed of anarchism, pacifism, and a wide open, non-academic poetry scene, provincial but liberating. There were two or three anarchist poetry magazines spasmodically published, but the central literary, political force in all this was the poet and polymath, Kenneth Rexroth who was active in the Anarchist Circle, waxed wroth regularly on KPFA/FM, and held Friday night soirées in his flat filled with apple-box bookshelves loaded with books he reviewed on every subject from anarchism to xenophobia.

The Beat poets, joining this San Francisco scene in the 1950s, furthered the postwar cultural synthesis, and "Howl" became the catalyst in a paradigm shift in American poetry and consciousness. The Beats were advance word slingers prefiguring the counterculture of the 1960s, forecasting its main obsessions and ecstasies of liberation, essentially a "youth revolt" against all that our postwar society was doing to us (even as Henry Miller in the 1940s had sensed that "another breed of men has taken over" in an air-conditioned nightmare.)

When the Beats—namely Ginsberg, Gregorio Nunzio Corso, Jack Kerouac, Neal Cassady, Peter Orlovsky—first appeared in San Francisco, they hardly looked like world shakers. When Ginsberg first walked into City Lights and handed me the manuscript of "Howl," I saw him as another of those far-out poets and wandering intellectuals who had started hanging out in our three-year-old bookstore, which the *San Francisco Chronicle* had already started calling the intellectual center of the city.

Bespectacled, intense, streetwise, Ginsberg showed me "Howl" with some hesitation, as if wondering whether I would know what to do with it. Later that month when I heard him read it at the Six Gallery, I knew the world had been waiting for this poem, for this apocalyptic message to be articulated. It was in the air, waiting to be captured in speech. The repressive, conformist, racist, homophobic world of the 1950s cried out for it.

That night I went home and sent Ginsberg a Western Union telegram (imitating what I thought Emerson had written Whitman upon first reading *Leaves of Grass*): "I greet you at the beginning of a great career," and adding, "When do we get the manuscript?" (Despite Allen's saving every scrap of writing, this telegram is not to be found in his archive.)

When City Lights published *Howl and Other Poems* in 1956, the holy unholy voice of the title poem reverberated around the world among poets and intellectuals, in countries free and enslaved, from New York to Amsterdam to Paris to Prague to Belgrade to Calcutta and Kyoto.

Ginsberg's original title was "Howl for Carl Solomon." Editing the poem, I persuaded him to call it simply "Howl," making "for Carl Solomon" a dedication, and thus implying a more universal significance. Putting the collection together, I talked him into including "In the Baggage Room at Greyhound." And still later, when I asked for more, he sent me "Footnote to Howl."

We had already published two books by Rexroth and poetic pacifist Kenneth Patchen, and they'd been printed in England by John Sankey. But the four-letter words (not including "love") in "Howl" would cause censorship to raise its lascivious head. British law held the printer liable for prosecution, and he elided certain words, with Allen's and my reluctant consent. (Later, after the trial, these so-shocking words were restored.)

Before sending the manuscript to the press, I showed it to the American Civil Liberties Union in San Francisco, since I suspected we would be busted, not only for four-letter words but also for its frank sexual, especially homosexual, content. And the ACLU promised to defend us. When we were indeed arrested, our little one-room bookstore would have been wiped out without the ACLU.

As for myself, I thought, well, I could use some time in the clink to do some heavy reading. But for Shigeyoshi Murao who actually sold the book to the police officers, it was a heavier story. A Nisei whose family had been interned with thousands of other Japanese-Americans during the war, he led me to understand that to be arrested for anything, even if innocent, was in the Japanese community of that time, a family disgrace. To me, he was the real hero of this tale of sound and fury, signifying everything.

In the trial itself we were defended *pro bono* by the famous criminal lawyer Jake Ehrlich, and Lawrence Speiser and Defense Counsel Albert Bendich of the ACLU. They were absolutely brilliant—Ehrlich especially so in his presentation of our case to the court and his devastating cross-examination of the prosecution's witnesses, and Bendich in his expert summation of the decisive Constitutional issues.

Among our witnesses, Professor Mark Schorer of the University of California, Berkeley, coolly defended "Howl" as "an indictment of those elements in modern society that, in the author's view, are destructive of the best qualities in human nature and of the best minds. Those elements are, I would say, predominantly materialism, conformity, and mechanization leading toward war." (Schorer also said "the picture which the author is trying to give us [is] of modern life as a state of hell," which reminded me of Bertolt's Brecht defining Los Angeles as a modern hell and Pier Paolo Pasolini saying the same of modern Rome.)

Allen himself was never arrested, though he wrote many supportive letters from abroad. We never had a written contract for "Howl, not even a handshake," but his letters more than once confirmed our agreement, assuring me also that he would not "go whoring around New York" for big money, and urging me to publish Kerouac, Corso, Bill Burroughs, so we could "altogether crash over America in a great wave of beauty."

When Judge Horn announced that we were innocent, a *San Francisco*

Chronicle reporter shoved a mike in my face, and I just stood there struck dumb, unable to articulate what I sensed might foreshadow a sea change in American culture. (Later I learned, from Allen himself, how to use such opportunities "to subvert the dominant paradigm.") I couldn't realize what was to happen in the revolution of the Sixties, but I suspected that this was just Allen's first strike as the conscience of the nation and a provocateur for peace.

Fifty years later, Ginsberg's indictment still rings in our ears, and his insurgent voice is needed more than ever, in this time of rampant nationalism and omnivorous corporate monoculture deadening the soul of the world.

Allen Ginsberg pointing at "Moloch whose eyes are a thousand blind windows!" This vision of the Sir Francis Drake Hotel was the inspiration for "Howl." © Harry Redl

ALLEN GINSBERG'S *HOWL*
A Chronology

1954

October 17   After taking peyote in his apartment at 755 Pine Street, in San Francisco, Allen Ginsberg has a vision in which the Sir Francis Drake Hotel and the Medical Arts buildings transform into the image of the ancient Phoenician god Moloch.

1955

August   While living in an apartment at 1010 Montgomery Street, Ginsberg writes the first part of "Strophes," which he soon renames "Howl," based on his Moloch vision.

August 30   In a letter to Jack Kerouac, Ginsberg mentions that City Lights might publish a small booklet of his poems to be called *Howl*.

October 7   Allen Ginsberg reads part of "Howl" for the first time in public at the Six Gallery, 3119 Fillmore Street.

October 8   Lawrence Ferlinghetti sends a telegram to Ginsberg asking for the manuscript of "Howl."

1956

March 18   Ginsberg reads the completed text of "Howl" for the first time at the Town Hall Theater in Berkeley, California.

March   Ferlinghetti asks the ACLU if it will defend the book in court if he is prosecuted.

March   William Carlos Williams writes an introduction for *Howl and Other Poems*.

May 16   Ginsberg mimeographs about 25 copies of "Howl" to give to his friends.

June	City Lights receives the first proofs of *Howl and Other Poems* from its British printer, Villiers.
August	A few advance copies of the book arrive from the printer and Ferlinghetti sends them to Ginsberg, who is working on a ship near the Arctic Circle.
November 1	Official date of publication for *Howl and Other Poems*, the fourth number in the City Lights Pocket Poets Series. The first printing is 1,000 copies.

1957

March 25	San Francisco Collector of Customs Chester MacPhee seizes 520 copies of the second printing of *Howl and Other Poems* on the grounds that the writing is obscene. ("You wouldn't want your children to come across it.") An additional 1,000 copies slip through undetected.
April 3	The American Civil Liberties Union informs Chester MacPhee that it will contest the legality of the seizure on the grounds that the book is not obscene.
May	Ferlinghetti does a third printing of 2,500 copies in the U.S., to circumvent the jurisdiction of Customs.
May 19	William Hogan of the *San Francisco Chronicle* writes a piece in favor of "Howl" in his column "Between the Lines" and lends it to Lawrence Ferlinghetti for the purpose of defending *Howl and Other Poems*.
May 29	Customs releases the copies of *Howl and Other Poems* after the United States Attorney in San Francisco, Lloyd H. Burke, refuses to institute condemnation proceedings against the book.
June 3	Shigeyoshi Murao is arrested for selling a copy of *Howl and Other Poems* to undercover inspectors, Russell Woods and Thomas Pagee, and a warrant is issued for the arrest of Lawrence Ferlinghetti by Captain William A. Hanrahan of the San Francisco Police Department's Juvenile Bureau.

June 6	Lawrence Ferlinghetti, who was in Big Sur when Murao was arrested, turns himself in to the police upon his return and is released after the ACLU posts $500 bail.
August 8	*Howl's* jury trial is scheduled to begin at the Municipal Court of the City and County of San Francisco, 750 Kearny Street, with Judge Byron Arnold presiding.
August 16	After a delay, trial by jury is waived and the case is switched to Judge Clayton W. Horn's court.
August 22	Charges against Shigeyoshi Murao are dismissed by Judge Horn, since the prosecution could not prove that Murao had read the publication or sold it "lewdly."
September 5	Nine witnesses for the defense testify on the literary merits of Ginsberg's *Howl and Other Poems.*
September 19	Rebuttal witnesses and closing arguments are given in the trial.
October 3	Judge Clayton W. Horn finds Lawrence Ferlinghetti not guilty of publishing and selling obscene writings, on the grounds that *Howl and Other Poems* was not written with lewd intent and was not without "redeeming social importance."
October	To meet the demand created by the trial, a fourth printing of 5,000 copies is ordered.

"Censorship reflects a society's lack of confidence in itself. It is a hallmark of an authoritarian regime. Long ago, those who wrote our First Amendment charted a different course. They believed a society can be truly strong only when it is truly free. In the realm of expression, they put their faith, for better or worse, in the enlightened choice of the people, free from the interference of a policeman's intrusive thumb or a judge's heavy hand. So it is that the Constitution protects coarse expression as well as refined, and vulgarity no less than elegance. A book worthless to me may convey something of value to my neighbor. In the free society to which our Constitution has committed us, it is for each to choose for himself."

—Potter Stewart, U.S. Supreme Court Justice

MILESTONES OF LITERARY CENSORSHIP
by Nancy J. Peters

During the century prior to the *Howl* decision in 1957, freedom of expression in America, with few exceptions, did not extend to any writing that contained overtly sexual references. No matter how beautifully written or ethical its viewpoint, if a work of literature employed frank sexual language or depicted sexual acts, it was considered obscene and banned in the U.S. Then, over the next decade, beginning in 1957, a series of court decisions began to remove restrictions on purportedly obscene literature. At the apex of legal tolerance, in 1966, the ban was finally lifted from John Cleland's 1749 novel *Fanny Hill: Memoirs of a Woman of Pleasure*, which had been, in 1821, the object of America's first known obscenity case.

Obscenity laws are concerned with prohibiting lewd or sexually charged words or pictures, and with determining what role the government should have in regulating what people should read and see. The U.S. Supreme Court has always held that the First Amendment does not protect obscene material that would present a clear and present danger to society. The problem is that there have always been disagreements about what constitutes obscenity. There is still a lack of clarity around the meaning of the words "indecent," "filthy," "lewd," "lascivious," and "obscene." Justice Potter Stewart memorably epitomized the problem when he admitted that he couldn't define "obscenity" but "I know it when I see it." In current Internet cases, deliberations of the Supreme Court focus on these same definitions. What is meant by "indecent"? Which "community" is being offended? These questions are still not resolved.

The intent of the authors of the Bill of Rights was to withhold the power to censor from the *national* government. Thus, the First Amendment: "Congress shall make no law respecting the establishment of religion, or prohibiting the free exercise thereof; or abridging the freedom of speech or of the press . . ." The idea was to leave decisions in these matters to the individual states. Today, American obscenity law is a patchwork of court decisions, made up of old British common law, federal, state, and local laws, as well as U.S. Customs and U.S. Postal Service regulations.

The law is not set in stone; it does not march in a straight line toward ever more liberty for all. Minority opinions remain on the record and decisions are subject to revision and change over time. New concepts are introduced; old precedents are weakened. The resulting laws may be more liberal and tolerant or they may support greater authoritarian control. By the time of the *Howl* trial, a century of obscenity prosecutions had produced a complex maze of contradictory decisions.

In spite of the standards set by Supreme Court rulings, books are still being challenged and banned at the local level, in schools and libraries across the country. Nearly every week somewhere in this country parents or religious organizations attempt to take a library book off a shelf or ban a book from a school curriculum. Often people take notice of banned books, protest, and the proscription is lifted. Sometimes nobody speaks up and the banned book stays banned. For better or for worse, the legal system depends on and is shaped by citizen involvement.

The American Library Association and the American Booksellers Association monitor challenged books and fight for the right to read educational and literary works of merit. The ALA reports that during the last twenty years, the themes most likely to arouse the censorious (in order of the number of complaints) are sexual explicitness, offensive language, occultism and Satanism, promotion of homosexuality, violence, anti-family values, and subject matter offensive to religion. Titles that almost always head the list of "dangerous" books are *Slaughterhouse Five* by Kurt Vonnegut (promoting deviant sexual behavior, sexually explicit), *Forever* by Judy Blume (sexual references), *Catcher in the Rye* by J.D. Salinger (sexual references, undermines morality), John Steinbeck's *Grapes of Wrath* (vulgar language), and *Of Mice and Men* (filth), *Harry Potter* by J.K. Rowling (anti-Christian Satanism), *I Know Why the Caged Bird Sings* by Maya Angelou (language and themes), and Toni Morrison's *The Bluest Eye* (language). A couple of classics that made recent lists are Chaucer's *Canterbury Tales* (lewdness) and Shakespeare's *Twelfth Night* (teaching alternative lifestyles).

Throughout the world, established institutions have tried to exert religious and government control over what people read. Today, sex is the big issue. However, in the past heresy and treason were the principal targets of the censors; if obscenity was a contributing factor in these crimes, the offense was worse and the punishment greater. As Gutenberg's invention of the printing press enlarged the potential readership for books, it also removed the written word from the control of church and state. As literacy spread, so did the danger of people thinking for themselves. The first printed book banned in England was William Tyndale's 1525 translation of the New Testament from Latin into the English. In 1536 Tyndale was imprisoned and burned at the stake along with those dangerous books that people might interpret without mediation by church and state.

Today, globalization, mass emigration, and electronic communication exert similar pressures on instilled cultural values in many parts of the world. To maintain control, governments and religious vigilantes alike respond. In 1987 the Salman Rushdie case shocked the world. Iranian authorities not only banned *The Satanic Verses* for blasphemy and obscenity but also issued a fatwa, condemning the author to death and putting a $2,500,000 price on his head. Closer to home, our own fundmentalists pursue their particular censorious agendas.

Historically, the Catholic Church persecuted early books and engravings of an obscene nature in the ecclesiastical courts of Europe; however, British secular authorities paid scant attention until the Victorian era. Bawdy poems, pornographic novels, erotic prints and etchings were freely circulated. It wasn't until the mid-19th century that concern began to grow about the effect of sexually explicit materials on the "public welfare."

In 1868, a case called *Queen (Regina) v. Hicklin* was heard in London. The decision, which became known as the *Hicklin Rule*, was that "the test of obscenity is whether the tendency of the matter charged is to deprave and corrupt those whose minds are open to such immoral influences," specifically, women, children, and the weak of mind. It allowed a publication to be judged on isolated passages of a work considered out of context and judged by their apparent influence on those presumed to need protection from sexually charged material. U.S. law is modeled on and incorporates much British law, so for many years the *Hicklin Rule* continued to echo through the American judicial system, even in the *Howl* case (1957) and the Communications Decency Act (1997).

Although "immoral" behavior was subject to trial and punishment in the American colonial era and the first century of independence, there were no laws prohibiting the expression of ideas about sex. Benjamin Franklin, for instance, wrote literary ribaldries that a century and a half later would have been, in all likelihood, condemned as obscene.

It wasn't until after the Civil War that, among various reform movements, there arose a moral purity movement committed to abolishing vice and obscenity. The leader of this movement, Anthony Comstock, was a fanatic crusader whose mission was to stamp out sex in all of its manifestations except what was unavoidable for procreation. In 1873, in an atmosphere of collective hysteria, he easily lobbied through Congress a draconian postal law with far-reaching prohibitions. Banned from publication and the mails were not only "dirty" books and pictures but also information about sex education, abortion, contraceptives, and sexually transmitted diseases. Individual states followed suit with strict laws of their own.

Comstock crusaded against women's suffrage, sex education, and preached that "free love and lust" were destroying the morals of the country. He also attacked the arts (all figures must be clothed, and all statues provided with fig leaves). As head of the New York Society for the Suppression of Vice, he was made a special agent of the Post Office, and wielded vast power. In the first six months of his national operation, he claimed that he seized 194,000 obscene pictures and photographs, 134,000 pounds of books, 14,200 stereopticon plates, 60,300 rubber articles, 5,500 sets of playing cards and 31,500 boxes of "aphrodisiacs."

Comstock died in 1915. His successor as head of the Society for the Suppression of Vice was John S. Sumner, less flamboyant than Comstock, but who nonetheless believed himself the embodiment of true Americanism, with a mission to uphold sexual propriety, patriotism, and Christian piety. The Society continued to have the statutory power to uncover violations of the Comstock Laws. And so it went, American law continuing to be shaped by a small group of evangelistic zealots who claimed to represent everyone in the country. Many of the Comstock laws are still on the books in the 21st century.

The Struggle for Free Expression

1821. *Fanny Hill: Memoirs of a Woman of Pleasure* by John Cleland, 1749. This is the first-known U.S. obscenity case involving a book, a novel about a the life of a prostitute. Charges were brought in Massachusetts against the book's U.S. publisher, Peter Holmes, who was convicted for corrupting, debauching, and subverting the morals of youth. It was finally cleared in 1966.

1842. The first federal obscenity law was passed, as the U.S. Tariff Act, which prohibited imports of obscene material from foreign countries and empowered U. S. Customs to seize offending books. This law was largely ignored.

1865. Sending obscene publications through the mail was made a criminal offence; this gave U.S. Postal authorities the power to censor, although they rarely did so.

1873. This is the momentous date when censorship got out of hand. Spearheaded by Anthony Comstock, the first federal anti-obscenity law was passed, a law that prohibited sending through the mail anything that had to do with sex (not just obscenity). State legislatures used it as a model for similar laws; the amalgam of all these laws came to be known as the Comstock Laws.

1881. *Leaves of Grass* by Walt Whitman was banned in Boston for sexually explicit language; the expurgation of offending passages was demanded. The poem was later published intact in Philadelphia.

1890. *The Kreutzer Sonata* by Leo Tolstoi. Forbidden by the U.S. Post Office. Theodore Roosevelt declared Tolstoi to be a "sexual and moral pervert."

1892. *Salome* by Oscar Wilde. Banned in Boston.

1915. *Hagar Revelly* by Daniel Carson Goodman. Warning the young of the dangers of vice, this book was attacked by Comstock because some of the vices were described. The publisher Mitchell Kennerly courageously defended the book and was acquitted. Federal Judge Learned Hand made the first legal challenge here to the Hicklin Rule.

1920. *Ulysses* by James Joyce. The book was published in installments, beginning in 1918, in Margaret Anderson and Jane Heap's *The Little Review* at the Washington Square Bookstore in New York. Copies were seized and burned by U.S. Post Office in 1920. Sylvia Beach published *Ulysses* in Paris at Shakespeare & Co. in 1922, but *Ulysses* was forbidden entry into the U.S. Not cleared until 1933.

1922. *Mademoiselle de Maupin* by Théophile Gautier. Bookstore clerk Raymond D. Halsey was nabbed in 1919 by Sumner's Society for the Suppression of Vice, tried for selling an obscene book, and acquitted. He then sued the Society for false arrest and malicious prosecution. The New York Court of Appeals read the book, which Gautier had frankly declared in his introduction made light of fornication, adultery, and homosexuality. The court decided in Halsey's favor. This important case established the precedent that literary experts could offer testimony in support of a book to guide the judge in assessing community opinion.

1927. *Elmer Gantry* by Sinclair Lewis. Banned in Boston because it depicted an "obscene" clergyman.

1927. *The Thousand and One Nights*. Seized by U.S. Customs as obscene.

1928. *The Well of Loneliness* by Radclyffe Hall. Cited by the New York Society for the Suppression of Vice for pleading tolerance of homosexuality, the book was seized in raids on the publisher's office and Macy's book department. The book was cleared in a courtroom victory in 1939.

1929. *Candide* by Voltaire. This classic was seized by U.S. customs as obscene on its way to a Harvard literature class. (It had been imported without hindrance for the preceding 170 years.) In 1944, the U.S. Post Office demanded that a mail order catalog omit this book. (All the works of Voltaire have been banned at one time or another, many of them burned.)

1929. *Confessions* by Jean Jacques Rousseau. Banned by U.S. Customs as obscene and injurious to public morality.

1929. *Lady Chatterley's Lover* by D.H. Lawrence. Written in 1928; although acclaimed as a literary masterpiece, the book was banned in England and in the United States for over thirty years.

1930. Amendment of U.S. Tariff Act of 1842 at last allowed a number of classics into the country, including Aristophanes' *Lysistrata*, Abelard's *Letters to Heloise*, Daniel Defoe's *Moll Flanders*, and Chaucer's *Canterbury Tales*.

1930. *An American Tragedy* by Theodore Dreiser and *The Sun Also Rises* by Ernest Hemingway banned in Boston.

1933. *Ulysses* by James Joyce. After Random House's four-year battle to publish the book, a landmark case (*United States v. One Book Called "Ulysses"*) was decided by the Federal Court in New York. Judge John. M. Woolsey wrote an eloquent and erudite opinion that esteemed the book as a work of art. He did not apply the *Hicklin Rule*, and judged the book not by its effects on children but on the average person and held that a work could not be judged on individual passages taken out of context. This effectively ended the *Hickin Rule* at the federal level.

1934. *Tropic of Cancer* by Henry Miller. Published in Paris in 1934, this book was banned in the U.S. for twenty-seven years. Brought to trial in 1953, the U.S. Customs ban was upheld by the court. Not cleared until 1961.

1946. Action was brought against Kathleen Windsor's restoration-era bodice ripper *Forever Amber*. The judge found it "conducive to sleep, but not to sleeping with a member of the opposite sex."

1946. *Memoirs of Hecate County* by Edmund Wilson. Banned in several U.S. cities. The New York Society for the Suppression of Vice brought suit against Doubleday, and the New York court found the book obscene. *Memoirs of Hecate County* then became the subject of the first U.S. Supreme Court obscenity case, heard in 1948. The justices split four to four, Felix Frankfurter abstaining because he knew the author personally. The earlier conviction was then upheld by New York Court of Appeals, which extended the ban through the 1950s.

1948. William Faulkner. Several novels banned in Philadelphia.

1954. *Wonder Stories* by Hans Christian Anderson stamped "For Adult Readers Only" in Illinois to prevent children from reading smut.

1954. *Decameron* by Giovanni Boccaccio was finally cleared by U.S. Customs.

1957. *Howl and Other Poems* by Allen Ginsberg. This is the earliest application of the Roth standard (*Roth v. United States*). Book dealer Samuel Roth had been prosecuted in New York for distributing such magazines as *American Aphrodite* and *Photo*. The U.S. Supreme Court upheld his conviction, but created an important new standard. Justice William J. Brennan, Jr. concluded that obscenity was not protected by the First Amendment but that literature was. The test of obscenity now became "whether to the average person, applying contemporary standards, the dominant theme of the material taken as a whole appeals to the prurient interest." The *Roth* case was argued in the U.S. Supreme Court in April 1957, just after *Howl* was seized, and decided in June, two months before *Howl* was tried. The *Roth* decision enabled the ACLU to argue that *Howl* as a whole had literary merit and did not appeal to prurient interest.

1960. *Lady Chatterley's Lover* by D. H. Lawrence. With this book, Barney Rosset at Grove Press began a long, costly campaign to clear outlawed works of significant literature. The importance of the case *Grove Press v. Christenberry* [the Postmaster General] is that it served as a platform for judges in the District Court and the Court of Appeals to emphasize the importance of artistic merit and the desirability of expressing controversial ideas in a free society.

1961. *Tropic of Cancer* by Henry Miller. Argued by First Amendment lawyers Edward de Grazia and Charles Rembar, the Miller case was finally won, and the book published by Grove Press. The decision was the high benchmark of First Amendment protection of literature: No book should be banned unless it was *utterly* without social importance. (This led to subsequent arguments that even hard-core pornography could be construed as important.)

1966. *Naked Lunch* by William S. Burroughs. Maurice Girodias published the first edition in Paris in 1959; the book was proscribed in the U.S. In 1962, after *Tropic of Cancer* was cleared, Grove Press published *Naked Lunch*. It was challenged and found obscene in Boston in 1965, but the Massachusetts Supreme Court reversed the finding the following year.

1973. *Miller v. California*. This is the present standard, reflecting the more prohibitive direction the Supreme Court took in the Nixon years. Under the *Miller* Test, to be obscene, a work's main theme must be prurient, it must offend contemporary community standards, and it must lack serious literary, artistic, political, or scientific value. This last point has been called the "SLAPS test." Community standards here replaced national standards, and the court attempted to remove hard-core pornography from First Amendment protections.

1978. *F.C.C. v. Pacifica Foundation*. The Court held that the F.C.C. could create time, place, and matter restrictions on literary and other material to be broadcast. For example, Ginsberg's "Howl" was among the works restricted to the early morning hours when children would presumably be asleep.

1997. *Reno v. ACLU*. The Supreme Court struck down the 1996 Communications Decency Act, ruling that it was an unconstitutional attempt to control communications on the Internet. The decision found that the law was too vague in defining obscenity.

1998. *National Endowment for the Arts et al. v. Finley et al*. The Supreme Court upheld a "decency" standard for NEA grants.

1999–. *ACLU v. Ashcroft*. Since the 2002 COPA [Child Online Pornography Act] victory of the ACLU in the Supreme Court, cases that concern the government's attempt to restrict access to "obscene" material on the Internet are still being contested. The ACLU is representing plaintiffs who publish literary and educational materials online, including Salon.com magazine,

Powell's Bookstore, and Lawrence Ferlinghetti/City Lights Books. The language of some of the laws' propositions could prevent access by everyone (not just children) to educational material on AIDS, for example, or to works of literature. The plaintiffs further assert that reliance on "community standards" improperly allows the most conservative communities to dictate what should be considered indecent. Under present law, Allen Ginsberg's "Howl" could be subject to censorship once again if offered on City Lights' web site.

References:

American Civil Liberties Union. www.aclu.org

American Library Association. www.ala.org

Clark, Allan. *Instances of Censorship throughout History*. Humanist Association of San Diego. www.godless.org

Ehrlich, J.W., ed. *Howl of the Censor*. San Carlos, CA: Nourse Publishing Co., 1961

Ernst, Morris L. and Alan U. Schwartz. *Censorship: The Search for the Obscene* [Milestones of Law Series]. NY: Macmillan, 1964

Haffercamp, Jack. "Studies in Erotology," *Libido*. www.libidomag.com

Kovarik, Bill. *Interactive Media Law*. Radford University, Radford, VA. www.radford.edu

Noble, William. *Bookbanning in America: Who Bans Books? and Why*. Middlebury, VT: Paul S. Eriksson, 1990

"The dirtiest book of all is the expurgated book."
                                          —Walt Whitman

THE POCKET POETS SERIES

HOWL

AND OTHER POEMS

ALLEN GINSBERG

Introduction by
William Carlos Williams

NUMBER FOUR

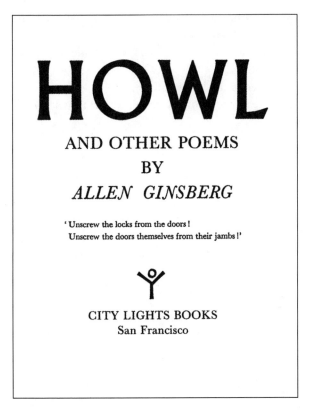

HOWL

AND OTHER POEMS
BY
ALLEN GINSBERG

' Unscrew the locks from the doors !
Unscrew the doors themselves from their jambs !'

CITY LIGHTS BOOKS
San Francisco

DEDICATION To—

Jack Kerouac, new Buddha of American prose, who spit forth intelligence into eleven books written in half the number of years (1951–1956)—*On the Road, Visions of Neal, Dr. Sax, Springtime Mary, The Subterraneans, San Francisco Blues, Some of the Dharma, Book of Dreams, Wake Up, Mexico City Blues,* and *Visions of Gerard*—creating a spontaneous bop prosody and original classic literature. Several phrases and the title of *Howl* are taken from him.

William Seward Burroughs, author of *Naked Lunch*, an endless novel which will drive everybody mad.

Neal Cassady, author of *The First Third*, an autobiography (1949) which enlightened the Buddha.

All these books are published in Heaven.

Lucien Carr, recently promoted to Night Bureau Manager of New York United Press.

Howl for Carl Solomon

Introduction by William Carlos Williams

When he was younger, and I was younger, I used to know Allen Ginsberg, a young poet living in Paterson, New Jersey, where he, son of a well-known poet, had been born and grew up. He was physically slight of build and mentally much disturbed by the life which he had encountered about him during those first years after the First World War as it was exhibited to him in and about New York City. He was always on the point of "going away," where it didn't seem to matter; he disturbed me, I never thought he'd live to grow up and write a book of poems. His ability to survive, travel, and go on writing astonishes me. That he has gone on developing and perfecting his art is no less amazing to me.

Now he turns up fifteen or twenty years later with an arresting poem. Literally he has, from all the evidence, been through hell. On the way he met a man named Carl Solomon with whom he shared among the teeth and excrement of this life something that cannot be described but in the words he has used to describe it. It is a howl of defeat. Not defeat at all for he has gone through defeat as if it were an ordinary experience, a trivial experience. Everyone in this life is defeated but a man, if he be a man, is not defeated.

It is the poet, Allen Ginsberg, who has gone, in his own body, through the horrifying experiences described from life in these pages. The wonder of the thing is not that he has survived but that he, from the very depths, has found a fellow whom he can love, a love he celebrates without looking aside in these poems. Say what you will, he proves to us, in spite of the most debasing experiences that life can offer a man, the spirit of love survives to ennoble our lives if we have the wit and the courage and the faith—and the art! to persist.

It is the belief in the art of poetry that has gone hand in hand with this man into his Golgotha, from that charnel house, similar in every way, to that of the Jews in the past war. But this is in our own country, our own fondest purlieus. We are blind and live our blind lives out in blindness. Poets are damned but they are not blind, they see with the eyes of the angels. This poet sees through and all around the horrors he partakes of in the very intimate details of his poem. He avoids nothing but experiences it to the hilt. He contains it. Claims it as his own—and, we believe, laughs at it and has the time and effrontery to love a fellow of his choice and record that love in a well-made poem.

Hold back the edges of your gowns, Ladies, we are going through hell.

HOWL

For
Carl Solomon

I

I saw the best minds of my generation destroyed by madness, starving
hysterical naked,
dragging themselves through the negro streets at dawn looking for an
angry fix,
angelheaded hipsters burning for the ancient heavenly connection to the
starry dynamo in the machinery of night,
who poverty and tatters and hollow-eyed and high sat up smoking in the
supernatural darkness of cold-water flats floating across the tops of
cities contemplating jazz,
who bared their brains to Heaven under the El and saw Mohammedan
angels staggering on tenement roofs illuminated,
who passed through universities with radiant cool eyes hallucinating
Arkansas and Blake-light tragedy among the scholars of war,
who were expelled from the academies for crazy & publishing obscene
odes on the windows of the skull,
who cowered in unshaven rooms in underwear, burning their money in
wastebaskets and listening to the Terror through the wall,
who got busted in their pubic beards returning through Laredo with a
belt of marijuana for New York,
who ate fire in paint hotels or drank turpentine in Paradise Alley, death, or
purgatoried their torsos night after night
with dreams, with drugs, with waking nightmares, alcohol and cock and
endless balls,
incomparable blind streets of shuddering cloud and lightning in the mind
leaping toward poles of Canada & Paterson, illuminating all the
motionless world of Time between,
Peyote solidities of halls, backyard green tree cemetery dawns, wine drunken-
ness over the rooftops, storefront boroughs of teahead joyride neon
blinking traffic light, sun and moon and tree vibrations in the roaring
winter dusks of Brooklyn, ashcan rantings and kind king light of mind,
who chained themselves to subways for the endless ride from Battery to
holy Bronx on benzedrine until the noise of wheels and children

brought them down shuddering mouth-wracked and battered bleak
    of brain all drained of brilliance in the drear light of Zoo,
who sank all night in submarine light of Bickford's floated out and sat
    through the stale beer afternoon in desolate Fugazzi's, listening to
    the crack of doom on the hydrogen jukebox,
who talked continuously seventy hours from park to pad to bar to
    Bellevue to museum to the Brooklyn Bridge,
a lost battalion of platonic conversationalists jumping down the stoops
    off fire escapes off windowsills off Empire State out of the moon,
yacketayakking screaming vomiting whispering facts and memories
    and anecdotes and eyeball kicks and shocks of hospitals and jails
    and wars,
whole intellects disgorged in total recall for seven days and nights with
    brilliant eyes, meat for the Synagogue cast on the pavement,
who vanished into nowhere Zen New Jersey leaving a trail of ambiguous
    picture postcards of Atlantic City Hall,
suffering Eastern sweats and Tangierian bone-grindings and migraines
    of China under junk-withdrawal in Newark's bleak furnished room,
who wandered around and around at midnight in the railroad yard
    wondering where to go, and went, leaving no broken hearts,
who lit cigarettes in boxcars boxcars boxcars rocketing through snow
    toward lonesome farms in grandfather night,
who studied Plotinus Poe St. John of the Cross telepathy and bop kabbalah
    because the cosmos instinctively vibrated at their feet in Kansas,
who loned it through the streets of Idaho seeking visionary indian angels
    who were visionary indian angels,
who thought they were only mad when Baltimore gleamed in
    supernatural ecstasy,
who jumped in limousines with the Chinaman of Oklahoma on the
    impulse of winter midnight streetlight smalltown rain,
who lounged hungry and lonesome through Houston seeking jazz or
    sex or soup, and followed the brilliant Spaniard to converse about
    America and Eternity, a hopeless task, and so took ship to Africa,
who disappeared into the volcanoes of Mexico leaving behind nothing
    but the shadow of dungarees and the lava and ash of poetry scattered
    in fireplace Chicago,
who reappeared on the West Coast investigating the F.B.I. in beards and
    shorts with big pacifist eyes sexy in their dark skin passing out
    incomprehensible leaflets,

who burned cigarette holes in their arms protesting the narcotic tobacco
    haze of Capitalism,

who distributed Supercommunist pamphlets in Union Square weeping
    and undressing while the sirens of Los Alamos wailed them down,
    and wailed down Wall, and the Staten Island ferry also wailed,

who broke down crying in white gymnasiums naked and trembling before
    the machinery of other skeletons,

who bit detectives in the neck and shrieked with delight in policecars for
    committing no crime but their own wild cooking pederasty and
    intoxication,

who howled on their knees in the subway and were dragged off the roof
    waving genitals and manuscripts,

who let themselves be fucked in the ass by saintly motorcyclists, and
    screamed with joy,

who blew and were blown by those human seraphim, the sailors, caresses
    of Atlantic and Caribbean love,

who balled in the morning in the evenings in rosegardens and the grass of
    public parks and cemeteries scattering their semen freely to whomever
    come who may,

who hiccuped endlessly trying to giggle but wound up with a sob behind
    a partition in a Turkish Bath when the blonde & naked angel came to
    pierce them with a sword,

who lost their loveboys to the three old shrews of fate the one eyed shrew
    of the heterosexual dollar the one eyed shrew that winks out of the
    womb and the one eyed shrew that does nothing but sit on her ass
    and snip the intellectual golden threads of the craftsman's loom,

who copulated ecstatic and insatiate with a bottle of beer a sweetheart
    a package of cigarettes a candle and fell off the bed, and continued
    along the floor and down the hall and ended fainting on the wall
    with a vision of ultimate cunt and come eluding the last gyzym of
    consciousness,

who sweetened the snatches of a million girls trembling in the sunset, and
    were red eyed in the morning but prepared to sweeten the snatch of
    the sunrise, flashing buttocks under barns and naked in the lake,

who went out whoring through Colorado in myriad stolen night-cars,
    N.C., secret hero of these poems, cocksman and Adonis of Denver—
    joy to the memory of his innumerable lays of girls in empty lots &
    diner backyards, moviehouses, rickety rows on mountaintops in caves
    or with gaunt waitresses in familiar roadside lonely petticoat upliftings

& especially secret gas-station solipsisms of johns, & hometown alleys too,

who faded out in vast sordid movies, were shifted in dreams, woke on a sudden Manhattan, and picked themselves up out of basements hungover with heartless Tokay and horrors of Third Avenue iron dreams & stumbled to unemployment offices,

who walked all night with their shoes full of blood on the snowbank docks waiting for a door in the East River to open to a room full of steamheat and opium,

who created great suicidal dramas on the apartment cliff-banks of the Hudson under the wartime blue floodlight of the moon & their heads shall be crowned with laurel in oblivion,

who ate the lamb stew of the imagination or digested the crab at the muddy bottom of the rivers of Bowery,

who wept at the romance of the streets with their pushcarts full of onions and bad music,

who sat in boxes breathing in the darkness under the bridge, and rose up to build harpsichords in their lofts,

who coughed on the sixth floor of Harlem crowned with flame under the tubercular sky surrounded by orange crates of theology,

who scribbled all night rocking and rolling over lofty incantations which in the yellow morning were stanzas of gibberish,

who cooked rotten animals lung heart feet tail borsht & tortillas dreaming of the pure vegetable kingdom,

who plunged themselves under meat trucks looking for an egg,

who threw their watches off the roof to cast their ballot for Eternity outside of Time, & alarm clocks fell on their heads every day for the next decade,

who cut their wrists three times successively unsuccessfully, gave up and were forced to open antique stores where they thought they were growing old and cried,

who were burned alive in their innocent flannel suits on Madison Avenue amid blasts of leaden verse & the tanked-up clatter of the iron regiments of fashion & the nitroglycerine shrieks of the fairies of advertising & the mustard gas of sinister intelligent editors, or were run down by the drunken taxicabs of Absolute Reality,

who jumped off the Brooklyn Bridge this actually happened and walked away unknown and forgotten into the ghostly daze of Chinatown soup alleyways & firetrucks, not even one free beer, who sang out of their windows in despair, fell out of the subway window, jumped in the filthy Passaic, leaped on negroes, cried all over the street, danced on broken wineglasses barefoot smashed phonograph records of nostalgic European 1930s German jazz finished the whiskey and threw up groaning into the bloody toilet, moans in their ears and the blast of colossal steamwhistles,

who barreled down the highways of the past journeying to each other's hotrod-Golgotha jail-solitude watch or Birmingham jazz incarnation,

who drove crosscountry seventytwo hours to find out if I had a vision or you had a vision or he had a vision to find out Eternity,

who journeyed to Denver, who died in Denver, who came back to Denver & waited in vain, who watched over Denver & brooded & loned in Denver and finally went away to find out the Time, & now Denver is lonesome for her heroes,

who fell on their knees in hopeless cathedrals praying for each other's salvation and light and breasts, until the soul illuminated its hair for a second,

who crashed through their minds in jail waiting for impossible criminals with golden heads and the charm of reality in their hearts who sang sweet blues to Alcatraz,

who retired to Mexico to cultivate a habit, or Rocky Mount to tender Buddha or Tangiers to boys or Southern Pacific to the black locomotive or Harvard to Narcissus to Woodlawn to the daisychain or grave,

who demanded sanity trials accusing the radio of hypnotism & were left with their insanity & their hands & a hung jury,

who threw potato salad at CCNY lecturers on Dadaism and subsequently presented themselves on the granite steps of the madhouse with shaven heads and harlequin speech of suicide, demanding instantaneous lobotomy,

and who were given instead the concrete void of insulin Metrazol electricity hydrotherapy psychotherapy occupational therapy pingpong & amnesia,

who in humorless protest overturned only one symbolic pingpong table, resting briefly in catatonia,

returning years later truly bald except for a wig of blood, and tears and fingers, to the visible madman doom of the wards of the madtowns of the East,

Pilgrim State's Rockland's and Greystone's foetid halls, bickering with the echoes of the soul, rocking and rolling in the midnight solitude-bench

dolmen-realms of love, dream of life a nightmare, bodies turned to
    stone as heavy as the moon,
with mother finally ******, and the last fantastic book flung out of the
    tenement window, and the last door closed at 4 AM and the last
    telephone slammed at the wall in reply and the last furnished room
    emptied down to the last piece of mental furniture, a yellow paper
    rose twisted on a wire hanger in the closet, and even that imaginary,
    nothing but a hopeful little bit of hallucination—
ah, Carl, while you are not safe I am not safe, and now you're really in the
    total animal soup of time—
and who therefore ran through the icy streets obsessed with a sudden flash
    of the alchemy of the use of the ellipse the catalog the meter & the
    vibrating plane,
who dreamt and made incarnate gaps in Time & Space through images
    juxtaposed, and trapped the archangel of the soul between 2 visual
    images and joined the elemental verbs and set the noun and dash of
    consciousness together jumping with sensation of Pater Omnipotens
    Aeterna Deus
to recreate the syntax and measure of poor human prose and stand before
    you speechless and intelligent and shaking with shame, rejected yet
    confessing out the soul to conform to the rhythm of thought in his
    naked and endless head,
the madman bum and angel beat in Time, unknown, yet putting down
    here what might be left to say in time come after death,
and rose reincarnate in the ghostly clothes of jazz in the goldhorn shadow
    of the band and blew the suffering of America's naked mind for love
    into an eli eli lamma lamma sabacthani saxophone cry that shivered
    the cities down to the last radio
with the absolute heart of the poem of life butchered out of their own
    bodies good to eat a thousand years.

II

What sphinx of cement and aluminum bashed open their skulls and ate
    up their brains and imagination?
Moloch! Solitude! Filth! Ugliness! Ashcans and unobtainable dollars!
    Children screaming under the stairways! Boys sobbing in armies! Old
    men weeping in the parks!

Moloch! Moloch! Nightmare of Moloch! Moloch the loveless! Mental Moloch! Moloch the heavy judger of men!

Moloch the incomprehensible prison! Moloch the crossbone soulless jailhouse and Congress of sorrows! Moloch whose buildings are judgment! Moloch the vast stone of war! Moloch the stunned governments!

Moloch whose mind is pure machinery! Moloch whose blood is running money! Moloch whose fingers are ten armies! Moloch whose breast is a cannibal dynamo! Moloch whose ear is a smoking tomb!

Moloch whose eyes are a thousand blind windows! Moloch whose skyscrapers stand in the long streets like endless Jehovahs! Moloch whose factories dream and croak in the fog! Moloch whose smokestacks and antennae crown the cities!

Moloch whose love is endless oil and stone! Moloch whose soul is electricity and banks! Moloch whose poverty is the specter of genius! Moloch whose fate is a cloud of sexless hydrogen! Moloch whose name is the Mind!

Moloch in whom I sit lonely! Moloch in whom I dream Angels! Crazy in Moloch! Cocksucker in Moloch! Lacklove and manless in Moloch!

Moloch who entered my soul early! Moloch in whom I am a consciousness without a body! Moloch who frightened me out of my natural ecstasy! Moloch whom I abandon! Wake up in Moloch! Light streaming out of the sky!

Moloch! Moloch! Robot apartments! invisible suburbs! skeleton treasuries! blind capitals! demonic industries! spectral nations! invincible madhouses! granite cocks! monstrous bombs!

They broke their backs lifting Moloch to Heaven! Pavements, trees, radios, tons! lifting the city to Heaven which exists and is everywhere about us!

Visions! omens! hallucinations! miracles! ecstasies! gone down the American river!

Dreams! adorations! illuminations! religions! the whole boatload of sensitive bullshit!

Breakthroughs! over the river! flips and crucifixions! gone down the flood! Highs! Epiphanies! Despairs! Ten years' animal screams and suicides! Minds! New loves! Mad generation! down on the rocks of Time!

Real holy laughter in the river! They saw it all! the wild eyes! the holy yells! They bade farewell! They jumped off the roof! to solitude! waving! carrying flowers! Down to the river! into the street!

III

Carl Solomon! I'm with you in Rockland
  where you're madder than I am
I'm with you in Rockland
  where you must feel very strange
I'm with you in Rockland
  where you imitate the shade of my mother
I'm with you in Rockland
  where you've murdered your twelve secretaries
I'm with you in Rockland
  where you laugh at this invisible humor
I'm with you in Rockland
  where we are great writers on the same dreadful typewriter
I'm with you in Rockland
  where your condition has become serious and is reported on
  the radio
I'm with you in Rockland
  where the faculties of the skull no longer admit the worms of
  the senses
I'm with you in Rockland
  where you drink the tea of the breasts of the spinsters of Utica
I'm with you in Rockland
  where you pun on the bodies of your nurses the harpies of the Bronx
I'm with you in Rockland
  where you scream in a straightjacket that you're losing the game of
  the actual pingpong of the abyss
I'm with you in Rockland
  where you bang on the catatonic piano the soul is innocent and
  immortal it should never die ungodly in an armed madhouse
I'm with you in Rockland
  where fifty more shocks will never return your soul to its body again
  from its pilgrimage to a cross in the void
I'm with you in Rockland
  where you accuse your doctors of insanity and plot the Hebrew
  socialist revolution against the fascist national Golgotha
I'm with you in Rockland
  where you will split the heavens of Long Island and resurrect your
  living human Jesus from the superhuman tomb

I'm with you in Rockland
    where there are twenty-five thousand mad comrades all together
    singing the final stanzas of the Internationale
I'm with you in Rockland
    where we hug and kiss the United States under our bedsheets the
    United States that coughs all night and won't let us sleep
I'm with you in Rockland
    where we wake up electrified out of the coma by our own souls'
    airplanes roaring over the roof they've come to drop angelic bombs
    the hospital illuminates itself imaginary walls collapse O skinny
    legions run outside O starry-spangled shocks of mercy the eternal
    war is here O victory forget your underwear we're free
I'm with you in Rockland
    in my dreams you walk dripping from a sea-journey on the highway
    across America in tears to the door of my cottage in the Western night

San Francisco 1955–56

FOOTNOTE TO HOWL

Holy! Holy! Holy! Holy! Holy! Holy! Holy! Holy! Holy! Holy! Holy!
    Holy! Holy! Holy! Holy!
The world is holy! The soul is holy! The skin is holy! The nose is holy!
    The tongue and cock and hand and asshole holy!
Everything is holy! everybody's holy! everywhere is holy! everyday is in
    eternity! Everyman's an angel!
The bum's as holy as the seraphim! the madman is holy as you my soul are
    holy!
The typewriter is holy the poem is holy the voice is holy the hearers are
    holy the ecstasy is holy!
Holy Peter holy Allen holy Solomon holy Lucien holy Kerouac holy
    Huncke holy Burroughs holy Cassady holy the unknown buggered
    and suffering beggars holy the hideous human angels!
Holy my mother in the insane asylum! Holy the cocks of the grandfathers
    of Kansas!

Holy the groaning saxophone! Holy the bop apocalypse! Holy the
   jazzbands marijuana hipsters peace & junk & drums!
Holy the solitudes of skyscrapers and pavements! Holy the cafeterias filled
   with the millions! Holy the mysterious rivers of tears under the
   streets!
Holy the lone juggernaut! Holy the vast lamb of the middleclass! Holy
   the crazy shepherds of rebellion! Who digs Los Angeles IS Los
   Angeles!
Holy New York Holy San Francisco Holy Peoria & Seattle Holy Paris
   Holy Tangiers Holy Moscow Holy Istanbul!
Holy time in eternity holy eternity in time holy the clocks in space holy
   the fourth dimension holy the fifth International holy the Angel in
   Moloch!
Holy the sea holy the desert holy the railroad holy the locomotive holy
   the visions holy the hallucinations holy the miracles holy the eyeball
   holy the abyss!
Holy forgiveness! mercy! charity! faith! Holy! Ours! bodies! suffering!
   magnanimity!
Holy the supernatural extra brilliant intelligent kindness of the soul!

Berkeley, 1955

THE *HOWL* LETTERS
edited by Bill Morgan

Editor's Note: By the summer of 1955, Allen Ginsberg had been living in San Francisco for nearly a year. During that time he had found a good-paying job in market research and moved in with his girlfriend, Sheila Williams. One night, high on peyote, Ginsberg had a vision. He witnessed the Sir Francis Drake Hotel transform itself from a solid brick and stone building into the image of the Biblical god, Moloch, a demonic power infamous for destroying human flesh and souls.

Not long after this vision, he met a young man, Peter Orlovsky, who was to become his lifelong companion. Depressed by the traditional lifestyle he had adopted, Ginsberg sought professional counseling and was surprised when the doctor suggested he follow his own desires to quit work, write poetry, and live with Peter if he wanted to. After about six months, Peter returned temporarily to New York, and in his absence Allen settled down alone and began to compose a long poem based on his Moloch vision of the previous fall. Ginsberg's plans for the future were to enter graduate school at UC Berkeley and perhaps become a teacher.

The following correspondence, much of it between Allen Ginsberg and Lawrence Ferlinghetti, covers the period from the creation of *Howl* through its publication and trial. Ferlinghetti's earliest letters to Ginsberg do not appear to have survived, but a clear picture emerges nevertheless. Passages in the letters not directly related to *Howl* have been omitted and replaced by the symbol ★★★. The first letter Ginsberg wrote that mentioned his new poem was to his brother, Eugene Brooks.

August 16, 1955. Allen Ginsberg [1010 Montgomery, San Francisco, CA] to Eugene Brooks [New York]

Dear Gene:
   ★★★ I'm expecting as of now barring troubles to settle at Berkeley for a year or so, have put in bid for $35 per mo. ivy-covered one room (plus kitchen & bath) cottage on side street, garden and apricot tree around, private and Shakespearean. Will have to get job, in hospital or restaurant nearby, work part-time. ★★★ Am over the hump on a collection of last 4 years work and writing in a new style now, long prose poem strophes, sort

of surrealist, & reading a lot of Spanish and French modern poetry, Lorca, Apollinaire, & some Latin, still on Catullus. Catullus really worth looking at in edition an anthology of all translations edited by someone named Aiken,[1] probably in Columbia library, if you liked Tacitus. The new style: example: referring to Carl Solomon[2]

". . . who presented himself on the granite steps of the madhouse with shaven head and harlequin speech of suicide demanding instantaneous lobotomy,

and who was given instead the concrete void of insulin Metrazol electricity hydrotherapy psychotherapy occupational therapy pingpong & amnesia,

and who in humorless protest overturned only one symbolic ping pong table . . ."

and other Who's Who's & images (this from a long catalogue)

"who screamed on all fours in the subway, and were dragged off the roof waving genitals and manuscripts,

who loned it thru the streets of Idaho seeking visionary Indian angels who were visionary Indian angels,

who copulated ecstatic and insatiate with a package of cigarettes a bottle of beer a chick or a candle and fell off the bed and continued on the floor and down the hall and ended fainting on the wall with an ultimate vision of cunt eluding the last come of consciousness,

who bit detectives in the neck and howled with delight in police cars for committing no crime but their own wild cooking pederasty and intoxication,

who digested rotten animals lung heart tail feet borscht and tortillas dreaming of the pure vegetable kingdom,

who plunged under meat trucks looking for an egg,

who tramped all night on the snowbank docks with bloody feet looking for a door in the East River to open to a room full of steam heat and opium,

who picked themselves up out of alleyways hung up with heartless Tokay and horrors of iron and stumbled off to unemployment offices,

who ate the lamb stew of the imagination or digested crabs at the muddy bottom of the rivers of Bowery,

---

[1] Aiken, W. Appleton (ed.). *The Poems of Catullus.* NY: Dutton, 1950.

[2] Carl Solomon (1928–1994), friend Ginsberg met in a psychiatric hospital ward and the person to whom *Howl* is addressed.

who chained themselves to subways for the endless ride from Battery to holy Bronx until the noise of wheels and children brought them down wide eyed and battered bleak of brain mouth wracked all drained of brilliance in the drear light of Zoo,"

etc. etc.

Goes on for 5 pages. This is more or less Kerouac's rhythmic style of prose, ends "the actual heart of the poem of life butchered out of their own bodies good to eat a thousand years." Elegy for the generation, etc.

Also, "who mopped all night in desolate Bickfords listening to the crack of doom on the hydrogen jukebox."

I have been looking at early blues forms and think will apply this form of elliptical semisurrealist imagery to rhymed blues type lyrics. Nobody but Auden's written any literary blues forms, his are more like English ballads, not purified Americana. Blues forms also provide a real varied syncopated metre, with many internal variants and changes of form in midstream like conversational thought. Most of my time is actually occupied with this type thought and activity, writing a lot and therefore beginning to change style, get hot, invent and go on interesting kicks thanks to courtesy of U.S. govt. leisure.[3] I never spent it better. ★★★

Love, Allen

August 25, 1955. Allen Ginsberg [San Francisco] to Jack Kerouac [Mexico]

Dear Jack:

★★★ The pages I sent you of "Howl" (right title)[4] are the first pages put down, as is. I recopied them and sent you the 100% original draft. There is no pre-existent version, I typed it up as I went along, that's why it's so messy. What I have here is all copies cleaned and extended. What you have is what you want.

I realize how right you are, that was the first time I sat down to blow, it came out in your method, sounding like you, an imitation practically. How far advanced you are on this. I don't know what I'm doing with poetry. I need years of isolation and constant everyday writing to attain your volume and freedom and knowledge of the form.

---

[3] Ginsberg was receiving unemployment checks during this period.

[4] Ginsberg had sent a few of the "Strophes," as he originally called them, to Jack Kerouac. Kerouac wrote back suggesting the poem be titled "Howl."

★★★ We wandered on Peyote all downtown, P&I [Peter and I], met Betty Keck and saw Moloch Molochsmoking building in red glare downtown St. Francis Hotel, with robot upstairs eyes and skullface, in smoke, again. And I saw in me and he a void under the knowledge of each other.

★★★ Bern Porter or City Lights bookstore here will publish a book of poems for me, possibly also for you, to be investigated.[5] I had a little poem in small magazine in Southern California[6] and my father sent me a copy republished from *NY Herald Tribune*, they do that every Sunday. Strange. Incomprehensible note about the Shrouded Stranger, of all things.[7] ★★★

Love, Allen

Late August 1955. Allen Ginsberg [San Francisco] to Robert LaVigne[8] [Mexico]

Dear Robert:

★★★ I am writing a big poem in prose poem strophes concerning adventures of my contemporaries, shorthand rhetorical form,

"who loned it through the streets of Idaho seeking visionary Indian angels who were visionary Indian angels

who howled with delight in police cars for committing no crime but their own wild cooking pederasty and intoxication,

who hiccupped endlessly trying to giggle but wound up with a sob behind a partition in a Turkish bath when the blond and naked angel came to pierce them with a sword.

who copulated ecstatic and insatiate with a cigarette a candle a bottle of beer and a lady and fell off the bed and continued on the floor and down the hall and ended fainting on the wall with a vision of cunt and come eluding the last hop of consciousness,

who let themselves be fucked in the ass by saintly motorcyclists and screamed with joy,

who blew and were blown by those human angels the sailors, caresses of Atlantic and Caribbean love,

---

[5] Ginsberg had shown his poetry to Lawrence Ferlinghetti, who recognized the power of the poetry at once. He offered to publish a book of Ginsberg's poems well before the Six Gallery reading that October.

[6] *Variegation* [Los Angeles], vol. 10, no. 39 (Summer 1955) pp. 50-51, published "Sunset" and "Fragment of a Monument."

[7] *New York Herald Tribune* (August 21, 1955) section 2, p. 4, published "Fragment of a Monument."

[8] Robert LaVigne (b. 1928), artist who first introduced Ginsberg to Peter Orlovsky.

who screamed on all fours in the subway and were dragged off the roof waving genitals and manuscripts,

who mopped all night in desolate Bickfords listening to the crack of doom on the hydrogen jukebox,

who chained themselves to subways for the endless ride from Battery to holy Bronx until the noise of wheels and children brought them down shuddering on Benzedrine mouth wracked battered bleak of brain all drained of brilliance in the drear light of Zoo (this being the Bronx zoo)

who presented themselves on the granite steps of the madhouse with shaven heads and harlequin speech of suicide demanding instantaneous lobotomy

and who were presented instead with the concrete void of insulin Metrazol electricity hydrotherapy psychotherapy occupational therapy pingpong and amnesia

and who in humorless protest overturned only one symbolic pingpong table"

etc. etc. I have 5 pages of this to read at the arts festival.[9] ★★★

As ever, Allen

August 30, 1955. Allen Ginsberg [San Francisco] to Jack Kerouac [Mexico City]

Dear Almond Crackerjax:

★★★ City Lights bookstore here putting out pamphlets—50 short pages—of local poets and one of WC Williams reprint and one of [e.e.] Cummings and will put out *Howl* (under that title) next year, one booklet for that poem, nothing else—it will fill a booklet. ★★★

"What Sphinx of cement and aluminum bashed in their skulls and ate their brains and imagination?

Moloch Moloch Solitude Ugliness! Ashcans and unobtainable dollars! Children screaming under stairways! Old men weeping in parks!

Moloch! Moloch! Skeleton treasuries! Ghostly banks! Eyeless capitols! Robot apartments! Granite phalluses and monstrous bombs!

Visions! Omens! Hallucinations! Gone down the American River! Dreams! Miracles! Ecstasies! The whole boatload of sensitive bullshit!" etc.

Love, Allen

---

[9] Ginsberg's first public reading was not at the Six Gallery as many believe, but actually a few weeks earlier at the San Francisco Arts Festival. It appears that he did not read "Howl" at the Arts Festival, but "Supermarket in California."

Mid-September 1955. Allen Ginsberg [1624 Milvia, Berkeley] to John Allen Ryan[10] [Mexico]

Dear Johnny:

★★★ Hendrix [sic: Hedrick][11] asked me if I wanted to organize a poetry reading at the Six, and I didn't several months ago, not knowing of any poetry around worth hearing, but changed my fucking mind, and so you will be glad to know the tradition continues with a gala evening sometime in a month or so or shorter, the program being Rexroth as introducer, McClure reading new poems (he thinks, it's partly true, he's found his own natural voice—it sounds a little tightassed to me but he is writing well and that's maybe the way god built him), Lamantia putting in an appearance to read John Hoffman's work (which I haven't really seen for years, if it isn't poetry it'll be a great social occasion), myself to read a long poem the first scraps of which I sent to Kerouac, you might look at it if you see him again. I don't have a copy or I'd send you a piece (its more or less up the alley of your SF recollections in tranquility), and a bearded interesting Berkeley cat name of [Gary] Snyder, I met him yesterday (via Rexroth suggestion) who is studying oriental and leaving in a few months on some privately put up funds to go be a Zen monk (a real one). He's a head, peyotlist, laconist, but warmhearted, nice looking with a little beard, thin, blond, rides a bicycle in Berkeley in red corduroy and levis and hungup on Indians (ex anthropology student from some Indian hometown) and writes well, his sideline besides zen which is apparently calm scholarly and serious with him. Interesting person. IF anybody else turns up along the way to read we may add somebody else. When Kerouac gets to SF probably I'll try set up another program, myself, Jack and Neal Cassady (whom you didn't know in SF?). You might send this bit of 6 gossip to [Jack] Spicer, he'll probably be pleased that something is being done to continue there. And you might send me any advice on organizing these readings that you can remember from previous experience. ★★★

Love, as ever. Allen

Editor's Note: The reading at the Six Gallery on October 7, 1955, was an unqualified success and is credited as being the high point of the San Francisco Renaissance. That evening, Ginsberg read his poem "Howl" for

---

[10] John Allen Ryan was one of the bartenders at The Place and a member of the Six Gallery. Allen had a brief sexual relationship with Ryan while Peter was back in New York that summer.

[11] Wallace Hedrick was another of the founding members of the Six Gallery.

the first time, and the poem so impressed Ferlinghetti that he sent a telegram to Ginsberg at once. "I greet you at the beginning of a great career. When do I get the manuscript?" it read, paraphrasing Emerson's letter to Walt Whitman after first seeing *Leaves of Grass*.

December 26, 1955. Allen Ginsberg [Berkeley] to Eugene Brooks [New York]

Dear Gene:

★★★ By the way I have a problem. Legal[12]—my own book is due, the mss. is due, before I leave here,[13] to be printed in England for economy's sake, costs only $150 there for 500 copies of 40 page booklet (comprising single poem, *Howl for Carl Solomon*, Lou saw it)—however City Lights, the people here publishing for me, are afraid it will be held up in customs for obscenity, since I use cunts, cocks, balls, assholes, snatches and fucks and comes liberally scattered around in the prosody—the question being, do you know anything about the customs law, appeals, etc. in case there is trouble, or (as I am told) are they likely if they notice it to forthwith burn the books without notice for appeal. The problem is whether I should cut out (which I don't want to do), chance it, or request book printed here, which City Lights is also willing to do. The problem is not with publisher but with possible customs laws, I expect there will be further use later, as I have been making arrangements for possible cheap publishing to be done for Self Jack and Bill in Japan, where a friend [Gary Snyder] is going next month—costs only $50 to print a book there. Amazing. Burroughs is getting fantastically dirty in his mss. but it is high art, but he doesn't shilly-shally, in fact he's been writing pornography with a vengeance lately, and my own work is full of orgies. ★★★

Love, Allen

January 16, 1956. Allen Ginsberg [Berkeley] to Lucien Carr [New York]

Dear Lucien:

Fast note on sudden impulse. Enclosed find copy of poem (new style, long lines, strophes). Write me what it looks like objectively from U.P.[14]

---

[12] Ginsberg's brother, Eugene Brooks, was a lawyer.

[13] Ginsberg was planning to leave San Francisco, either to go to Los Angeles to find employment or ship out with the Merchant Marine.

[14] Carr was working for the United Press in New York at the time.

or whatever angle. It's very good read aloud cause it's got swing. I have a publisher for this as the notice I sent you several days ago can prove. Uncensored no less. ★★★

Love, Allen

Late March 1956. Allen Ginsberg [Berkeley] to Louis Ginsberg [Paterson, New Jersey]

Dear Louis:

W. C. Williams read "Howl" and liked it and wrote an introduction for the book; and meanwhile there is the possibility of expanding and making a whole book of poems. We put on another reading in a theatre here in Berkeley,[15] I read some other poems, Whitman ["Supermarket in California"], "The Sunflower" [Sutra], and a new poem called "America"— a sort of surrealist anarchist tract—all of which came off very well, so the publisher is now interested in a book full of representative work not just the one poem. The reading was pretty great, we had traveling photographers, who appeared on the scene from Vancouver to photograph it, a couple of amateur electronics experts who appeared with tape machines to record, request from state college for a complete recording for the night, requests for copies of the recordings, even finally organizations of bop musicians who want to write music and give big west coast traveling tours of "Howl" as a sort of Jazz Mass, recorded for a west coast company called Fantasy Records that issues a lot of national bop, etc. No kidding. You have no idea what a storm of lunatic-fringe activity I have stirred up. On top of that the local poets, good and bad, have caught up and there are now three groups of people putting on readings every other week, there's one every weekend, all sorts of people—this week Eberhart (Richard) arrived in town for readings at State, there is a party for him tonite, I was invited to give a private reading, refused (sheer temperament), and so the recordings will be played. Tomorrow night Rexroth invited me over to meet a group of jazz musicians and discuss the possibility of making some form of jazz-poetry combo. There is also another group of musicians, the leader of which used to arrange for Stan Kenton who wants to record with me. Finally I was asked to write an article which I haven't gotten around to do for *Black Mountain Review*, & also contribute to 2 literary magazines starting here. Bob LaVigne, a painter whose work I've been

---

[15] On March 18, 1956, the Town Hall Theater in Berkeley reenacted the Six Gallery reading with the same poets except Philip Lamantia, who was out of town.

buying and digging, has been putting up wild line drawings to plaster the walls of the readings and painting fantastic 7 foot posters *à la* Lautrec. Really a charming scene. My big problem now is not having enough time to do all I could, working at Greyhound[16] and not having moved out of Berkeley, so I get little time for actual writing anymore—it will be a relief to get out from under and away on a ship or up to Alaska possibly on a fishing industry job.

English publishers want [sic: won't] handle *Howl*, that is English Printers (Villiers) and so there is now difficulty in getting it through unexpurgated. I revised it and it is now worse than it ever was, too. We're now investigating Mexico, if necessary will spend extra cost and have it done here tho. Civil Liberties Union here was consulted and said they'd defend it if it gets into trouble, which I almost hope it does. I am almost ready to tackle the U.S. Govt out of sheer self delight. There is really a great stupid conspiracy of unconscious negative inertia to keep people from "expressing" themselves. I was reading Henry Miller's banned book *Tropic of Cancer*, which actually is a great classic—I never heard of it at Columbia with anything but depreciatory dismissal comments—he and Genet are such frank hip writers that the open expression of their perceptions and real beliefs are a threat to society. The wonder is that literature does have such power.

Allen

April 26, 1956. Allen Ginsberg [Berkeley] to Louis Ginsberg [Paterson]

Dear Louis:

Have laid off teaching for this week and am revising final mss. for the booklet but not getting very far, tho I set a deadline for this weekend for City Lights & said I'd bring it all in. I don't seem to be able to do any imaginative work till I've slept and read and goofed for a week or more in complete timeless bored meditation. I have a longish absurd poem on America to finish:

"Are you going to let your emotional life be run by *Time* magazine?
I'm obsessed by *Time* magazine.
I read it every week.
Its cover stares at me every time I pass the N.W. corner of Sutter Montgomery streets.

---

[16] For a short time Ginsberg worked in the baggage room of the San Francisco Greyhound bus depot.

I read it in the basement of the Berkeley public library.
They're always telling me about responsibility. Businessmen are serious.
Movie producers are serious. Everybody's serious but me.
It occurs to me that I am America.
I'm talking to myself again."
etc. for 7 pages. I cover everything from international relations to the
dope problem. ★★★
Write — love, Allen

Editor's Note: Richard Eberhart was asked by the *New York Times* to write
an article on the S.F. Poetry Renaissance and Ginsberg wrote him a long let-
ter to explain the composition of *Howl*. The following is a short excerpt of
that letter. The complete letter was published by Penmaen Press in 1976 in
To Eberhart From Ginsberg.

May 18, 1956. Allen Ginsberg [San Francisco] to Richard Eberhart [New York]

Dear Mr. Eberhart:
★★★

Summary
I. Values

1) *Howl* is an "affirmation" of individual experience of God, sex, drugs,
absurdity etc. Part I deals sympathetically with individual cases. Part II
describes and rejects the Moloch of society which confounds and suppresses
individual experience and forces the individual to consider himself mad
if he does not reject his own deepest senses. Part III is an expression of
sympathy and identification with C.S. [Carl Solomon] who is in the
madhouse — saying that his madness basically is rebellion against Moloch and
I am with him, and extending my hand in union. This is an affirmative act
of mercy and compassion, which are the basic emotions of the poem. The
criticism of society is that "Society" is merciless. The alternative is private,
individual acts of mercy. The poem is one such. It is therefore clearly and
consciously built on a *liberation* of basic human virtues.

To call it work of nihilistic rebellion would be to mistake it completely.
Its force comes from positive "religious" belief and experience. It offers no
"constructive" program in sociological terms — no poem could. It does offer
a constructive human value — basically the *experience* — of the enlightenment
of mystical experience — without which no society can long exist.

2) *Supermarket in California* deals with Walt Whitman, Why?

He was the first great American poet to take action in recognizing his individuality, forgiving and accepting *Him Self*, and automatically extending that recognition and acceptance to all — and defining his Democracy as that. He was unique and lonely in his glory — the truth of his feelings — without which no society can long exist. Without this truth there is only the impersonal Moloch and self-hatred of others.

Without self-acceptance there can be no acceptance of other souls.

3) *Sunflower Sutra* is crystallized "dramatic" moment of self-acceptance in modern terms.

"Unholy battered old thing, O sunflower O my soul, I *loved* you then!"

The realization of holy self-love is a rare "affirmative" value and cannot fail to have constructive influence in "Telling *you* (R.E.) [Richard Eberhart] how to live."

4) *America* is an unsystematic and rather gay exposition of my own private feelings contrary to the official dogmas, but really rather universal as far as private opinions about what I mention. It says — "I am thus and so I have a right to do so, and I'm saying it out loud for all to hear."

II. Technique

A. These long lines or Strophes as I call them came spontaneously as a result of the kind of feelings I was trying to put down, and came as a surprise solution to a metrical problem that preoccupied me for a decade.

I have considerable experience writing both rhymed iambics and short line post-WCW [William Carlos Williams] free verse.

Howl's 3 parts consist of 3 different approaches to the use of the long line (longer than Whitman's, more French).

1. Repetition of the fixed base "Who" for a catalogue.

    A. building up consecutive rhythm from strophe to strophe.

    B. abandoning of fixed base "who" in certain lines but carrying weight and rhythm of strophic form continuously forward.

2. Break up of strophe into pieces within the strophe, thus having the strophe become a new usable form of stanza. Repetition of fixed base "Moloch" to provide cement for continuity. *Supermarket* uses strophe stanza and abandons need for fixed base. I was experimenting with the form.

3. Use of a fixed base, "I'm with you in Rockland," with a reply in which the strophe becomes a longer and longer streak of speech, in order to build up a *relatively* equal nonetheless free and variable structure. Each reply strophe is longer than the previous I have measured by ear and speech-breath, there being no other measure for such a thing. Each

strophe consists of a set of phrases that can be spoken in one breath and each carries relatively equal rhetorical weight. Penultimate strophe is an exception and was meant to be—a series of cries—"O skinny legions run outside O starry spangled shock of mercy O victory etc." You will not fail to observe that the cries are all in definite rhythm.

The technical problem raised and partially solved is the break-through begun by Whitman but never carried forward, from both iambic stultification and literary automatism, and unrhythmical shortline verse, which does not yet offer any kind of *base* cyclical flow for the build up of a powerful rhythm. The long line seems for the moment to free speech for emotional expression and give it a measure to work with. I hope to experiment with short-line free verse with what I have learned from exercise in long.

B. Imagery—is a result of the *kind* of line and the kind of emotions and the kind of speech—and interior flow-of-the-mind transcription I am doing—the imagery often consists of 1920s W.C.W. [Williams] imagistically observed detail collapsed together by interior associative logic—i.e., "hydrogen jukebox," Apollinaire, Whitman, Lorca. But *not* automatic surrealism. Knowledge of Haiku and ellipse is crucial.

Editor's Note: To earn enough money to live on after his unemployment ran out, Ginsberg signed up with the Merchant Marine. He was assigned first to the USNS *Joseph Merrell,* which was in dry dock, and later to the USNS *Sgt. Jack J. Pendelton*, then resupplying bases along the D.E.W. [Distant Early Warning] line in Alaska.

Late May 1956. Allen Ginsberg [USNS *Joseph Merrell*] to Jack Kerouac [Mill Valley, CA]

Jack:

★★★ Received proofs on my book and Ferling [Ferlinghetti] asked for extra poems to include so I sent him Holy! ["Footnote to Howl"] etc. and a new 4 page Greyhound poem ["In the Baggage Room at Greyhound"] you haven't seen yet. [line from poem] ★★★

I sent copies of *Howl* to T.S. Eliot, Pound, Faulkner, Van Doren, Meyer Schapiro, Eberhart, Trilling, till they were exhausted (the copies). I wonder what T.S. Eliot will do. I wrote them each about you too. Funny letters to each. Imagine to T.S. Eliot. ★★★

Love, Allen

June 22, 1956. Allen Ginsberg [USNS *Sgt. Jack J. Pendleton*] to Lawrence Ferlinghetti [San Francisco]

Dear Larry:

Well what news? I am in Seattle, will be here over weekend and thru next Friday, will return to SF next weekend for a few days — arrive sometime Sunday I expect, around the 30th or 31st. If therefore you got or will get proofs hold on to them, I'll look them over myself.

Generally speaking the Greyhound poem stinks on ice, at least the end does — that won't last no 1000 years — I had a nightmare about it standing on the prow several days ago. I dunno what to do, haven't written anything better on it since leaving town. Maybe later.

As ever, Allen

Editor's Note: After seeing the proofs Ginsberg was disappointed by the printer's re-alignment of the left and right margins.

July 3, 1956. Allen Ginsberg [USNS *Sgt. Jack J. Pendleton*] to Lawrence Ferlinghetti [San Francisco]

Dear Larry:

This being my first book I want it right if can. Therefore I thought and decided this, about the justifications of margins. The reason for my being particular is that the poems are actually sloppy enough written, without sloppiness made worse by typographical arrangement. The one element of order and prearrangement I did pay care to was arrangement into prose-paragraph strophes: each one definite unified long line. So any doubt about irregularity of right hand margin will be sure to confuse critical reader about intention of the prosody. Therefore I've got to change it so it's right.

It looks like the whole book will have to be reset practically. Find out how much it costs to reset the first proofs we received, which is my fault for not having followed precisely thru and made sure in advance it was understood. I will pay that no matter how much up to $200.00, which I guess it may well cost. For the material they received subsequent to the first proofs, that's their look-to, I think. Can we get them to change that on their own? Sankey [the printer at Villiers] did right on pages 2 & 3 of "Transcription of Organ Music," so he did have an idea what we wanted, but was confused and didn't check with you after you'd raised the point so I think he can be held up for it — for he screwed up everything else, page one of same poem, and "Greyhound" and "Footnote."

I have marked on the copy exactly what needs justifying page by page.

This will be sure to delay things longer but the more I look at it the worse it seems, it's real bad this way, I mean you can't tell *what* I'm doing, it looks like just primitive random scribblings in pages. I had not intended the prosody to be *that* arbitrary.

Specific notes: If he is confused by the *left-hand* appearance of margin in "Transcription," the erratic jumps to new paragraph as in "to think at the sun" are intentional and should be kept. The problem is to iron out the right hand margin—not flatten the left hand margin in that poem is my worry. In case there should be confusion. (My reason incidentally for the erratic is simple, most of it's prose but wherever it struck me as really poetic as I was writing I would indent all of a sudden.)

Allen

Late July 1956. Allen Ginsberg [USNS *Sgt. Jack J. Pendleton,* Seattle] to Lawrence Ferlinghetti [San Francisco]

Dear Lawrence:

I have not yet had time to put together another copy of the mailing list I spoke of but will in a week or so after we sail, and will mail it then, you'll have it in time.

Enclosed find a note to my brother, Eugene Brooks, 505 West 125 Street, New York City.

When the bill comes in for the changes I ordered and said I would pay for, send it on to him with instructions how and where to pay it, whether to send you a check or else to Villiers directly, whatever way is most convenient or efficient for you to handle it. In any case send him instructions what to do. He has my money in the bank. If any legal problems rise up to bug us also, consult him, as he is an attorney-at-law. I have already written him of this arrangement, about paying for changes, etc. so he will wait to hear from you.

I leave here in 3 days (Friday or Saturday) (from here, is Seattle) finally for Arctic. Sorry I wasn't able to be around for final OK on proofs so I guess you came in drunk and couldn't stay. ★★★ Back I guess Sept. or Oct. maybe earlier. Drop me a line and let me know what's happening with the book—send me a card for sure when you see the proofs and tell me if it came out alright.

As ever, Allen

PS: I know this is another strange request—but if we still have extra pages why not have an illustration by Robert LaVigne? Peter Orlovsky saw them and wrote me they were great. If this is possible get a hold of LaVigne at Clayton Shaw's on Hyde or Leavenworth, have him draw something, preferably the Sunflower Sutra scene. (I think he knows where it is, back of SP [Southern Pacific] depot by the river one block in from 3rd Street, tell him to ask Phil Whalen where) and make a plate. I'll pay for that naturally, the plate, it probably wouldn't be more than $50 do you think? If this is possible to do let's do it unless it involves hassle and delay and absurdities etc. Add that to the bill for my brother. If can, let me know.

August 4, 1956. Allen Ginsberg [USNS *Sgt. Jack J. Pendleton*, Wainwright, AK] to Lawrence Ferlinghetti [San Francisco]

Dear Larry:

Enclosed find:

1. Mailing list I said I'd copy for you. I've already or will soon in near future send the announcement you sent me to these, so add them to your list for any other future uses.

2. 13 copies of a mimeographed pamphlet of the Mexican poem I made up here on ship last weekend.[17] Keep one yourself and put the other dozen on sale at 50¢ each if you think you can sell them. Give the proceeds to Mike McClure for use for *Moby* magazine. You can advertise them as a charity type shot for *Moby*. I made up another 40 and am keeping them or sending them out as whim strikes me.

Have you heard from Villiers as to the revisions? Was it possible to do anything about LaVigne? Have you yet sent the bill to my brother in NY? ★★★

As ever, Allen

Did you receive my letter with instructions to collect for extra Villiers bill from my brother Eugene Brooks, who has my money in the bank? If not, can do so whenever ready.

Editor's Note: Ginsberg asked that complementary copies of *Howl* be sent to everyone on the following list.

---

[17] Ginsberg printed up his own first book, fifty copies of the long poem *Siesta In Xbalba*, while stationed on board the ship off the coast of Alaska on July 28-29, 1956.

Alan Ansen, Walter Adams, David Burnett, Eugene Brooks, Martin Baer, Marius Bewley, Justine Brierley, Lucien Carr, Haldon Chase, Donald Cook, Elyse Cowen, Peter Caswell, Richard Davalos, Harry Wigham, Jim Fitzpatrick, Burton W. Forman, Lenore Grunes, Donald Gaynor, Ruth Goldenberg, John Clellon Holmes, Berthel Hoeniger, Theodore Hoffmann, John Hohnsbean, Robert Howard, John Kingsland, Robert Merims, Charles Peters, Jethro Robinson, Meyer Schapiro, Louis Simpson, Parker Tyler, Charles Boultenhouse, Lionel Trilling, Rufino Tamayo, Alan Temko, Mark Van Doren, Malcolm Cowley, A.A. Wyn, Seymour Wyse, Esq., Louis Zukofsky, Louis Ginsberg, Jason Epstein, Eugenio Villacana, Joseph Wood Krutch, Andrew Chiappe, Robert Cantwell, Irita Van Doren, Louise Bogan.

Editor's Note: A few advance copies arrived in August from the printer and Ferlinghetti sent one on to Ginsberg.

August 9, 1956. Allen Ginsberg [USNS *Sgt. Jack J. Pendleton*] to Lawrence Ferlinghetti [San Francisco]

Dear Larry

Received the copy of the book you sent me promptly—and was excited to see it. Everything worked out fine with the typography—it looks much better this way and it seems to have been real cheap to do— $20 is nuthin. I shuddered when I read the poetry tho, it all seems so jerry-built sloppy and egocentric, most of it. "Greyhound" looks fine, I'm glad you told me to put it in. Reading it all through I'm not sure it deserves all the care and work you've put into it and the encouragement you've given me, in fact to tell you the truth I am already embarrassed by half of it, but what the hell, thank you anyway for all your courtesy and I hope few people will see it with such jaded eyes as I do, tho I guess it's best the poems have a truthful fate than an over-sympathetic one. I wonder if we will actually sell the thousand copies.

Did Villiers send back the spare and extra MSS? hold on to them for me please—the poem's not printed. The choice is fine, tho since the "Dream Record" poem is, I think of early poems, the best, I wish it were there too. ★★★

Editor's Note: Ferlinghetti had decided to leave out "Dream Record," but later included it in Ginsberg's *Reality Sandwiches*.

"Transcription of Organ Music" I still like, I'm not sorry. It's not revised so it's not bad "Art" like the rest of the writing. It's ineptness is its own and nature's not mine.

Keep hold of my copies—the fifty—till I return but out of them hand out free copies to
Peter Orlovsky—2 (or as many as he wishes), Robert LaVigne, Phil Whalen, Sheila Williams Boucher, John Ryan, Mike McClure, Neal Cassady, Kenneth Rexroth ★★★.

September 1956. Gregory Corso [San Francisco] to Allen Ginsberg

Read HOWL and said Allen is Allen still and better. America cry was embarrassing . . . but so was Novalis and Wackenroder. And Kliest had the Amazon eat her lover raw right on stage . . . and He, Kliest, double-suicided with Eva Schmidt. The German poets are the end.

Read HOWL and thought why when Rimbaud put us all down by 19ing himself. Read HOWL and said why when Chatterton rat-poisoned us by 17ing himself. You are old. I am old. Our cries sound more like cracked wheezes than GRRRRRRRRRRRRRS. And LOVE. We are too old to say what love is. Easily enough we can call it Zen Polemic Boycock . . . ★★★

Read HOWL and liked it because it's almost like my WAY OUT. Two old men who cupped their farts in an organ. E. Power Briggs plays Bach's Tocata in Fugue. ★★★

goodbye, Gregory Corso

Editor's Note: The following is Corso's review of *Howl.*

"Howl" is the howl of the generation, the howl of black jackets, of James Dean, of hip beat angels, of mad saints, of cool Zen, the howl of the Withdrawn, of the crazy Sax-man, of the endless Vision whose visionary is Allen Ginsberg, young sensitive timid mad beautiful poet howler of Kerouac's Beat Generation.

"Howl" is essentially a poem to be read aloud, but only by the Howler . . . any other Howler would screw it up, thus for those who are unable to hear Ginsberg read his "Howl" will have to settle for its visuality. And visuality it has, that is, if you're hip enough to visualize it. If you're a drag go read Wilbur or something.

But for the hipsters, the angels, the Rimbauds, etc. etc., I, and all the Universe, recommend HOWL.

Technical notes: Style, romantic, after a long dry classical necessary spell of Eliot, Pound, Williams. Tradition, Christopher Smart, Lorca, Apollinaire, Crane, Whitman. Rhetoric: Prosaic, rising into elliptical messianic imagery. Line: Long, a development out of short-line W.C. Williams practice to accommodate sudden burst of exclamatory energy. Structure: Part I, Random, catalogue of spiritual excesses of legendary anonymous personal heroes, variations on a fixed base, "Who" (did this, who did that etc.). Part II, Contrived, variation on a fixed base with strong repetitive rhythm, mainly dactylic, with great syncopated jumps. Part III, Further experiment in variation on fixed base, employing a response to base, beginning with response equal in length to base, each response gradually extended longer and longer ending in outsize fantastic streaks of thought—still held down to base by elastic of breath.

Editor's Note: By the publication date in early November, Ginsberg had found several typos and changes he wanted to make in the next printing. He began a lifelong habit of keeping a list of corrections and changes to each of his books.

Early November 1956. Allen Ginsberg [San Francisco] to Lawrence Ferlinghetti [San Francisco]

Larry,

Re Changes in *Howl*: they are indicated in this copy of the book.
Explained in book on pages

12 "A. ." not ". . ."
12 "F. . . ." not ". . . . ."
15 ★★★★★ not . . . . .
17 "!" not "."
18 "!" not " " (blank)
20 shock not shocks
28 clanking Joes not clanking, Joes
37 ride not take
rear cover: comma not period.

I think that all except p. 37 were their [the printer's] inconsistencies or mistakes, not mine, except as with 12, misunderstandings. If there's any extra bill for these, charge me c/o my brother whose address you have.

Forward mail to Allen Ginsberg, c/o U.S. Embassy, Mexico D.F., please until November 16, 1956. After November 16, 1956, forward mail to my permanent family home address which is Allen Ginsberg, 416 East 34 Street, Paterson, New Jersey. I have taken 29 more copies of *Howl* to Mexico with me so that I now owe you for 75 of them. If you're ordering another printing I guess that's OK. When the printing comes thru, you can send the last 25 copies to my permanent address for me.

I'll send another book whenever ready if you're still game.

Love, Allen

December 7, 1956. Allen Ginsberg [Paterson] to Lawrence Ferlinghetti [San Francisco]

Dear Larry:

★★★ Well anyway, this letter from Laughlin.[18] Open all letters you think necessary, personal or not, I don't care. I hope to give him something new, rather than reprint "Howl." So the reprint of 1500 *Howls* is safe. Grove Press has an *Evergreen Review* upcoming and they asked for reprint of "Howl" too, but I'll give them other material.[19] Maybe later on if there's still demand, in a year or so, I don't know. Why [reprint] 1500 copies?? Can you sell them? There are a number in the 8th St. Bookshop, buried under Rexroth's title, but nobody I know in the Village has seen or bought it. So I don't imagine you'll dispose of many in the Village. Need some kind of advertising or distribution but that's out of the question.

Send me please the remaining 25 copies (as per 1000 reprint) due me, I can use them here now. I keep giving them away. If any more are due me since the reprint is 1500 send them too, to bring to Europe. Or do you have any now, and are you waiting for reprint to arrive? If have few send me 5 at least if you have them. ★★★

Allen

---

[18] James Laughlin, the publisher of New Directions, had asked Ginsberg for a poem to print in his *New Directions in Prose and Poetry* series. He included Ginsberg's "Sunflower Sutra" and "Psalm III" in issue no. 16.

[19] Grove persisted and Ginsberg allowed them to reprint "Howl" in *Evergreen Review* (May-June 1957), the special San Francisco Renaissance issue.

The room at 1010 Montgomery Street in which Allen Ginsberg wrote the first draft of "Howl," in August 1955. © Allen Ginsberg Trust

Allen Ginsberg in Merchant Marine uniform, Lafladio Orlovsky (seated), and Peter
Orlovsky, in front of Peter's apartment at 5 Turner Terrace on Potrero Hill, 1956.
© Allen Ginsberg Trust

December 20, 1956. Allen Ginsberg [Paterson] to Lawrence Ferlinghetti [San Francisco]

Dear Larry:

★★★Went to *NY Times* and bearded them for a review, got interviewed by Harvey Breit, and will, I think, get *Howl* reviewed there.[20] Few stores carry City Lights, generally unobtainable unless you know where, but one review in *Times* or *Tribune* or *Saturday Review* could break the ice maybe. ★★★

As ever, Allen

January 15, 1957. Allen Ginsberg [Paterson, NJ] to Lawrence Ferlinghetti [San Francisco]

Dear Larry:

Jan 9 letter received, as well as clipping from *Chronicle*.[21] I was going to write [Norman K.] Dorn the reviewer a letter but I tried several each a different tone and they all sounded goofy so I gave up. If you see him ever say we collectively rarely have lice, and I hope he drops dead of clap. No, wasn't really discouraged, just realized what a weird place NY book reviewing works like. ★★★

Listen, great tragedy. My friend Lucien Carr objects violently to using his name in dedication.[22] His reasons are varied and personal and real enough for him—I had never asked his OK, and he has reasons why not. What can be done about omitting that line in the dedication in the second printing? Is it too late? for immediate action—I'd write Villiers but don't know.

It's my fuck up, but I have to straighten it out. Therefore if the whole thing is printed and bound already, have it done all over again and bill me for the second printing. It's about $100 more or less? Write them immediately and find out how far they've gone and to suspend operations, and what will it cost to eliminate the line, in toto. I dunno. Anyway I am bound by honor to DO something about it no matter how much it fucks everything up. So please write them and tell them send me carbon of answer, so can send you immediate cash or advice whatever necessary. I

---

[20] Harvey Breit did not review *Howl* but he did mention Ginsberg in one article about the new literature in the *New York Times Book Review* (January 20, 1957).

[21] Norman K. Dorn's review appeared in the January 6, 1957 issue of the *San Francisco Chronicle*.

[22] Originally *Howl and Other Poems* was dedicated to Jack Kerouac, William Burroughs, Neal Cassady and Lucien Carr.

know this sounds crazy and probably it is but I have to. Please don't flip. I got the money so it won't screw you up. ***

As ever, Allen.

February 5, 1957. Lawrence Ferlinghetti [San Francisco] to Allen Ginsberg [New York]

Dear Allen,

HOWL will be delayed an extra two weeks due to deletion of Lucien Carr, and I have been completely out of it for almost a month. However, it should be here in bulk by February 20 at the latest. I caught them in the last stage — the book had already been folded and gathered, but not stitched. Therefore, one section could still be taken out, reprinted, and regathered etc. The total extra cost comes to $25, which I could use as soon as possible, to pay the bill. I'll send you the 5 copies you asked for, as soon as the shipment arrives. I have backorders from all over the country now — including big orders for Paper Editions. [Ted] Wilentz at the Eighth Street Bookshop in NY has ordered 100 copies. I sent him the last five I had. Gotham Book Mart has also put in a big standing order, and I sent them five of yours as a stop-gap. You will note that the second edition carries note that the book is distributed nationally to bookstores by the Paper Editions Corp. in NY and Redwood City, etc. I had even received advance airmail copy of your second edition (without Carr deletion)

We all got photographed for *LIFE* Sunday night at a mass reading at Kenneth's [Rexroth]. I am sick of all these con operations, and I hope every photog in the country crawls in a hole somewhere and drops dead. It all has nothing to do with poetry. I am not sending my poetry anywhere unsolicited, and frankly I don't give a good shit if they come and get it or not. I wasted enough post on *Partisan* [*Review*] 20 years ago. However, as for your book, I will continue to push and will send copy to Lisa Dyer at *Hudson Review* as soon as I get a copy to send. *POETRY* writes me that they will include it in a review early this summer, by [Frederick] Eckman. ***

Best, regards, etc, Larry

Mid-February, 1957. Allen Ginsberg [Paterson] to Lawrence Ferlinghetti [San Francisco]

Dear Larry:

*** Thank God you caught *Howl*, now the gods are appeased, send me the bill whatever it may be. Sorry the hassle and the delay and thanks for being so good about it.

Re, Grove. Don Allen says he would like to reprint "Howl" poem complete in *Evergreen Review*. I told him I had promised you no. He said he'd write you. I have various thoughts, but I leave it completely up to you, do whatever you think best for sale of City Lights edition and cause of Frisco publishing. It may be you can sell your edition enough before *Evergreen* comes out; it may be that reprint in *Evergreen* will help sell complete book; or it may be the converse that reprint will kill sales of *Howl* pocket book. Figure it out and make decision yourself. I'm not too personally eager yet to reprint like in *Evergreen*, since if I wait maybe someday I can sell it to *New World Writing* for some loot when I'm starving in Europe. On the other hand, Don Allen has been very hep with Kerouac, myself, Snyder, Whalen and the West Coast, and cooperated like a dream, liking everything and digging everybody — so I wish him well with *Evergreen* project and would like on principle to cooperate with his project. If you say yes to him it's OK by me; if you say no, equally OK. I told you originally I wouldn't fuck up your publishing with reprinting, so that is why I refuse to make decision now one way or the other and leave it in your hands. ★★★

Grove also thinking of record business, I'm supposed to see them Monday for arrangements for them to underwrite recording of "Howl." I already had arranged for kicks to make a tape with friends at Esoteric [Records]. I'll ask [Barney] Rosset at Grove to arrange tie-up of some kinds with City Lights, if they go thru with it.

Saw Bogan at *New Yorker*, she'll review *Howl* and West Coast.[23] ★★★

As ever, Allen

Editor's Note: Ginsberg wrote to Ferlinghetti asking what his policy was on foreign rights. He planned to visit Burroughs in Tangiers and then stay on in Europe for an extended visit; and he hoped to get some European publishers to translate *Howl* while he was there. He found some interest in reprinting "Howl" in magazines and anthologies in both the U.S. and Europe, and he wondered what percentage City Lights would expect from those, since there had been no formal contract.

---

[23] *New Yorker* never reviewed *Howl*. Their first mention of Ginsberg was in 1961 when they published an Ogden Nash poem called "Eh?"

February 1957. Lawrence Ferlinghetti [San Francisco] to Allen Ginsberg [New York]

Dear Allen,

The hell with contracts—we will just tell them you have standing agreement with me and you can give me anything you feel like giving me on reprints whenever you get back to States and sit in Poetry Chairs in hinterland CCNYs and are rich and famous and fat and fucking your admirers and getting reprinted in all of seldenrod-man's[24] anthologies, until then, natch, the loot shud be yours since as you say I am getting famous as your publisher anyway. Do you want more *HOWLs* and other PP [Pocket Poets] sent now (which ones?) and charged against you? How many? ★★★ Max Weiss at Fantasy here is already to do *HOWL* recording and knows lots of recording facilities in Paris and is going to write you or get me addresses and instructions for you very soon. Let him arrange it. He is great and honest. He will probably want contract and will send. (Re contracts, you see whut happens after one week in NY—I am talking just like all the other literary detectives there before I leave—contractsconttractscontracts . . . well fuckem and fuck the partisanreview whom I've never sent anything to and we'll make it here in SF . . . I am going into publishing prose books and got printers lined up in east and have some really great ideas on reprints of long-out-of-print authors and new authors etc.) Sending copy to Bremser in reformatory,[25] as you request. WILL SOON SEND addition on *HOWL* sales to-date. OK? G'bye.

Larry

March 3, 1957. Allen Ginsberg [Paterson] to Lawrence Ferlinghetti [San Francisco]

Dear Larry:

Have investigated but as far as I know, the book can't be copyrighted here because printed in England.[26] If you know a way it can be, please do so in my name and send me bill for what it costs.

The best way, lacking possibility of US copyright, is to copyright it in England. For that, Villiers would have to put I believe 6 copies on sale in

---

[24] Selden Rodman was the editor of several poetry anthologies.

[25] Ginsberg had met poet Ray Bremser earlier in New York City. Bremser was now back in jail in New Jersey.

[26] Since the book had been printed in England, the copyright registration presented a problem. Ginsberg had his brother, Eugene, look into their various legal options.

England, and send it to certain prescribed British Libraries. If this is the best way, could you write and ask them to do that in my name and send me the bill?

If necessary, can copyright it in your name or City Lights or whoever, with the understanding that it's my copyright to use as I wish and get whatever loot I can.

Though actually I guess no copyright is necessary and it's all just a bunch of bureaucratic papers so no point actually in doing anything, nobody has anything to steal except in paranoiac future lands.

If it seems like too much trouble don't bother doing anything but if you know a simple way, please try it. ★★★

I gave *Hudson* [*Review*] a copy of my book so forget them. Also gave them a pack of poems by Gregory and Whalen, and McClure. As far as I know, there should be review there, as well as *Partisan* this summer, *New Yorker, Poetry* you mentioned, and photos also in *Esquire* (me and Gregory and man from Grove).

When you get copies, send five to my father, at above address and 10 to me in Tangiers. Allen Ginsberg c/o U.S. Embassy, Tangier, Morocco. Also one each to the following, free. Lucien Carr, Bert Hoeniger, Max Frohman, John Ashbery, Kenneth Koch, John Ciardi.

Send me bill for all of these, as I've now gotten above my author's quota—unless you can afford to give them away free. I haven't got too much money. But send bill to me if appropriate. ★★★

I wrote awhile back that Don Allen at Grove wants to reprint "Howl" in *Evergreen Review*, but I told him to consult you and take your decision. Let me know what you think, so I can give him something else if not. My guess is it wouldn't hinder sale of the book, but I don't know, so as I said I won't intrude on your business. ★★★

As ever, Allen

April 3, 1957. Allen Ginsberg [Tangiers, Morocco] to Lawrence Ferlinghetti [San Francisco]

Dear Larry:

Received your letter of March 27 and was surprised by news of Customs seizure.[27] As to the $25 I owe you, I had told my brother to send

---

[27] On March 25, 1957, the U.S. Department of Customs seized part of the shipment of the new printing of *Howl and Other Poems* as it came into the country from Ferlinghetti's British printer, Villiers. They found the contents of the book obscene.

it before I left the States and presumed that he had. I'll write him today to check on it and I guess you'll get it in a week. You might check if he hasn't sent it to you—a check from Eugene Brooks. Maybe he sent it without saying it was connected to Ginsberg. Offhand I don't know what to say about MacPhee.[28] I don't know what the laws are and what rights I got. Is it possible to get them in at New York P.O. and have them shipped on to you under other label or address? Transshipped from NY that is? Is it also possible to have any copies sent to me here from England? I suppose the publicity will be good I suppose. I have been here with Jack [Kerouac], Peter [Orlovsky] and Bill Burroughs all hung-up on private life and Bill's mad personality and writings and on digging the Arab quarter and taking majoun (hashish candy) and opium and drinking hot sweet delicious mint tea in Rembrandt dark cafes and long walks in lucid Mediterranean coast green grassy brilliant light North Africa that I haven't written any letters (this is the second in 2 weeks) or thought much about anything. I'll write to Grove to Don Allen and let him know, and he'll tell the lady from Time-Life. If you can mimeograph a letter and get some kind of statement from WC Williams, [Louise] Bogan, [Richard] Eberhart and send it around to magazines might get some publicity that way. Also let Harvey Breit at *NY Times* know for sure definitely—he'd probably run a story maybe. My brother is a lawyer and has recently done some research on the subject, I'll write him to get in touch with you and provide any legal aid—if any is useful from him in New York. I guess this puts you up shits creek financially. I didn't think it would really happen. I didn't know it was costing you 200$ for reprint, I thought it was $80.00 each extra thousand. Sorry I am not there, we might talk and figure up some way for a U.S. edition, I guess that would be expensive tho. Be sure let the *Life* people in SF know about situation, they might include it in story. The woman in NY is Rosalind Constable c/o Time-Life, Rockefeller Center. She is very simpatico and would immediately call it to attention of Peter Bunzell who is (I heard) writing up the story for *Life* in NY. Send story too to *Village Voice*, they've been digging the scene. By the way I heard there was a lukewarm review in *Partisan Review*,[29] could you send it to me? Might let them know, too, as they took a poem of mine for later. I guess the best way publicity wise is prepare some sort of outraged and idiotic but dignified statement, quoting the Customs man, and Eberhart's article and Williams,

---

[28] Chester MacPhee was the U.S. Customs Collector in San Francisco.

[29] John Hollander's review appeared in *Partisan Review*, vol. 24, no. 2 (Spring 1957).

and *Nation* review, mimeograph it up and send it out as a sort of manifesto publishable by magazines and/or news release. Send one to Lu Carr at United Press, News Bldg., 42 Street NYC too. If this is worthwhile. Also write, maybe, [Randall] Jarrell, at Library of Congress and see if you can get his official intercession. I imagine these Customs people have to obey orders of their superiors; and that superiors in Wash. D.C. might be informed and requested to intercede by some official in Lib. of Cong. Maybe I'll write my congressmen—is there a friendly congressman in SF? This might be more rapid than a lawsuit. Copyright it under City Lights name—only thing is, if you ever make your money back and make some profit from all your trouble, and we go into a 4th or 17th edition, we divvy the loot. I don't think Grove book will knock out sales. They'll probably carry note about the full book. Send me clippings of reviews—I haven't got anything besides the *Nation*, if anything comes through; also any further news of The Cellar etc. sounds charming.[30] Everybody must be having a ball. ★★★ I must say am more depressed than pleased, [more] disgusted than pleased, about Customs shot, amusing as it is—the world is such a bottomless hole of boredom and poverty and paranoiac politics and diseased rags here *Howl* seems like a drop in the bucket-void and literary furor illusory—seems like its happening in otherland—outside me, nothing to do with me or anything. ★★★ I'll write Señor MacPhee myself, ask him to let my copies go, big serious poignant sad letter.

Write me and I'll answer, let me know how things go, if there's anything you want me to do let me know and send along any clippings if you can. These aerogrammes are only 10¢ postage if there are no enclosures.

Thank Kenneth [Rexroth] for efforts and say I hope he enjoys the scene—it is pretty funny, almost a set-up, I imagine they can't bug us forever, and will have to give in. Let me know what the law is. ★★★

As ever, Allen Grebsnig

April 18, 1957. Allen Ginsberg [Tangiers] to Don Allen [New York]

Dear Don:

★★★ I don't know if you've heard about the Customs problem, but I got a letter from Ferlinghetti 2 weeks ago saying 500 copies of 2nd printing of my book sent to him from Villiers in England were seized by customs inspector at SF Post Office. Says he's reprinting 2500 copies photo-offset

---

[30] Ferlinghetti joined Kenneth Rexroth in a series of readings with jazz accompaniment at The Cellar, a popular North Beach night club.

in US and ACLU is taking court action — they had been consulted before he published book and had ok'd the mss. for action if it did get stopped. I find it hard to believe this unlikely eventuality actually has happened. But so much the better all the way around I guess. Please let Rosalind Constable know about this if she doesn't already since if there's time and they are actually doing the *Life* article it might give it some spicy news value, and get some good publicity for the book, or your reprint.[31] ★★★

Later, Allen

Late April 1957. Allen Ginsberg [Tangiers] to Robert LaVigne

Dear Bob:

★★★ *Howl* was seized by customs, second edition coming over from England. So much court action with Civil Liberties Union in SF, which I guess will be successful; and City Lights made phototype or whatever of 2500 more, selling well he says. I haven't and won't see any loot from that, but I ran out of money here and got $200 grant from Amer. Academy of Arts and Letters thru [William Carlos] Williams, a grant. ★★★

Love. As ever, Allen

May 6, 1957. Gregory Corso [Barcelona] to Allen Ginsberg

Dear Allen —

★★★ Ferl sent me Ban of *HOWL* — how absurd of that man to seize the books — how many children will read *HOWL*? He is afraid of what it might do to children — but children read nothing! Children know nothing — children are nothing! Was any other POET banned from American kids before, but the poet of Batman, The Human Torch, The Joker and The Penguin? ★★★

Love. Gregory

May 10, 1957. Allen Ginsberg [Tangiers] to Lawrence Ferlinghetti [San Francisco]

Dear Larry:

★★★ Please tell Villiers send me 25 copies here care of US Embassy. I don't know what I'll do with them here tho. Please send 25 copies to my father of the new American edition,[32] and send me one or two here, also.

---

[31] *Evergreen Review,* no. 2.

[32] Ferlinghetti proceeded with his plan to print future copies of *Howl* in the U.S. as a photo-offset edition and thus circumvent any interference from U.S. Customs agents.

I hope to God that new edition has Lucien Carr's name off it. Whalen wrote you hocked your back teeth to put it out, I hope you don't lose out on it—tho he said it was selling well SF and NY. Thanks for so rapid action, I guess it will be alright and Grove won't do no harm, especially if Customs story makes *Life*. Anyway what's new? How's ACLU doing? Have you got your money back on photocopy, and what cost was it?

Will there be any difficulty about copyrights if *Evergreen* [*Review*] reprints the poem "Howl?" You took *ad interim*[33] copyright on book? Can Grove take US copyright out for me in my name for the separate poem if they print it in states? They haven't written or asked me, and I wouldn't have thought of it but Whalen wrote and said there was some difficulty or decision to make. Is there any, or what's the situation? ★★★ If you need me I'm reachable here in case it's anything I'm supposed to decide. ★★★

As ever, Allen

Send me sample of new edition. Oh, also send copies to people I wrote you to, please and add: Charles Reznikoff. *Commentary* magazine wrote me they'd do review and maybe an article. Send a pile of books for them to review.

May 31, 1957. Allen Ginsberg [Tangiers] to Lawrence Ferlinghetti [San Francisco]

Dear Larry:

Received photocopy of *Howl* here two days ago—mailed a month earlier, that's why I never wrote you about it, I only just got it. It looks fine, all the changes seem to be there and no screw-up on Lucien Carr deletion, what a sigh of relief I breathed over that. But changes in text are right as I indicated, thanks. Looks like a fine job of printing too, not suffer much from photo process at all. How are they selling now? Can you unload them? Seems there are now 5000 in print in all 3 editions, that's a remarkable lot. I hope the *Evergreen* "Howl" doesn't screw things up— I thought when I wrote you it might even help, but I don't know. What does it seem like from SF? I hear *Evergreen* will copyright their magazine as a unit; and then turn copyright of "Howl" over to me by letter. Does that work in alright with *ad interim* arrangements you made alright? ★★★ Are you still in hock from the photocopy or have sales made up at all yet? I ran out of loot but WCW came to rescue with 200 from Academy Arts

---

[33] An *ad interim* copyright was a special short-term copyright that applied to certain books and periodicals that were first manufactured and published outside the U.S.

and Letters. That should get me to Paris or Venice, wherever it be. No plans yet. Mail for me will be forwarded. Did you write Villiers to send me some copies? How are court proceedings proceeding? And was there any reaction to your mimeographed bulletin? I haven't seen anything in the *Times*, but I don't see *Times* regularly. Is anything going to happen with *Life* after all the fuss. May seems past and no story. ★★★

Love, as ever, Allen

Larry—also—is there anything I can or should do re court scene? I've been too occupied here to be in better touch. ★★★ I wrote Rosset asking what's happening with his record. Who's supposed to be on? Too many and the boat will sink. ★★★

P.S. Received also today your article in *SF Chron*. Just got it before seeing this. No, not too stuffy and thanks for all the kind words, and thank also Duncan and Witt D. [Ruth Witt-Diamant] for their kindness. Looks like a good move, if *Poetry* will carry a defense as you write and the *Nation*. Can you send me the *Poetry* and *Partisan* articles when they come? Hollander's particularly I'd like to see—your reference made me wonder. Who else did you hear from? Sure got lots of space—looks like things roll easier now than when we first started—glad also you quoted some of actual poem in your piece. Is there anyplace or anything you'd like me to write that would be useful? I've apparently been singularly removed and silent in all this, but if all these others can put their 2 cents in maybe I should too, some kind of mad blab full of obscene vitriol. ★★★ If you have an extra copy of your article, can you send one to my papa Louis? OK, later. Write, as I say mail will be forwarded.

Editor's Note: Ferlinghetti was correct about printing the books in the U.S., for this took them out of the jurisdiction of the Customs censors. That wasn't the end of the matter, however, for on the evening of June 3, 1957, two plainclothes policemen from the City's Juvenile Department came to the store and purchased copies of *Howl And Other Poems* and a little magazine, *The Miscellaneous Man*, from Shig Murao, the store manager. They returned later to arrest Shig and swear out a warrant for the arrest of Ferlinghetti on charges of selling and publishing obscene material. Ferlinghetti turned himself in and then both men were released pending trial.

Dear Larry:

Received your June 4 letter today, with clipping. I guess this is more serious than the customs seizure since you can lose real money on this deal if they find you guilty.[34] What does it look like? I guess with ACLU should be possible to beat—except this is local law—does that give police complete discretion to decide what's obscene? If so that may make it difficult.

Presumably a matter of local politics—therefore can anything be done to call off police through politicians at City Hall thru State College thru Poetry Center thru [Ruth] Witt Diamant? [35] If it is a matter of purely interpretive local law and juvenile bureau, perhaps somebody at Berkeley and State Coll. know *somebody* at City Hall that can call a halt. But arrest and formal charges have been filed already, so I guess open showdown is inevitable.

I remember your speaking of troubles with local police on Henry Miller—and not being able to beat the cops on that—is it possible also in this case? It was all funny before but could be very difficult, for you, you actually stand to risk so much, money. In any case if you get fined I'll try to help raise loot to pay it—you've put yourself out financially very far already.

Had awful fantasy of being in SF and putting on big reading sponsored by State College at museum and inviting cops and ending in big riot scene. I wish I were there; there could really, we could really have a ball, and win out in the end inevitably.

There seems to be good ground for expecting to win out—but I haven't seen the *Miscellaneous Man*[36]—if you can convince them my book is "Art" will you get hooked on *M.M.*? I wonder if that will prove a stumbling block—you didn't seem to think much of the *MM* story when you mentioned it sometime back. Does it make things harder or more confused with two separate issues to deal with?

---

[34] In the case of the customs seizure, City Lights could have lost all the books impounded, but in this case a heavy fine and/or prison time was a possibility.

[35] Ruth Witt-Diamant was the director of the San Francisco Poetry Center at San Francisco State College.

[36] Charges related to *The Miscellaneous Man,* which was also purchased by the police, were dropped later.

Who or what is behind all this attention? It appears like Customs were burned up when they had to let go and someone must have called juvenile police from customs, and asked them to take up and carry the ball from there.

Well these are just vague ramblings, I don't know the situation, you must have chewed it all over already.

One thing occurs to me—re *Evergreen Review*. They're carrying "Howl" complete and are due out soon if not now. Will they get carried in SF bookstores? Will you be able to carry them (Are you still selling *Howl* from the store)? And if Grove can't distribute *Evergreen* in SF for their special SF issue, Grove will be in a hell of a spot and the police are likely to have the whole poetry population of SF personally with all their mothers and aunts up in outraged arms. Well I guess the more the merrier. Really it's a ridiculous mess. Have you got in touch with Grove? Or maybe they can just slip thru unnoticed and not ask for trouble. Too bad Gregory Corso is not there to make an anonymous phone call to the juvenile authorities tipping them off that Paul Elder[37] is carrying same obscenity in *Evergreen*—infiltrating thru every channel—by the way is Elder selling *Howl* or any other store in town—and what are they doing about it—pulling their necks back in or continuing to sell? I'm really sorry I'm not there to take part in this latest development. I never thought I'd want to read "Howl" again but it would be a pleasure under these circumstances. It might give it a reality as "social protest" I always feared was lacking without armed bands of outraged Gestapo. Real solid prophetic lines about being dragged off the stage waving genitals and mss., biting detectives in the neck, etc. . . . I wonder by the way if the communist propaganda in America will further confuse the issue, the police, the judges and even ACLU. I really had some such situation as this in mind when I put them in, sort of deliberately saying I am a communist to see what would happen . . . burning bridges (not Harry [Bridges]) you might say. Well if they do send you to jail I'll make haste to return to SF and wage war in person, join you in next cell. Poor Shig, after his motorcycle bust up[38] to get busted on this kind of bum rap . . . give him my thanks and apologies . . . I hope it was not grim. Strange to see his name in the paper.

I don't know what to suggest, I guess you already got testimonials from WCW and *Poetry*, etc., judging from the article you sent me. Are local

---

[37] Paul Elder, a San Francisco book dealer.
[38] Shig Murao had been involved in a motorcycle accident which left him with a limp for the rest of his life.

newspapers being sympathetic? I have a friend on the *Oakland Tribune*, named Jim Fitzpatrick, who is quite literate . . . might try calling him for some kind of local pressure publicity—give him a statement or something. Did Harvey Breit carry anything on the original customs seizure? He ought to be informed about this, I guess he'd write something and you might get in further angles there about what is Grove *Evergreen* going to do—and the fact that you've put out the Levertov and Ponsot[39] and are expecting Gregory[40] next. As far as testimonials and official types, I imagine Jarrell might be rung in and make himself useful. He don't approve of the dirty words in my book so I understand, but he is Poetry Consultant at Library Congress and gets paid for it and he has visited your store and he did dig it as cultural center and he is interested in Gregory publication, so he should be conscience bound to make some kind of official Federal statement for you to use in court. With testimony from someone with his *official* title and ACLU backing you would have strong case, even if the judge had never heard of WCW Patchen Jarrell or Rexroth or anyone since Ambrose Bierce. I'll write him; it might be good for you to get in touch with him and tell him what you need. Has *Village Voice*, who knew me and Greg in NY, followed the case?

Who else—man I got the greatest—get Josephine Miles—no one can suspect her of any but most respectable judgment—to court in person— star witness. Well I'm rambling.

I haven't received 25 copies yet, nor the Ponsot and Levertov (5 and 6), and did get the single copy of photo offset edition. Yes it looks excellent, as I wrote last note—I didn't think it could be done so neatly. What did it cost? Is that cheaper than Villiers reprint? You now have 5000 copies— 2500 distributed—will you be able to unload the rest or is it going to be a white elephant? Very relieved you caught Lucien as per request.

Would like to see the Hollander review in *Partisan*. Any other reviews I don't know of, of interest? ★★★

Regards and thanks. Hope all works out well—keep in touch, mail will be forwarded wherever I am—write me and I'll pick up letter at American Express Madrid, in 2 weeks. If there's anything I can do tell me. What does Kenneth R. say? Give him regards, I still have to write and will. Hello to jailbird Shig.

As ever, Allen

---

[39] City Lights also published Denise Levertov's *Here and Now* and Marie Ponsot's *True Minds* in 1957 as part of the same Pocket Poets series.

[40] Gregory Corso's *Gasoline*.

P.S. What do you hear about that *Life* story? Is that going to happen and how much of this in? Rosalind Constable c/o Time Life Rockefeller Center is interested in developments. Send her review copies of all your books as you issue them—she cares.

P.S. Was interviewed here sometime back by *Variety* correspondent from Madrid—he said they were always interested in civil liberties and censorship stories—have you tried them for publicity?

July 10, 1957. Allen Ginsberg [Venice, Italy] to Lawrence Ferlinghetti [San Francisco]

Dear Larry:

Received copies of Ponsot and Levertov today—took that long to get forwarded and will read them again. Still like Levertov tho she seems a little indecisive, but individual poems are all sharp and hep. Ponsot I hardly read well, when I saw the mss. but it seems better now and tougher. Will they be reviewed?

Haven't heard from you since your letter describing arrest—that's over a month ago—have you been in jail? Am eager to hear what's happened. Please write fast aerogram and say what's up—and I read of recent adverse-type supreme court decisions about obscene. I wrote Jarrell asking him give you official help but no reply has he got in touch with you? What's happening?

Saw Stock's broadside[41] and some pictures in *Esquire*[42] of NY. I gave them a pitch about City Lights but they didn't use it, being hung up on NY social life. Is there anything to come from *Life*?[43]

★★★ Venice is beautiful; big heat wave all last first week; now great rain. Living with friend Ansen who has an apartment, and he threw a party when we came and invited Peggy Guggenheim and Peter and I talked about T and masturbation and wiped our brows with big sweaty towel so she rushed away angry and didn't invite us to her big surrealist party that weekend. So I'm left lone in Venice to cook food and read about Fra Angelico and dig the great cathedral and row around in gondolas alas. ★★★ Meanwhile I'm set here awhile, so write me. I have no copies of my book—you sent them, or asked Villiers to? I haven't received them in any case.

---

[41] Robert Stock, "Letter From San Francisco." *Poetry Broadsides*, vol. 1, no. 2 (June 1957) p. 3+.

[42] Burt Glinn, "New York's Spreading Upper Bohemia." *Esquire*, vol. 48, no. 1 (July 1957) pp. 46-52.

[43] Eventually *Life* ran an article, "Big Day For Bards At Bay," in the September 9, 1957 issue.

*** How are sales now, and how is *Evergreen* doing? Out yet? Do you ever see Jack Kerouac?

Waiting to hear—tho I may get a letter from you before this reached you—if so will reply immediate.

As ever, Allen

Late July 1957. Gregory Corso [Paris] to Lawrence Ferlinghetti [San Francisco]

Dear Ferl—

Allen tells me you have been arrested. Are you in jail? If so, say nothing until you see a lawyer. Don't incriminate yourself. You must be careful because I once knew a man who was sentenced to 30 years for selling children dirty books with pictures—thank God you didn't have pictures in your book. I guess you must feel terrible—now all your neighbors will whisper, "There goes Ferlinghetti, he sells dirty postcards." Actually for a man in your position the only honorable thing to do would be to take to the knife—alas, suicide might erase the shame. You know, of course, that the writer of the book is immune to shame—that only the peddler of said book is mune—and, I must say that the most shameful person or persons involved are those that condone—such as Mr. Rexroth, and Miss Diamatt—Too bad that such a nice guy like you got mixed up with such a lot. ***

Seriously, I think that you are perhaps the only great publisher in America and will have to suffer for it. ***

Love to both you & your wife, Gregory

July 26, 1957. Allen Ginsberg [Venice] to Louis Ginsberg [Paterson]

Dear Lou:

Received your 2 last letters, including the page from *Poetry* magazine. I guess the seizure works out fine as publicity; except that I am afraid of what will happen in court—trial set for August 6—maybe City Lights lose, be out dough, & screw up the whole publishing deal. Jarrell been no help according to Ferlinghetti who's written him several times asking for official Library of Congress statement but no answer. ***

Love, Allen

August 21, 1957. Allen Ginsberg [Venice] to Lawrence Ferlinghetti [San Francisco]

Dear Larry:

Not heard from you since July 17 letter—thought trial was due sometime round Aug. 8 and so have been waiting on edge going down to American Express daily since the 13th hoping for news. I guess you must be pretty busy what with work at store and frazzle of law, but wish you'd let me know what's up as soon as you are able. I can't wait. Someone wrote me you had an extra good lawyer volunteer but beyond that haven't heard a thing.

Not yet received any copies of book from Villiers. I think I could sell some in Venice and Milan. How are sales? *Evergreen* cutting in or not?

Been here all along except for wild trip with Orlovsky through Florence and Rome and we ran out of money and went to Assisi and were broke and happy and argued with monks and slept out at night, warm, on the lawn in front of their monastery and acted like wild Franciscans and begged food and talked about poetry and gave them a copy of *Evergreen Review*. Then hitched back to Venice and sneaked on trains. While in Rome I ran into Louis Simpson, a poet, who said he'd written a parody of my style which was upcoming in *Hudson*. I told him book was banned and he said he felt like shit adding trouble and I rather agreed, tho I like his poetry.

Back here a week, and heard from *Time* correspondent in Rome, they are doing, he said, a story on SF literature in *Time*, wanted to come up here and interview me and was looking for Kerouac who's in Florida. I made arrangement with him to come down to Rome (by air) and stay a few days for the interview at *Time's* expense. He didn't want to leave office there and was relieved at my suggestion. They gave me $17.50 a day for 2 days expenses. I'm broke and can live on about 2 bucks daily comfortably so it's a great deal—expect to spend maybe 2 weeks screwing around and go down to Naples and really see some more Italy—at Naples will see if I can get job shipping. ★★★

Writing a good deal of prose and some fragmentary poetry but nothing good. Vatican has fig leaves on all the statues—I almost flipped there it is maddening after all the beautiful nakedness of *David* in Florence. Also been digging a lot of Giotto in Assisi and Padua and Fra Angelico in Florence and got high in the Forum and in the Vatican and have been having a fine time. I eat well because have kitchen and cook all meals in and so spend very little time in any kind of society except household or Ansen's guests. But been seeing a lot of different kinds of people. But for Christ's sake write me what's happening with the law, the trial, etc. Is there anything I should do? Orlovsky sends regards. Girl I knew Elise Cowen, from NY now in SF living at 1010 Montgomery—do you ever see her? Very interesting girl. I hear Ron Loewinsohn[44] got hitched, congratulate him if you see him and usual regards to Du Peru[45] if he's around. As I said, have received nothing yet from Villiers and will be leaving here in 3 weeks.

As ever, Allen

September 3, 1957. Allen Ginsberg [Venice] to Lawrence Ferlinghetti [San Francisco]

Dear Larry:

Received your two letters of Aug. 28 and 29. Thanks for the check. I have been very broke—this gets me to Paris. Glad you are able to afford it. I had thought earlier you would use any profits to plough back into the City Lights series investment so could publish things like Gregory. But I'm too broke to send it back now. Is there any possibility of any further money in several months if you're able to sell out the fourth magical printing? How many you printing by the way? The Time-Life stories should maybe sell more too I guess, if they only mention your address in the story. Well things look fine. I got back here broke from 10 day trip to Naples wondering what next and your check was the answer. Are you out of red really?

Still in Venice, leave in a few days for Vienna to see Breughels and then direct to Paris, so can reach me there—be there by Sept. 15.

God knows where and whether Villiers copies will reach me, since I'm leaving here. I'll write them a note directly saying I'm going to Paris and giving new address. Probably it's too late. I'll be at American Express Paris. I doubt my father received his either. I'll check and let you know.

I've only been here so long because have had place to stay free and refuge and Venice is great. But have been waiting to head for France. No, no Arab boys tho there were plenty; strangely no nooky in Venice either—been very shy and almost subdued—hope Paris can make it.

But still wondering what happened to the trial?? Isn't it over yet?

---

[44] Ron Loewinsohn, poet and author of *Watermelons* published in 1959 with an introduction by Allen Ginsberg.

[45] Peter du Peru, a San Francisco hustler and underworld connection for many of the beat writers.

And glad *Evergreen* didn't cut into sales, I didn't think it would. ★★★

I have started writing a lot and wrote a good new poem. Wieners has one about Seattle which isn't so good, and *Evergreen* has another about Sather Gate which is better. It'll be another half year or year however before I settle down and produce anything good enough for a book. However there's lots of time. I'm feeling fine, got enough loot now for a few more months and am going to Paris.

Please write me what the legal situation is tho up to date. Someone wrote me that Karl Shapiro [is] writing a favorable review for *Prairie Schooner* and there was a strange discussion in *London Times Supplement* Aug. 16 that I saw. Maybe Shapiro be help on trial if it's not too late, and if he isn't the kiss of death.

Carl's [Solomon] letters—what's his address?? I had letter from him or family saying it was OK to use name—god it would be mad if he sued too.

If possible in 4th printing, there's still one typographical problem—which is, that on the dirty words we've replaced by dashes, some of the words have the first letter, and some don't. All should have the first letter, like

who got f. . . in the a. . . instead of total blank.

For that matter, if we win the trial—is it possible to put in the whole words now??? If so that would be worth doing, as far as I'm concerned. I never liked the blanks and think they actually weaken the effect and make it shocking where it should be powerfully hip. We put the blanks in to evade customs and protect Villiers—if we win have we green lite? Or is this just making trouble when we got enough already. The book look less "rebellious" and more poetic without the asterisks, in actual effect. Asterisks look like you're self-conscious and scared to say what you're saying. ★★★

Get more from Corso?? Says he sees Genet and had big argument with him about Gregory painting in oils on some friends apartment walls—so Genet insulted American boors and Gregory called him a frog creep, or some such Gregorian scene.

Glad you wrote, Allen

Saw Caresse Crosby, tell Kenneth [Rexroth]—she spoke of Venice trip with him. Interviewed by *Time*. FBI agent in Rome, came away depressed. Sleeping in hostels and in fields and eating cheap pizzas in Naples and climbed Vesuvius and saw Pompeian pornography in Naples Museum and dug Capri and Ischia and ruins of Cuma (Cumaean Sybil) and also saw the Pope in Rome same day Vatican Square got filled with thousands of people—and before that made it all around Rome and Florence and Assisi. Please think over Kerouac poems and Burroughs prose excerpt possibility.

Do you know anyplace I could stay cheap in Paris?

September 1957. Allen Ginsberg [Italy] to Jack Hirschman [San Francisco]

Dear Jack:

There has been at this point almost embarrassing amount of publicity about "Howl." I [am] afraid the poem almost too slight to support the enormous pile of bullshit piled over it—tho that's probably my own fault. Thanks for your letter. (I mean I have written very little this last year and feel ashamed and self-conscious.)

About Shapiro—dammit I bet you it's the kiss of death. Almost afraid to say things like this now (since you know him). I mean what I wish is that while he were editor of *Poetry* (and rejecting my poems) he had paid more attention to a sort of hep or hip literature that was and still is flourishing almost neglected—and unreviewed by *Poetry* magazine—I'm referring to writings in *Origin, Black Mt. Review*, the unreviewed books of Charles Olson, Robert Creeley and a lot others. I don't know I suppose I'm a little confused. ★★★

Allen

September 17, 1957. Lawrence Ferlinghetti [San Francisco] to Allen Ginsberg [Paris]

Dear Allen,

Got your last and guess you are now in Paris. I am working on Gregory's book right now, and he agrees with me that you should do Introduction. You can write anything up to about 900 words, though just a couple of hundred will do if you want to keep it short . . . I wd like to send this book off to the printer by the end of September—or by October 5th—so let me have it by then for sure . . . I've just sent you, by surface mail, a copy of the Fourth Printing of *HOWL*. The *LIFE* article on Sept 9, with your pict, is causing the national distributor to take two or three hundred copies a week . . . though this probably won't keep up indefinitely! *Time* article, on general scene here, is due out in another week . . . Have you seen any of the articles on the trial, except what I sent? Am saving clips, so you can go over them when you hit town again. ★★★ Trial is not over yet—we're in court again this Thursday. ★★★ Typos in *HOWL* can't be changed now, without much expense, since photo offset plates are 16 pages to one plate, and one change means 16 pages redone . . . (I found one typo—"solipisisms"—which slipped thru all these printings)—Question of Fucked in the Ass not yet settled in court—so had to let that stand again . . . Got to go. ★★★

Later dad, Larry

September 23, 1957. Allen Ginsberg [Paris] to Lawrence Ferlinghetti [San Francisco]

Dear Larry:

Received your letter today. Paris a great ball—later on that. Business— (ugh). ★★★

Thanks for sending 4th printing *Howl*—surface mail is so slow, I won't see it for months though.

I haven't seen any articles on anything, except what's been in *Life* so far and what you've sent me, I'm completely out of touch—but would like some details of what's gone on—can't you send me a few clips in chronological order covering the various trial days?—I won't be back there for awhile. Let me know what the final decision is with court.

Records—haven't heard Grove record [*San Francisco Poets*]. The record is probably a fuckup no doubt—they ignored my advice as to which recording and which part of "Howl" to print on record. However it was then too much effort to otherwise advise them, I tried by mail. But it doesn't make much difference, they're the only ones who'll be screwed. No, I didn't sign any exclusive contracts, nor any contracts for that matter— contracts are too hung-up and legal and if possible would prefer never signing any even if it means losing control over my own scribblings. Money: They gave me $40, 6 months ago and another $54 one month ago—I don't know whether for the record or for *Evergreen* reprint. In sum they've given me 94 dollars, but I'm not sure exactly what for. I asked them about pay for records and Rosset wrote me they were paying per page on the review; per time or something equally divided on the record; and also that he'd sent Kenneth R. $200 for expenses. Whether they actually did or not, or why or what for, I dunno.

At the time they reprinted "Howl," I hadn't made any other money (like from you) on the poem, and it wasn't much money anyhow, and I needed it, so I didn't assume they'd have to pay you for rights. Should they have? Too complicated—it wouldn't have been much anyway and no

Allen Ginsberg's Merchant Marine identification photo. © Allen Ginsberg Trust

Peter Orlovsky probably took this picture of Allen Ginsberg typing in the kitchen of Peter's apartment at 5 Turner Terrace, 1956. © Allen Ginsberg Trust

point worrying about it now. (In future you're welcome to any rights money anybody wants to give, so long as it isn't subtracted from any sum that would go into my starving pocket, and so long as it isn't unwilling payment on the part of some penniless entrepreneur who's not in the business to make money anyway.)

Re Fantasy Record deal—that sounds fine, I will do anything anytime except maybe come back prematurely to US. Perhaps we can make decent recording here. Make whatever arrangements you think wise and by all means get me any money you can. I don't have specific plans, other than that I want to stay here for at least six months and dig Paris and read and write—so I don't want to plan on coming to US just to make another fucking recording of that fucking poem (which I'm positive was written 2 years ago in limbo by somebody else not me, maybe Carl Solomon). Fantasy people will know how to arrange good studio here; if they don't, let me know, and I'll contact Newman of Esoteric who may be here soon or will know a good tape set up here for trustworthy hi fi—he's an expert in the business and's been in and out of Paris making records for his own company. In other words try arrange recording here, the sooner the better; or let me know and I'll try.

No word from my father on receipt of books. I'll let you know. However I haven't received any copies, and haven't any, and there are none in Paris. Does Villiers still have that stock of them? I'd like to circulate some around here. I looked up George Whitman at the bookstore Mistral and I live around the corner from him. He has idea what's happening but hasn't seen any of the books and his bookstore is filled with old musty copies of *Epoch* and 1945 *Partisan Reviews*. Yet there are plenty of live interested cats here in Paris who would absolutely dig *Howl* and SF scene. A few copies of *Evergreen* sold out here and all sorts people stop me in American Express recognizing picture; and I've talked to a few French types, etc.—and there is a large market here—unexplored so far partly because of full impact of SF scene not hit here, where it would be gobbled up, and the texts not here either. Whitman said if he had material he'd make a window display, books articles and pictures, whatnot. His bookstore is pretty central like yours is and would reach most of the hip English speaking French poets, and all the US and British local cats. So, please make arrangements—would definitely suggest you round up all the material you can, as inclusive as possible—get a few copies of *Arks*, *Needles*, [Michael] Grieg's Kerouac issue [of *Mademoiselle*] if out, all your series, ask perhaps McClure for his and Duncan and make up a big care package to send to Whitman for his window and reading room. Honestly, it's a mad opportunity to make it an international scene, very rapidly. I don't know how much Whitman be able to sell, or what money terms you can make with him, but it be great advertising. In any case whatever you do with everything else, send him a number of copies of my book as soon as you can—either from Villiers or from you. I'm sure we can start disposing of them here. There's also, after Gregory's visit, a market for his book here, when it comes.

The impression, I mean, is that if our books were here they would stir and sell, just as in SF. I'm thinking of looking around for a French translator, you know any? ★★★

You sent me so much money, do I still have any copies due me at all?? If so please send them or cause them to be sent fast as you can.

Let me know, in a general way, without committing yourself, if you think they'll be any more money for me from 4th printing—I'm trying to figure out next 6 months. ★★★

Anyway, I'll leave for Amsterdam later this week. If there's immediate trial news, send me a fast note c/o Gregory in Amsterdam, where I'll be for 2 weeks. Otherwise for anything that can wait, American Express, Paris. I've located a room here near Seine, Rue Git Le Coeur, I can move in Oct. 15,—it's dirty and small but it's got a gas stove to cook in. Costs I'm afraid it will be almost $35 a month for 2 of us (me and Peter O.) but it's all I can find so far and I have to have a place I can boil eggs potatoes and tomatoes or I'll starve entirely. Great central location tho. Leaving Paris to save loot till the gas stove is ready. Later—

Yours from the banks of the Seine, Goon. ★★★

Thanks, Allen

September 28, 1957. Allen Ginsberg [Amsterdam, The Netherlands] to Lawrence Ferlinghetti [San Francisco]

Dear Larry:

Am in Amsterdam sleeping on Gregory's floor, waiting for your list of poems so I can write introduction [for Corso's *Gasoline*]. If you haven't sent them send them immediately yes? Also please airmail here all the excess Corso manuscripts. We will be here till Oct. 14—(then American Express in Paris)—hope to receive lists and material in a week from you tho.

Gregory will send a (final) dedication page also, scrapping previous— same time I send intro. He will also send you a few more poems this week.

Can you send us a copy of *Coastlines* too? Haven't seen it. Did *Ark II* come out?

What's with trial?

Finally have room in Paris Oct. 15 with gas stove so will settle there then. Lots Dutch hipsters here, read Artaud. Windmills, cows, green fields, Van Gogh and Vermeer, art cafes, canals, museums, cheap Indonesian restaurants, no housing shortage much in Amsterdam. How strange to be in Holland with the ducks. And great Red Light district, girls are like wax dolls in bright windows.

I know everybody puts Gregory down there and am glad you don't, I am amazed by his genuine genius and originality.

Gregory says right color for *Gasoline* cover is bright-solid red letters on white background. Have you used this already? (Red border?, with label like mine, red letters on label.) Is it possible to get a red explosive and solid like an Esso sign?

I'll send the introduction in a few days—hoping to receive your table of contents here as per your last letter.

Allen

September 28, 1957. Lawrence Ferlinghetti [San Francisco] to Allen Ginsberg [Paris]

Dear Allen,

Got yours of the 23d. Have sent out 50 *HOWL* c/o American Express, Paris, and they really shouldn't take more than 3 weeks, four at the very most. ★★★ Will send you clips on final action on *HOWL* trial next week, when judge brings in his written decision and opinion. I am writing it up for next issue of *Evergreen*, per request of Don Allen. Great picture of you in *Life*. Where was it taken? Wd like to get it for cover of Fantasy Record. Could you trace down negative of it and get it and send it to us? Re: Fantasy Record, yes why don't you go ahead and get studio in Paris for recording, and I will foot bill for it, until Fantasy forks over, that is if you can rent a sound studio for an hour or two for under $25. The idea is to make the sharpest clearest livest recording, uninterrupted by remarks or extrapolations etc. (You should undoubtedly get in touch with Newman of Esoteric, since he is coming to Paris, since Fantasy has no contacts there, except for distribution. If you get a chance, make a couple of readings of "Howl," as well as recording all the other long poems in the book (or at least "America" and "Supermarket") and be sure to include

"Footnote to Howl." This will have to be a LP which means you need enough tape to fill both sides of a 12-inch disk, which is about three times as much as "Howl" by itself. That's what FANTASY wants. ★★★ At Art Festival here this week, there was Grand Guignol puppet type show, with puppets of you and Corso and Rexroth, with scene at The Place for backdrop, lampooning all and fingerlike penis flopping out and Kenneth intoning and Lawrence F and the Police Inspector and the Cellar jass scene with Kenneth on the podium with Brooks Brothers suits and you get the idea anyway. ★★★

Yours trooly, write, LF

Editor's Note: On October 3, 1957, Judge Horn handed down his verdict on the trial: Not guilty.

October 9, 1957. Allen Ginsberg [Amsterdam] to Jack Kerouac [New York]

Dear Jack:

★★★ No news on Trial, tho I guess it's over. Is Lucien carrying the story at all? I wish he would, his name's out. [Henry] Miller attended trial—and later developments may wind up freeing Miller's books—and maybe Bill's [Burroughs]—not inconceivable—maybe Ferl try other test cases in SF. ★★★

Re *Howl*, Ferl sent me 100 dols., has 4th printing, sold 5000 already, will sell more,—it's circulating a lot. Could Viking or Grove actually do better? I wonder. However I don't know. But City Lights took it, way back, and fought trial, and Ferl went into red once for it, so I have already told him I won't go whoring around NY. Tell Lord,[46] if he can reprint "Howl" itself (or any other poem) anywhere, and get me some loot—in *Life* (maybe Rosalind Constable would even back that you know) or *Look* (who knows?) or *New World Writing* (more likely) to do try do so and be agent if he cares and will. That won't fuck up Grove, since their issue is over, and will only help City Lights sales. Anyway, tell Lord, and ask him to inquire around and think it over if he will. ★★★

Love, Allen.

---

[46] Sterling Lord was Jack Kerouac's literary agent.

October 10, 1957. Allen Ginsberg [Amsterdam] to Lawrence Ferlinghetti [San Francisco]

Dear Larry:

Got your note with *Chronicle* decision page today, natch was glad and thankful and also surprised to see you've got 10,000 in print, that's fantastic. Well that's all great. ★★★

Was decision news carried nationally anyway? Look up Harvey Breit on *Times*, he'll probably want to interview you. Also phone Rosalind Constable on Time-Life, who's very sympathetic. ★★★ Also try arrange thru Breit, or see Brown the editor at *Times*, that they begin reviewing City Lights.

I hear from Jack that both Viking and Grove interested in hardcover *Howl*, however that be wrong etc so don't worry as I said I won't go whoring in NY. If you follow Corso with Kerouac and Burroughs you'll have the most sensational little company in US, I wish you would dig that, anyway—we could all together crash over America in a great wave of beauty. And cash. But do you think you can sell 5,000 more actually? How mad.

When I was in NY I saw Rhav and Phillips at *Partisan*, Morgan at *Hudson*, Bogan at *New Yorker*, spoke to somebody (Mrs. Abel) at *Commentary*; Porter at *New World Writing*. I yelled at all, about reviewing books. You might contact them (they all know about City Lights) and make sure they are getting books and insist on them reviewing—particularly Gregory's upcoming *Gasoline*. Breit too. With Porter above I yakked about SF, Black Mt. and Boston poets; you might talk to her and see if she'll start printing us, or get someone to edit a mad poetry section in one of the *New World Writings*.

If possible, now that *Evergreen Review* issue is over, would like to get the single poem "Howl" reprinted more widely, perhaps in *Time, Life, Look, Cong. Record*, or more likely *New World Writing*. It would not hurt the book. Sterling Lord, Jack's agent, address above, may be (maybe not) working on this. If you can get in touch with him and see if some deal to make us all some more money can be made, this way.

I will try arrange a decent tape in Paris when I'm there in a week. Phone Jerry Newmann at Esoteric on 28th Street, he's not coming to Paris, ask him advise on who I should contact in Paris. Let's see what else. You ought to get yourself interviewed by the *Village Voice*, Ed Fancher there a friend of Gregory's interviewed us once. They would carry story on conclusion of trial. Was decision carried anywhere but in SF? ★★★

Is there chance of continuing the fight and freeing Miller, Lawrence, and maybe Genet etc? That would be really historic and worth the trouble. ★★★ Later, Allen.

Thanks for all trouble, is there anyone I should write thank you notes to??

P.S. Do me favor, phone my papa Louis G. and tell him trial news— please. He'll be proud to hear, etc.

November 6, 1957. Allen Ginsberg [Paris] to Louis Ginsberg [Paterson]

Dear Lou:

★★★ Got the record from Evergreen, it certainly is terrible, in fact it stinks. Fortunately I can put a full 12 inch LP out thru City Lites that will come off better I hope. Grove screwed up that deal, took wrong tapes, wrong sections, wrong people. I got news of trial from S.F., the *Chronicle* there had it in headline on first page. He's sold 5000 & has another 5000 in print he says. He'll send me more money when there is some, he's quite honest, he sent me the last hundred at time I didn't know I had it coming. I wouldn't shift publishers in any case, since no NY publisher would go to court, as he did, nor would a NY publisher manage to print & sell 10,000 copies cheap, as he can do. Like I say, all NY has is prestige, but not much of that—since it's mainly a money-prestige racket they're in, not the poetry racket as City Lights is. ★★★

December 3, 1957. Peter Orlovsky, Gregory Corso and Allen Ginsberg [Paris] to Neal and Carolyn Cassady [Los Gatos, CA]

Dear Neal and Carolyn:

Saw your picture in *Life*, Neal, you were in the court room looking in on how Allen's *Howl* was progressing, just the side of your face with your hair back. Yes it was you, Gregory just discovered it and told us. We all said together, "Ha, Neal was there seeing how things was going." ★★★

February 1, 1958. Lawrence Ferlinghetti [San Francisco] to Allen Ginsberg [Paris]

Dear Allen,

FANTASY RECORDS is making up contract and you will get about a $100 advance for recording *Howl and Other Poems*. You can add some new stuff if you want, in place of shorter poems in Pocket Poets book, since you will have to fill up both sides of an LP. More specific instructions are coming from Fantasy, along with studio name and address in Paris for you to contact. Contract will be signed between Fantasy and City Lights Books but with your copyright. I shd be getting the papers from Fantasy tonight and will send you the doe right away. ***

Will send the copies of *HOWL* to Sterling Lord, as you say, but I don't have his address, so send it and I'll do the mailing. ***

I hear from Don Allen that you have new long poem in next *Evergreen Review* (due out April 1), same issue as my article called HORN ON HOWL (Horn was name of judgeman). So it looks like you will be growing still more famous like. Let me know whut you think of Horny on Howl when you git it. What about this "new long poem" of yours?[47] Do I get it as part of new book soon? I hope so. But did you let Grove acquire full rights to it, so that I could not reprint it? Am counting on another book of yours for next year's list. OK? The excerpt you sent me from long poem on FALL OF AMERICA really flips me over, and I hope you'll give me first shot at it. It doesn't have to be in the same same pocket series but a largersize, more Grove Press and ND type-book, if you wd rather, although having it in a series helps a book sell a great deal. Let me know. Wdn't FALL OF AMERICA be great title for book. THE Fall?

Yurn, Larry

February 14, 1958. Lawrence Ferlinghetti [San Francisco] to Allen Ginsberg [Paris]

Dear Allen

Finally, and I hope yer still there [Paris], no word since my last letter of a couple of weeks ago. Here's the dope for recording for Fantasy Records (Max Weiss is the man working on it from this end of Fantasy): Contact Mr. Delaunay, Vogue Records, who will handle arrangements to record you. He has been informed about it. You're getting a $150 advance, which I will send you by check as soon as Max Weiss gives it to me this week. The contract from Fantasy is not quite ready but will be executed between Weiss and myself anyway, since I am operating the way most larger publishers do in matters of reprints and "secondary rights." I'll send you the whole $150 advance royalty, since you need it now to live on, but I would like to

---

[47] "Siesta in Xbalba and Return to the States" was published in *Evergreen Review,* no. 4 (Winter 1957).

split the total royalties with you, as is usually done by publishers and authors, on reprints. Now the idea is for you to record both sides of an Lp, and I would suggest all the long poems in our Pocket Poets book, plus whatever new long poems you would like to get on record. *HOWL* of course will be the main part and the title of the record. Please follow the book. Nothing need be "censored," natch. I will write the jacket blurb for the record if you would like, but I would just as soon you got Kerouac or somebody else to write it if you wanted to. On the other hand, a jacket full of quotes from all the famous critics and cats who testified at the trial or wrote us letters would make some display, and I can furnish all this material. Let me know what you prefer on this, and I'll suggest same to Max Weiss who naturally has the say on this. A lot of this material is in the *Evergreen Review* article I wrote. ★★★

Trooly, Larry

May 8, 1958. Lawrence Ferlinghetti [San Francisco] to Allen Ginsberg [Paris]

Dear Allen,

★★★ HOWL HORN article was a deaddog by the time it came out— shud have been in previous issue, written for square consumption, pretty corny. Latest printing of *HOWL* does not have any change indicating it is a new printing, since a whole new cover plate wd have had to be made just to change words from Fourth to Fifth Printing. Hope you don't mind much. Do you have any desire to have a hardcover City Lights edition? Cd do. ★★★

LF

August 30, 1958. Lawrence Ferlinghetti [San Francisco] to Allen Ginsberg [Paris]

Dear Allen,

Just back from Big Sur, got yours. Will have more loot for you in 8 weeks. Reprinting *HOWL* again late in October. Have arranged sale of German bilingual edition with big German publisher. They will advance $80 on publication, based on 7 1/2 % royalties on retail sales; so that much more money would be forthcoming later. Am figuring to continue splitting loot with you on all such reprints. (This is what New Directions does with me). Will, however, wait to hear from you before signing contract for German edition (not for sale in USA). I can get you much more long green in the long run, if you refer all reprint requests to us; I think you should have gotten much more for reprint in *Beat Gen & Angry Young Men*. Maybe you don't care. But there's no reason you can't live off *HOWL* for a long time to come, especially if I continue to uncover new reprints. We've got Canadian distributor now. And German one, for our own editions. ★★★

Larry

September 12, 1958. Lawrence Ferlinghetti [San Francisco] to Allen Ginsberg [Paris]

Dear Allen,

Don't worry about recording *HOWL*. Max is relaxed. Whenever you can, do it. Five Spot,[48] with audience? Fantasy coming out with my IMPEACHMENT of IKE, with Cal Tjader making with a funereal drum all thru it. Out in 3 weeks now. It shakes; in spots.

Will have new printing of *HOWL* within three more weeks. That makes total of 20,000 in print! (In other words, am getting 5000 more in October). Am adding list of all printings on verso of title page, and making slight change in back cover blurb, all of which means three new plates; but this will keep it fresh.

Larry

Editor's Note: *Horizon* magazine reprinted "Howl" but they decided to cut all the "dirty" words without consulting Ginsberg or Ferlinghetti.

October 3, 1958. Lawrence Ferlinghetti [San Francisco] to Barney Rosset and Don Allen [New York]

Dear Barney & Don,

The manner in which *HORIZON* has censored the text of *HOWL* in their reprint is very disturbing, particularly after the fight we put up over the censorship of it, and I hope you'll let them know it was a cynical thing to do. I am unable to do anything about it at this end, as you can see from the following quote from their legal counsel's opinion on the subject:

"If, however, as Mr. Ginsberg alleges, the material was originally copyrighted in his name (assuming it validly copyrighted) the copyright was lost by giving permission to Grove Press Inc. to publish the material

---

[48] The Five Spot was a legendary New York jazz night club on the Lower East Side.

under its own copyright, unless at the same time the ownership rights in the material were transferred to the Grove Press Inc. If the ownership was not transferred (as Mr. Ginsberg states) Mr. Ginsberg's copyright notice should have been reproduced on page 137 of the *Evergreen Review*, and the failure to do so put the material in the public domain . . ."

My letter to Don [Allen] of May First, 1957, gives permission to reprint but asks that you reprint the copyright notice (c) 1956 by Allen Ginsberg, an *ad interim* copyright for material originally printed and published in England. Unfortunately you did not reprint this copyright, but we didn't transfer the "Ownership rights" to you, and I hope in the future you'll help us in preventing the kind of thing HORIZON has done. (As you may know Ginsberg was paid very little for the material they used, which is pretty poor for such a wealthy magazine). But it's the censorship that really bugs me.

In any case, as far as Allen G. and I are concerned, he still has the "ownership rights" to this material and any future requests for reprintings should, in all fairness and on all ethical and moral grounds, be referred to us as his original publisher. I imagine and trust that you do not intend to claim future rights to *HOWL* based upon that blanket copyright covering all contents of the *Evergreen Review* #2, in as much as neither Allen nor myself gave you anything in writing as to "ownership rights." I am doing my best by Allen G., in the way of financial help, and we have the standard arrangement as to payment on reprints, etc.

Enclosed is a copy of the brand new printing of *HOWL* just off the press. ★★★

Best regards and salutations, Lawrence Ferlinghetti

October 1958. Lawrence Ferlinghetti [San Francisco] to Allen Ginsberg [New York]

Dear Allen,

Horizon says *HOWL* is in public domain since Grove did not print your copyright in *Evergreen* but covered it with their own copyright on entire contents. But ownership of work should still be yours! (When I wrote [Donald] Allen to give him written permission for *Evergreen* reprint, I specifically said your copyright should be reproduced, but it wasn't, altho they gave City Lights "credit" for reprint). Is Allen figuring on using "Howl" again in his new anthology? Or what of yours is he going to use? Did you know that you should not get a flat fee for anthology use from them but royalties on all above first 50000 copies? This is what shud have been done in SF *Evergreen* issue but wasn't.

MacGregor at ND [New Directions] has told Allen that they wd have to give me royalties as above, and Mc refused to accept $3 a page for my work from ND book. If they are figuring on using "Howl" or anything else from *Howl and Other Poems*, I'd like to get you that royalty instead of that flat little fee. (Do you realize how many copies of *ER* were sold, not to mention the record?) For an unknown poet, that's all right, but maybe you don't realize you are the famousest young poet in America and shud be getting some of that real gold like Kerouac, not $3 a page. (I read that drivel in *THIS WEEK* about goodbye to the beatniks because they make too much money, merde). Anyway, this is just to let you know whut you shud be getting, accdg to ND standards, and I hope it's not already too late and that you've not already let Grove have it. They HAVE to have you in their book, you know.

Editor's Note: Allen Ginsberg wrote at least two epic letters concerning *Howl*. The first was to Richard Eberhart in advance of Eberhart's article on the writers of the San Francisco Renaissance. The second was to John Hollander, and this letter followed Hollander's review that was critical of *Howl and Other Poems*. John Hollander was born in 1929, three years after Ginsberg. The two had been classmates for a while at Columbia University, where they shared an interest in literature. Hollander's book *A Crackling of Thorns* (1958) had been selected by W.H. Auden for the Yale Series of Younger Poets and Hollander was well on his way professionally, following a more traditional, academic path than Ginsberg.

Sept. 7, 1958. Allen Ginsberg [New York] to John Hollander [New York]

Dear John:

Got your letter, slow answering since writing a little and invasion of people in apartment and too much mail, a lady in Michigan wanting to know if I believe in God, I have to answer everything, it's difficult. No, of course, communication's always there why not, only a shit would be bugged, besides I've seen too much, I'm tired. It's just that I've tried to do too much explaining and get overwhelmed by the vastness of the task, and sometimes what seems to be all the accumulated ill-will and evil vibrations in America (Kerouac got beaten up at the San Remo for his trouble in coming down there and making himself available.) But to begin somewhere, I should might begin with one thing, simple (I hate to go back to it over and over, like revolving around my corpse, the construction of "Howl"). This may be corny to you, my concern with that, but I've got to begin somewhere and perhaps differences of opinion between us can be resolved by looking at that. See, for years before that, thinking in Williams' line, which I found very helpful and quite real for what it is doing, the balance by ear of short lines formed of relatively natural ordinary notebook or conversation speech. "[Siesta in] Xbalba" is fragments of mostly prose, written in a Mexican school copybook, over half a year—then rereading, picking out the purest thoughts, stringing them together, arranging them in lines suitably balanced, mostly measured by the phrase, that is, one phrase a line—you know it's hard to explain this because its like painting and unless you do it like practicing a piano, you don't think in those terms and get the experience of trying to work that way, so you don't notice all the specific tricks—that anyone who works in that field gets to be familiar with—that's why I'm interested in Blackburn, Levertov, Creeley, Oppenheimer, all the Black [Mountain] lit people—they work steadily consistently trying to develop this line of goods, and each has a different interesting approach—they all stem out of Williams—but I can tell their lines apart, they really are different, just as you can tell the difference between styles and approaches of abstract painters. When you tell me it's just a bore to you, that just cuts off communication, I mean I don't know what to say, I get embarrassed to retreat and go about my work and stop explanations. Of course you may not be interested in this field of experiment, but that doesn't mean it's uninteresting to others, that it's categorically a bore. I ALSO believe it's the main "tradition," not that there is any tradition except what we make ourselves. But basically I'm not interested in tradition because I'm more interested in what I'm doing, what it's inevitable for me to do. This realization has given me perspective on what a vast sad camp the whole literary-critical approach of school has been—basically no one has insight into poetry techniques except people who are exercising them. But I'm straying at random. But I'm now getting bugged at people setting themselves up as scholars and authorities and *getting in the way* of continuous creative work or its understanding or circulation—there is not one article on the Beat or SF scene yet that has not been (pro or con) invalidated (including yours)[49]

---

[49] Hollander, John. [review of *Howl and Other Poems*]. *Partisan Review,* vol. 24, no. 2 (Spring 1957) pp. 296-298, in which he calls the book a "dreadful little volume."

by the basic fact that the author is just a big windbag not knowing what he's talking about—no technical background, no knowledge of the vast body of experimental work, published and unpublished (the unpublished is the best), no clear grasp of the various different schools of experiment all converging toward the same or similar end, all at once coming into intercommunication, no knowledge of the letters and conversations in between, not even the basic ability (like [Norman] Podhoretz) to tell the difference between prosody and diction (as in his *Partisan Review* diatribes on spontaneous bop prosody confusing it with the use of hip talk not realizing it refers to rhythmical construction of phrases and sentences). I mean where am I going to begin a serious explanation if I have to deal with such unmitigated stupid ignorant ill willed inept vanity as that—someone like that wouldn't listen unless you hit him over the head with a totally new universe, but he's stuck in his own hideous world, I would try, but he scarcely has enough heart to hear)—etc. etc.—so all these objections about juvenile delinquency, vulgarity, lack of basic education, bad taste, etc. etc., no form, etc. I mean it's impossible to discuss things like that— finally I get to see them as so basically *wrong* (unscientific) so dependent on ridiculous provincial schoolboy ambitions and presuppositions and so lacking contact with practical fact—that it seems a sort of plot almost, a kind of organized mob stupidity—the final camp of its announcing itself as a representative of value or civilization or taste—I mean I give up, that's just too much fucking nasty brass. And you're guilty of that too John, you've just got to drop it, and take me seriously, and listen to what I have to say. It doesn't mean you have to agree, or change your career or your writing, or anything hideous, it just means you've got to have the heart and decency to take people seriously and not depend only on your own university experience for arbitrary standard of value to judge others by. It doesn't mean you have to agree that free verse is the only path of prosodic experiment, or that Williams is a saint, or I have some horrible magic secret, tho god knows I have enough, this week with that damned Buddhist laughing gas, everybody has. Just enough to dig, you to dig, what others besides yourself are trying to do, and be interested in their work or not, but not get in the way, in fact even encourage where you can see some value. And you're in a position to encourage, you teach, you shouldn't hand down limited ideas to younger minds—that was the whole horror of Columbia, there just was nobody there (maybe except Weaver)[50] who

---

[50] Raymond Weaver, one of Ginsberg's English professors at Columbia.

had a serious involvement with advanced work in poetry. Just a bunch of dilettantes. And THEY have the nerve to set themselves up as guardians of culture?!? Why it's such a piece of effrontery—enough to make anyone paranoiac, it's a miracle Jack or myself or anybody independent survived— tho god knows the toll in paranoia been high enough. All these grievances I'm pouring out to you. Well, why revise?

Back to "Howl": construction. After sick and tired of short line free verse as not expressionistic enough, not swinging enough, can't develop a powerful enough rhythm, I simply turned aside, accidentally to writing part I of "Howl," in solitude, diddling around with the form, thinking it couldn't be published anyway (queer content my parents shouldn't see, etc.) also it was out of my short-line line. But what I did about my theory, I changed my mind about "measure" while writing it. Part one uses repeated base "who" as a sort of kithara BLANG, Homeric (in my imagination) to mark off each statement, each rhythmic unit. So that's experiment with longer and shorter variations on a fixed base—the principle being, that each line has to be contained within the elastic of one breath—with suitable punctuatory expressions where the rhythm has built up enough so that I have to let off steam by building a longer climactic line in which there is a jazzy ride. All the ear I've ever developed goes into the balancing of those lines. The interesting moments when the rhythm is sufficiently powerfully pushing ahead so I can ride out free and drop the "who" key that holds it together. The method of keeping a long line still all poetic and not prosy is the concentration and compression of basically imagistic notations into surrealist or cubist phrasing, like hydrogen jukeboxes. Ideally anyway. Good example of this is Gregory's great (I swear) Coit Tower ode.[51] Lines have greater poetic density. But I tried to keep the language sufficiently dense in one way or another—use of primitive naive grammar (expelled for crazy), elimination of prosy articles and syntactical sawdust, juxtaposition of cubic style images, or hot rhythm.

Well then Part II. Here the basic repeated word is "Moloch." The long line is now broken up into component short phrases with ! rhythmical punctuation. The key repeat BLANG word is repeated internally in the line (basic rhythm sometimes emerging /—/—) but the rhythm depends mostly on the internal Moloch repeat. Lines here lengthened—a sort of free verse prose poetry STANZA form invented or used here. This builds up to climax (Visions! Omens! etc.) and then falls off in coda.

---

[51] Reference to "Ode to Coit Tower," published in Corso's book, *Gasoline*.

Part III, perhaps an original invention (I thought so then but this type of thinking is vain and shallow anyway) to handling of long line (for the whole poem is an experiment in what you can do with the long line—the whole book is)—::: that is, a phrase base rhythm (I'm with you, etc.) followed as in litany by a response of the same length (Where you're madder, etc.), then repeat of base over and over with the response elongating itself slowly, still contained within the elastic of one breath—till the stanza (for it is a stanza form there, I've used variations of it since) building up like a pyramid, an emotion crying siren sound, very appropriate to the expressive appeal emotion I felt (a good healthy emotion said my analyst at that time, to dispose once and for all of that idiotic objection)—anyway, building up to the climax where there's a long long long line, penultimate, too long for one breath, where I open out and give the answer (O starry spangled shock of Mercy the eternal war is here). All this rather like a jazz mass, I mean the conception of rhythm not derived from jazz directly but if you listen to jazz you get the idea (in fact specifically old trumpet solo on a JATP [*Jazz at the Philharmonic*] "Can't Get Started" side)—well all this is built like a brick shithouse and anybody can't hear the music is (as I told you I guess I meekly informed Trilling, who is absolutely lost in poetry) is got a tin ear, and that's so obviously true, I get sick and tired I read 50 reviews of *Howl* and not one of them written by anyone with enough technical interests to notice the fucking obvious construction of the poem, all the details besides (to say nothing of the various esoteric classical allusions built in like references to Cézanne's theory of composition etc. etc.)—that I GIVE UP and anybody henceforth comes up to me with a silly look in his eye and begins bull-shitting about morals and sociology and tradition and technique and JD [juvenile delinquency]. I mean I *je ne sais plus parler*—the horrible irony of all these jerks who can't read trying to lecture me (us) on FORM.

Kerouac has his own specific method of construction of prose which he has pursued for a decade now and I have yet to see one piece of criticism taking that into account, or even interested enough to realize he has one and its implications and how it related to the rhythm of his prose,—much less how his method alters and develops chronologically from book to book, and what phases it goes thru, what changes one would encounter in so prolonged and devoted an experiment as his (rather like Gertrude Stein)—but nobody's interested in literature, in technique, all they think about is their goddam lousy ideas of what they preconceive writing to be about and I'M SICK OF LISTENING TO THAT AND READING ABOUT THAT AND UNLESS THERE IS

MORE COOPERATION FROM THE SUPPOSEDLY RESPONSIBLE PARTIES IN UNIVERSITIES AND MAGAZINES I ABSOLUTELY CUT OUT AND REFUSE TO SUBMIT MY HEART WRUNG PSALMS TO THE DIRTY HANDS AND MINDS OF THESE BASTARDS AND THEY CAN TAKE THEIR FUCKING literary tradition AND SHOVE IT UP THEIR ASS—I don't need them and they don't need me and I'm sick of putting myself out and being put down and hit on the head by jerks who have no interests but their ridiculous devilish social careers and MONEY MONEY MONEY which is the root of the EVIL here in America and I'm not MAD.

"Footnote to Howl" is too lovely and serious a joke to try to explain. The built-in rhythmic exercise should be clear, it's basically a repeat of the Moloch section. It's dedicated to my mother who died in the madhouse and it says I loved her anyway and that even in worst conditions life is holy. The exaggeratedness of the statements are appropriate, and anybody who doesn't understand the specific exaggerations will never understand "Rejoice in the Lamb" or Lorca's "Ode to Whitman" or Mayakovsky's "At the Top of My Voice" or Artaud's "Pour En Finir Avec Le Judgment de Dieu" or Apollinaire's "inspired bullshit" or Whitman's madder passages or anything, anything, anything about the international modern spirit in poesy to say nothing about the international tradition in prosody which has grown up nor the tradition of open prophetic bardic poetry which 50 years has sung like an angel over the poor soul of the world while all sorts of snippy cats castrates pursue their good manners and sell out their own souls and the spirit of god who now DEMANDS sincerity and hell fire take him who denies the voice in his soul—except that it's all a kindly joke and the universe disappears after you die so nobody gets hurt no matter how little they allow themselves to live and blow on this earth.

Anyone noticing the constructions and the series of poems in *Howl* would then notice that the next task I set myself to was adapting that kind of open long line to tender lyric feelings and short form, so next is "Supermarket in California" where I pay homage to Whitman in realistic terms (eyeing the grocery boys) and it's a little lyric, and since it's almost prose it's cast in form of prose paragraphs like St. Perse—and has nobody noticed that I was aware enough of that to make that shift there. Nor that I went on in the next poem "Transcription of Organ Music" to deliberately write a combo of prose and poetry some lines indented which are poetical and some lines not but paragraphed like prose to see what could be done with absolute transcription of spontaneous material, transcription of sensual data (organ) at a moment of near ecstasy, not, nor has anybody noticed that I have technically developed my method of transcription (as Cézanne developed sketching) so that I could transcribe at such moments and try to bring back to the poor suffering world what rare moments exist, and that technical practice has led to a necessary spontaneous method of transcription which will pass in and out of poetry and so needs a flexible form—its own natural form unchanged—to preserve the moment alive and uncensored by the arbitrary ravenings of conceptual or preconception or post-censoring-out-of-embarrassment-so-called intelligence? Anyway there is a definite experiment in FORM FORM FORM and not a ridiculous idea of what form *should* be like. And it is an example that has all sorts of literary precedents in French poetry, in Hart Crane, in—but this whole camp of FORM is so ridiculous I am ashamed to have to use the word to justify what is THERE (and only use it in a limited academic context but would not dream of using this kindergarten terminology to poets from whom I *learn*—Kerouac, Burroughs or Corso—who start to new worlds of their own academic tribe that is so superciliously hung on COLLEGE that it has lost touch with living creation.)

The next problem attacked in the book is to build up a rhythmical drive in long lines without dependence on repetition of the words and phrases, Who's, Moloch's, or Holy's, a drive forward to a climax and conclusion— and to do it spontaneously . . . well I've broken my typewriter on this explanation I continue on Peter's—a twenty minute task ("Sunflower Sutra")[52] with fifteen years practice behind—to ride out on the breath rhythm without any artificial built-in guides or poles or diving boards or repetition except the actual rhythm, and to do it so that both long long lines, and long lines, and shorter ten-word lines all have roughly the same weight, and balance each other out, and anybody take the trouble to read Sutra out [loud] will see it does that and the come of the rhythmic buildup is "You were never no locomotive Sunflower, you were a sunflower, and you locomotive (pun) you were a locomotive, etc." And furthermore at this point in the book I am sick of preconceived literature and only interested in writing the actual process and technique, wherever it leads, and the various possible experiments in composition that are in my path—and if anybody still is confused in what literature is let it be hereby announced once for all in the Seven Kingdoms that that's what it is—Poetry is what poets write, and not what other people think they should write.

---

[52] Ginsberg wrote this poem in one twenty-minute sitting.

The next poem "America" takes off on the free line and is an attempt to make combinations of short and long lines, very long lines and very short lines, something I've always wanted to do but previously had to depend on sustained rhythmical buildup to carry the structure of the poem forward. But in "America" I rely on discrete separate statements, rather than one long madbreath forward. Here as always however the measure, the meter, of each line, the think, the thing that makes it a complete line, and the thing that balances each line with its neighbors is that each (with tactical exceptions) is ONE SPEECH BREATH — an absolute physical measure as absolute as the ridiculous limited little accent or piddling syllable count. And in this I've gone forward from Williams because I literally measure each line by the physical breath — each one breath statement, dictated by what has to be said, in relation and balance to the previous rhythmic statement.

The next task the book includes is the Greyhound poem[53] which is attempt to apply the method with all tricks, long with short lines mixed, some repetition some not, some lyric, some Bardic, some surrealist or cubist phrasing, some pure imagistic-Williams notation — to apply all this to a realistic solid work proletarian common experience situation and come up with a classical type elegiac poem in modern rhythm and tricks etc. Also to make a nonhowling poem with separate parts, etc.

So all this adds up to handbook of various experiments with the possibilities of an expressive long line, and perhaps carries on from where Whitman left off with his long lines. At least I've (in part III of "Howl") attempted one visible organic stanza construction. Pound complains that Whitman was not interested enough in developing his line, I have tried to rescue long line for further use — tho at the moment (this last year I've abandoned it for a totally different mode than I've ever used, a totally wild page of free verse dictated by the immediate demands of spontaneous notation, with its appearance or form on the page determined by the structure of thought, rather than the aural quality primarily.

Latter's unclear I'll start over. Tho poetry in Williams has depended a lot on little breath groups for its typographical organization, and in "Howl" an extension into longer breaths (which are more natural to me than Williams short simple talks) — there is another possible approach to the measure of the line — which is, not the way you would *say* it, a thought, but the way you would think it — i.e. we think rapidly, in visual images as

---

[53] "In the Baggage Room at Greyhound."

well as words, and if each successive thought were transcribed in its confusion (really its ramification) you get a slightly different prosody than if you were talking slowly.

This still not clear—if you talk fast and excitedly you get weird syntax and rhythms, just like you think, or nearer to what you think. Not that everybody's thinking process is consciously the same—everybody's got a different consciousness factory—but the attempt here is to let us see—to transcribe the thought all at once so that its ramifications appear on the page much as the ramifications of a sentence appear on the page when it's analyzed into a paradigm in grammar books—example, from last poem ("Laughing Gas"—an attempt to transcribe that experience of the disappearance of chilicosm[54] when consciousness is anesthetized, as an instance of what maybe happens at death).

See [the following] for example:
The Bloomfield police car
   With its idiot red light
   Revolving on its head
   Balefully at eternity
     Gone in an instant
        —simultaneous
        appearance of bankrobbers
  at the Twentieth Century Bank
The fire engines screaming
   Toward an old lady's
   Burned-in-her-bedroom
   Today apocalypse
    Tomorrow
   Mickey mouse cartoons

I'm disgusted! It's unbelievable!
How could it all be so
   Horrible and funny?
    It's a dirty joke!
The whole universe a shaggy dog story
   With a weird ending that
    Begins again
       Till you get the point

---

[54] "Chilicosm" may be defined as the interpenetration of many different levels of cosmic creation.

"IT was a dark and gloomy night"
   "in every direction in and out"
      "You take the high road
   and I'll take the low"
      everybody in the same
fantastic Scotland of the mind—
   consciousness

Gary Snyder, Jack, thou Zens
   Split open existence
   And laugh and cry—
What's shock? What's measure?
   When the mind's irrational
   —following the blinking lights
   of contrariety—
(etc. etc.)

Well, I haven't done enough work yet in this direction, I want to get a wild page, as wild and as clear (really clear) as the mind—no forcing the thoughts into straightjacket—sort of a search for the rhythm of the thoughts and their natural occurrence and spacings and notational paradigms. Naturally when you read it aloud it also turns out to have intricate aural rhythm. But this is just an experiment—and naturally, this type writing gives thought an artificial form—the mere crystallizing it on page does—but to attempt to reproduce the droppings of the mind on the page—to work freely with this kind of direction—you see—you see—it's fascinating to me.

Now if I have you at all intrigued with this as a possibility—to spread out into the field—there's Olson's interesting essay on projective verse, and Kerouac's handmaiden article on approaches to prose—and all his experience in organizing whole novels with mad complicated structures (*tres* formal you see) built on the process of his mind in composition—novels say about Neal (unpublished *Visions of Neal*)[55] which take off from the first shining memory, (irrespective of chronology) and take their form from the deep sublime symmetries that are to be found in following from naked recollection instance to another one to another I mean. I mean that in watching natural thought (like in meditation Buddhist type) you see the structure of your random seeming thought and you can build whole prose

---

[55] Published after Jack Kerouac's death as *Visions of Cody.*

or poetry structures on it. Not without effort at first, for it takes immense self discipline and effort to learn to not think (IBM) but to meditate and <u>watch</u> thought without interrupting it by literary self-consciousness and embarrassed preconceptions and rules.

So the most authoritative handbook of forms for me in modern poetry is Kerouac's immense sonnet sequence *Mexico City Blues*, they're not sonnets, they're a series of 280 short (10-30 line) poems written sequentially in Mexico City, each has its own form-universe, all interrelated, being pieces of the same mind. They look roughly like the piece of verse above I typed out—very weird and zigzag on the page—tremendous rich language and imagery too—nobody except the poetic hepcats in SF and *Chi Review* picked up on this yet, nobody will publish it, a dirty rotten shame, but fuck everybody, they don't deserve it, it's their Karma and they'll never learn how to write. (This is for real and important.)

Gary Snyder and Phil Whalen from SF we lived with, they're learned Zens, Gary speaks Chinese and Jap and translates and taught anthropology and just got back from monastery etc. and specialized in comparative mythology, etc etc. and peyote and T [marijuana] etc. He has a little beard, 27 years old rides a bicycle and has vow of poverty and likes girls—well him and Whalen (who just sits like a Buddha) also have vast unpublished mss. Well, their work is great too, tho who would know because who's interested except those advanced enough in same line and similar experiences in composition. Jack myself Gary and Phil originally read together in SF and that was the renaissance and any evaluation of the poetry is incomplete without FULL authoritative account of their work and one of these shits who presumes to write on the subject for MONEY or EGO reasons has taken the trouble to investigate, and I've tried some of their work out on *Hudson* and *Partisan* and all the so called responsible journals and been put down so I conclude the whole official publishing scene in the US is a vicious camp and Rahv[56] and etc and Morgan at *Hudson* [*Review*] etc etc and all those people are ENEMIES of culture and civilization and a bunch of perverted fairy amateurs and will get theirs anyway when the universe collapses on them so why worry in any case.

Then we have the case of Gregory [Corso] who has absolute genius at elliptical hilarity, great natural phrasing, and is as good a poet now as Dylan Thomas. His great "Bomb" poem and "Army" and "Coit Tower" in his book [*Gasoline*] which is powerful and pure and rich like [Thomas' poem]

---

[56] Philip Rahv was an editor of the *Partisan Review.*

94

"Fern Hill" and why nobody gives him the respect and money he deserves I'll never understand except a peculiar kind of ungrateful ill will of mediocrity which is always the enemy of the muse and will wind up poisoning Corso except that he's too mad—yet I haven't seen one responsible review of his book, an epoch making original book, tho much richer and better has already been composed by him—we are living in a very rich period of poetry in the US, it may be the very cracks in consciousness appearing over the fall of America is the concomitant of such a flowering— and his book's been out years now, a year and half—without official notice people have picked up on it, about 2,000 copies already—not one review. I can't stand the pharisaical attitude of the whole treasonable intellectual group who think they are the civilization—basically the problem is they are not free, they have all sold their souls for money ego security conformity prestige university maturity social integration of the most spiteful and chicken kind—to have to endure the attacks and ignorance of these people is more than I should have to bear with the load I have to carry already it's not fair and it's asking too much of me, and to do that and have done that in a kind of ridiculous self imposed safety-poverty where I don't have stamps to communicate with Corso half the time. Oh well, I'm complaining like Hitler. But not one inch of understanding! And the vulgarity of the kind of opportunistic publicity so called friendly from the same intellectual types—in another guise or job—at *Esquire* or *Time*—stories which ball up the real prosodic and spiritual issues—halfwit interpretations of "negative values" of "Howl"—all the Highets[57] that are paid thousands of dollars a year to sit there and yatter out their opinions opinions opinions the screwy band of opinionated clunkheads that run everything from the *Daily News* to the *Hudson Review*—you should see the insulting letters I get from that Morgan lame duck poet. And Simpson reviewing "Howl" and an inept and prosodaically inaccurate parody and rejoicing (with Podhoretz) that Burroughs and Kerouac and other SF mss. are unavailable and unpublished— and you resolving your conflict by taking the angle that "Howl" is rather "vulgar"—I mean I sent it to you hoping you'd have the technical knowledge to deal with it as a piece of construction and that you'd fuck the whole sociological-tone-revolut whatever bullshit that everyone else comes on with—and to have Gold (Herb) mocking me for dragging myself around the magazines and publishers trying to go out of my way to introduce new materials, explain, spread some light—in the face of the worst civilized shits

---

[57] Gilbert Arthur Highet (1906-1978), professor of Greek and Latin at Columbia.

that ever ran so monstrous a conspiracy as America mass communication at all—to have to tackle all that single-handed practically and then be put down for all that—I DIDN'T HAVE TO TAKE THE TROUBLE—to have to listen to Rahv in Venice giggling that there's no poetry in US so that's why they didn't have a poetry editor at all 2 years ago—which was just his ignorance and the ignorance of all non-poets—yet he's RUNNING this so called mental newssheet!? and to call *that* responsible culture? And to have them and everybody else ignoring totally the productions of the Jno Williams' Jargon series which for 8 years was the only respectable publishing company for experimental poetry—and total ignorance of all the work developed out of Black Mt—the fucking sneers if anything—total incomprehension of Creeley's funny volumes of verse, nobody reviewed or heard of Blackburn's book, *The Dissolving Fabric*—not GREAT but *real*, nor Levertov's nor Zukofsky's books there reviewed, *Black Mt Review* the only decent mag operating for poets in America circulating 300 copies and nobody supposedly responsible at Columbia or anywhere taking the trouble to HELP, and the other BM poets minors, Oppenheimer, Perkoff, maybe Duncan, etc.—and the great new young ones John Wieners and Edward Marshall—whom nobody every heard of—or will investigate—and don't think I haven't written this to anybody I could get hold of, Gold, Rahv, *Mademoiselle*, *Hudson*, *New World Writing*, endless conversations and letters and explanations and trying to spread some good news, *Life*, and have them fuck it all up with their indifference or vulgar money journalism—and the whole problem of the Burroughs mss. legally uncirculatable here in the US—to say nothing of the great unknown Boston Group around John Wieners (got a magazine *Measure* out in SF now)—and the beginning of interconnection of all these with the NY people, O'Hara, Ashbery and Koch—at least these latter three pick up on something, and have some sympathy and openness, and respond to original attempts at composition.

The key and interest of Creeley's verse incidentally is this. Whereas in short line, Williams generally, or mine, runs forward in the line like actual speaking, Creeley has an ear of his own that's peculiar and laconic. He has got lately to using the most simplified forms, two lines together, free verse type couplets, trying to listen and balance them—his line tends to run backward, so to speak, rhythmically, the words very separate from each other and halting and stoic, effort of difficult nuts of speech, little pure sayings. A very peculiar subtle ear I'd say, NOT AT ALL like Williams, more like Pound writing Williams. Also a great historic literary grasp, used well and incisively as editor of the *BMR*—he's a great figure—sort of the great connection between the BM-Olson-Williams school and the SF Williams-Beat-Zen types—and also the Bostonians, (Wieners and Marshall and others). That you say these people have poor or inadequate preparation, education, to write poetry—considering their individual respective learnings, languages, skills, etc. etc. educations (to say nothing of their radical approach)—I mean I don't see how you come on like that, or why. They're all perfectly literate. Snyder is more learned than you or anybody, except maybe Ansen. Creeley teaches Latin. Blackburn Provençal. Olson you know. Whalen's reading everything both occidental and Oriental. Kerouac knows everything intuitively. But also he's read extensively in Buddhist specialties. I don't see where you think you're better educated particularly than, well I was going to say me, but that gets us into tendentiousness. I mean it isn't really education that's at issue, never was, I don't know what illiterate jerk brought that point up, probably Podhoretz. But this kind of incredible corny crap has served for literary discussion at endless length. The scene is too corrupt.

Well what's all this leading up to? I don't know yet, I'm just obviously blowing off steam. Yes, back to "[Siesta in] Xbalba." If you, one, is interested in a certain awkward natural style, for reasons, then the fact the Xbalba is "carefully made" is its most minor virtue—it's technically no improvement on Williams, except it's application of free verse to Wordsworthian meditation long poem—Tintern Abbey type, or Byronic meditation on ruins. But the real technical advance is in the long line poems, they proceed inevitably and naturally from the earlier poems, it's just a sort of COMPOUND imagism—compounded cubist images, and compounded rhythmic long lines. By hindsight. If I ever worried about technique in advance I wouldn't be able to write a line—THAT kind of worry. My worries are more practical having to do with the problem of breath and notation and the freeing of myself from preconceptions as to literary style. The beauty of writing is as Williams says, the invention, the discovery of new appropriate forms, the discovery of something you DON'T know, rather the synthesis repetition of things you do already know. It's a jump up forward into life, unknown future life, not—not an old spinster hung up on her one virgin experience and endlessly crooning it to herself (while the robber unknown's waiting under the bed). Any poem I write that I have written before, in which I don't discover something new (psychically) and maybe formally, is a waste of time, it's not living. I mean to get to the point of finally being frank and including queer material in the poems was a liberation, socially and psychically etc.—of expanding the area of reality I can deal with in the poems rather than shrinking back—(one reason I dig Gregory—he'll write about *anything*, socks, army, food, Arnold, Loony—so he also now writes the One Great Poem about the Bomb. He's extended the area of poetic experience further out than anyone I know—my own area is still rather limited to literary aesthetic hangovers from stupid education experiences. At least he writes (as Koch co-incidentally demanded in poem "Fresh Air") a poem about pants. Williams precise real images are such a relief after affected iambics, but pants is such a relief after hard real Williams—a new Romanticism in bud. But expanding the area you can deal with directly, especially to include all the irrational of subjective mystic experience and queerness and pants—in other words individuality—means again (as it did for Whitman) the possibility in a totally brainwashed age where all communication is subject to mass control (including especially including offbeat type talks in universities and places like *Partisan*)—means again at last the possibility of prophetic poetry—it's no miracle—all you have to know is what you actually think and feel and every sentence will be a revelation—everybody else is so afraid to talk even if they have any feelings left. And this kind of bardic frankness prophecy is what Whitman called for in American poets—them to take over from priests—lest materialism and mass production of emotion drown America (which it has) and we become what he called the fabled damned among nations, which we have—and it's been the cowardice and treason and abandonment of the poetic natural democratic soul by the poets themselves that's caused the downfall and doom of the rest of the world too—an awful responsibility. It's not that Podhoretz and the rest of the whores are just a passing phenomenon of vulgarity, like transient editorials in the *Daily News*, it's the very poison that'll permanently sicken the mental soul here and has sickened the nation beyond recovery already—simply nobody taking responsibility for their own real thought—nothing but a lot of Trillinguesque evasions with communist doubletalk about moral imagination, a cheap trick to suppress their own inside irrational Life and Poetry and reduce everything to the intellectual standard of a *Time* magazine report on the present happiness and proper role of the American Egghead who's getting paid now and has a nice job and fits in with the whole silly system. Well, it's no loss to have it already blown out from under them by the ridiculous collapse of the American Century after Sputnik. I suppose there's a new "examination of conscience" going on somewhere in their heads and they'll come up with a new worried bald set of polemics while gay prophet Corso starves ignored in Paris. And I'm not overstating Corso's magical importance. So anyway there is this Grove anthology [*The New American Poetry: 1945-1960*] of all these poets (about 30) coming out in a year and if you call that a BORE again I swear I'll write you a letter goofier than this and twice as exasperated—unless you really *believe* that— in which case I give up but god knows I have tried—and while I'm on the subject, I'm sick of reading articles on Beat or SF poetry accusing me or anyone of inability to express myself, incoherence or jimmydeanesque oral blocking, inability to communicate, etc. I certainly refuse to get any more involved with the stupidity of other people in petty mad literary arguments and so for that reason have refrained (tho god knows I get messianic critical article impulses) from writing insane long articles refuting this and that misunderstanding, etc etc. better save my energy for god knows what, at least something real, a letter, or a poem, agh, I wind up fuming in solitary. Well I know I'm raving, but I've saved it all up for you. And is Trilling behind all this mass stupidity about poetry, at least in NY?

Then there is McClure who started out as a narcissist but seems to have grown some, there was a gleam in him earlier, now it's a fire. Long poems this last year very good. He has his own way.

All these people should have long ago been having books out in NY and reviewed seriously everywhere and the lack of their material has left the atmosphere poisoned by bad poetry and bad people and bad criticism— and the criticism! Incredible after two decades of new criticism and the complete incompetence to evaluate and recognize anything new—nothing but lame sociological bullshit in response to Jack's prose or my poetry—or total amnesia with Gregory's or Creeley's and Olson's, etc. All the universities been fucking dead horses for decades and this is <u>Culture</u>!? Yet prosody and conceptions of poetry been changing for half a century already and what a Columbia instructor can recognize in Pound he can't see in Olson's method, what he can see in Lorca or Apollinaire he can't see in "Howl"— it's fantastic. You call this education? I call it absolute brainwashed bullshit. Not saying that either Olson or "Howl" are Lorca or Pound—I'm saying there's a recognizable continuity of method—yet I have to listen to people giving me doublethink gobbledygook about why don't I write poems with form, construction, something charming and carefully made. O Lawrence thou should be living at this hour! And Diana Trilling in public correspondence with that eminent representative of the younger generation Podhoretz about Lawrence! It's a vast trap. And god save the poor young students who know nothing but that mad incestuous atmosphere.

99

I could go on all night. What else, what else? I don't have your review here or I'd try and work in and out of that. And some jerk named Brustein who TEACHES at Columbia writing in a new money money money magazine *Horizon* attacking the Cult of Unthink,[58] grandscale vicious attack on Stanislavsky Method, abstract painting (bedfellow!) and beat writing drooling on about how I express every degradation except the one humane one, loneliness—I mean some completely inaccurate irrelevant piece of journalism! Ignoring bi queer lonely lyrics about Whitman and Moloch in whom I sit lonely cocksucking—just goes on and says this here vicious incoherent Ginsberg refuses to admit he's lonely. He TEACHES! Is such shit allowed on this earth? The whore of Babylon's befallen us! Run for your life! And in highclass *Partisan*, Podhoretz (I keep coming back to him it seems he has collected all the garbage in one mind, archetype) quoting me about Jack's "spontaneous bop prosody" proceeds to attack it instead of trying to figure what I mean—because I put it there as a tip, a helpful hint to criticism, a kindly extraverted gesture—and winds up all balled up confusing Jack's *diction* and use of the mind's hip talk to itself with the *rhythm* of the consequent sentences. This sort of ignorant babble in *Partisan Review*—and they tell me he'll be editor someday? Could that be true? Well they deserve it if they put up with that yahoo type creepy mentality. I'm sick of the creeps bugging the scene, my scene, America's scene, we only live once, why put up with that grubby type ambitious vanity. Ugh. It's too ignoble. Take it away. I'll take a sick junky any day to this horde of half educated deathly academicians. Not one yet, not ONE in all the colleges, magazines, book pages has said anything real, has got the point, either of spirit or prosody prosody (what a campy word—I'm sorry I keep using it—it really is that—but *another* way) NOT ONE. And this is the product of the schools of the richest nation of the earth, this is the intelligentsia that's supposed to run the world, including the moon? It's a monster shambles.

Complaints, complaints, you hear them on a summers day. Pound is absolutely right . . . with usuria. The whole problem is these types want money and security and not ART.

Well, I don't know where to go from here, I've unloaded it all on your head . . . tho you asked for it . . . on the other hand, that's what we're here for, why not have a ball. I did all this so I wouldn't be involved in endless statements when we met, explanations, better shit it all out at once.

---

[58] Brustein, Robert. The Cult of Unthink. *Horizon*, vol. 1, no. 1 (September 1958) pp. 38–45, 134–135.

Yours in the kingdom of music.
Nella Gregsnig, Allen

The birds have eaten the berries. Haven't I sent this letter before in another life? And haven't you received it?

CHESTER MACPHEE, SAN FRANCISCO COLLECTOR OF CUSTOMS, 1957

MARCH: POETRY SEIZED

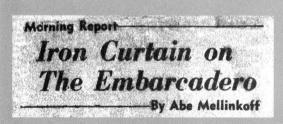

Iron Curtain on The Embarcadero
By Abe Mellinkoff

COLLECTOR OF CUSTOMS Chester MacPhee is a nice guy and a good public servant. I've known him for years and as far as I could ever find out, he knows no more about modern poetry than I do. What I mean [is that] he is ignorant on the subject. That's why I think he has a lot of nerve in confiscating 520 copies of a book by an unknown poet named Allen Ginsberg.

The thing was printed in England and picked up on the local docks as being too dirty for Americans to read. The book is titled: "Howl and Other Poems."

I am happy to report that I have not read "Howl" or any of the "Other Poems." Mr. MacPhee has but, modern poetry being what it is, I'm not sure this gives him any advantage over me.

In his literary criticism of the volume, the customs collector said: "The words and the sense of the writing is obscene. You wouldn't want your children to come across it." Assuming all of this to be correct, I don't see that this is any justification for grabbing the books.

The collector of the customs has a very important job. He and his men patrol the docks to keep opium from sneaking across. They also are there to keep fine citizens honest by making them declare various knick-knacks they have picked up on cruises.

But the collector has no duty to protect my children. I sometimes wish he had. If he is going to pick up everything that is a menace to them, he is going to be confiscating night and day.

This would include, in addition to dangerous books, such lethal instruments as knives, high-speed can openers, and, of course, guns of all kinds.

What is more, if a literary iron curtain is to be erected along the Embarcadero, let's put some professors of literature down there to patrol it.

Morning Report: Iron Curtain on The Embarcadero
By Abe Mellinkoff, SAN FRANCISCO CHRONICLE
March 28, 1957

In response to the seizure of HOWL AND
OTHER POEMS and THE MISCELLANEOUS
MAN, the following letters were published in the
SAN FRANCISCO CHRONICLE in April 1957

LETTERS TO THE EDITOR

The people of San Francisco are fortunate indeed to have in their midst a man so devoted to the promotion of the arts as Collector of Customs Chester MacPhee. In the past, I have wondered about Mr. MacPhee's motives, but his recent confiscation of the book, "Howl and Other Poems," by Allen Ginsberg, which he termed obscene, convinces me, at least, that he is secretly sympathetic to avant-garde poetry . . .

The publicity attendant on confiscation ought to be of great aid to Mr. Ginsberg.

BERKELEY. BARBARA FRIED

I think 95 per cent of the decent people of this area support Collector of Customs Chester MacPhee, in his efforts to keep cheap, vulgar, pornographic books from entering the U.S.A

OAKLAND. C.N. SOARES

The fact that the eminent literary feinschmecker and arbiter, Mr. MacPhee, was quoted as saying, "You wouldn't want your children to come across it" ("it" being "Howl and Other Poems") indicates that the masterpiece was definitely on the level of child understanding.

I have never heard of an adult work of literary art — sacred or profane — containing questionable passages or words which would not be thoroughly boring to children. They can pick up a finer batch of pornography at almost any newstand.

BERKELEY. JOSEPH A. BABANDO

As a parent of teen-age children, I wish to support Mr. MacPhee in his attempt to keep dirty books out of this country. If the people who oppose this filth sit quietly by while a minority of liberalites shout to open the gates to obscene books and poems it may well be that this minority will soon swamp the country with the filth and dirt they love so well.

OAKLAND. J. LESLIE JENSEN

> ## "The major principle involved is whether a collector of customs is a suitable person to select the reading material of the general public . . ."

As I remember, MacPhee did a lot of work with kids when he was a Supervisor. He initiated the Master Plan for Youth which developed the many San Francisco playgrounds. He had a big family himself and took a great interest in kids . . .

I have two teen-age youngsters of my own and if MacPhee says something is obscene I think I'll string along with him . . .

SAN FRANCISCO. HERBERT H. FLING

I don't know whether "Howl and Other Poems" is suitable for a kindergarten book report or not, and frankly I care even less. The major principle involved is whether a collector of customs is a suitable person to select the reading material of the general public . . . The man is being paid out of public funds as a customs collector and should confine his activities to just that.

We have suffered too much in recent years from the clumsy antics of ignorant do-gooders. Tolerance of such upstarts can only breed what John Adams chose to call "the wrath of an exasperated people."

SANTA CLARA. F.W. DOREY

I must protest Chester MacPhee's pronouncement that Allen Ginsberg's "Howl" is obscene . . . .

I should say that when Mr. MacPhee saw too many four-letter words, he neither saw nor read anything else. Allen Ginsberg's poem may be a lot of things — bitterness bleeding and crying, a rapture and rupture of pain, a malaise given to melody — but it is not obscene. I ask, in a loud and angry voice: What does Mr. MacPhee think he is doing?

SAN FRANCISCO. MARK S. WITTENBERG

We believe there are certain standards that all sensible and decent persons accept, and it is no violation of our cherished American liberty for Mr. MacPhee to utilize these standards in judging whether or not this sort of printed matter should get across the docks.

BURLINGAME. ED ARNOLD

Our customs house has arrogated to itself the guardianship of what one should read and what one should admire in literature and art . . .

Yet who are these guardians of our moral and political outlook? They do not possess any degrees in art nor any broad political worldviews that would enable them to say what people should read or think in our world, where new standards are being established . . . and moss-grown ethics are being discarded.

Must our America be subject to censorship by the ninnies of the San Francisco customs house?

DALY CITY. PETE MORGAN

I cannot understand why The Chronicle opens its pages to the writers who want the Federal Government to open our gates to obscene and pornographic books and poems.

Since this country was born, we Americans have rejected this type of junk. I called the Customs office and found out that under Section 305 of the Tariff Act the Government is required to stop this stuff from coming into our country.

I say thank God for Section 305 and thank God for a guy like Mr. MacPhee who has the guts to stop this obscene material . . .

REDWOOD CITY. MRS. H. LAURIENTI

In the March 26 Chronicle Customs Collector Chester MacPhee is quoted as saying that he confiscated 520 copies of Allen Ginsberg's "Howl and Other Poems" because "you would not want your children to come upon it."

This is, of course, precisely the reasoning of the Michigan obscenity statute which the U.S. Supreme Court, on February 25, declared unconstitutional.

"Quarantining the general reading public against books not too rugged for grown men and women in order to shield juvenile innocence," wrote Justice Frankfurter, "is to burn the house to roast the pig."

This procedure, the unanimous opinion continues, tends "to reduce the adult population . . . to reading only what is fit for children." and is in clear violation of the due processes clause of the 14th Amendment. . . .

BERKELEY. ANTHONY BOUCHER, CENSORSHIP COMMITTEE: MYSTERY WRITERS OF AMERICA

THIS WORLD   SAN FRANCISCO CHRON

Between the Lines

LAWRENCE FERLINGHETTI, San Francisco bookseller, poet and publisher, was the central figure in the recent action by the local Collector of Customs who seized 520 copies of the paper-bound volume "Howl and Other Poems," by Allen Ginsberg. The books, seized last March 22, were being shipped to Ferlinghetti's City Lights Book Shop by the British printer, Villiers. A first edition passed through U.S. Customs in October 1956 and was released without incident by Ferlinghetti. The March shipment was halted by Chester MacPhee, Collector of Customs for San Francisco . . . ."

The following is a statement by Mr. Ferlinghetti in defense of "Howl."

The San Francisco Collector of Customs deserves a word of thanks for seizing Allen Ginsberg's "Howl and Other Poems" and thereby rendering it famous. Perhaps we could have a medal made. It would

have taken years for critics to accomplish what the good collector did in a day, merely by calling the book obscene. Since City Lights Books has now had an entirely new edition printed locally and thereby removed it from Custom's jurisdiction, I should like to justify this action by defending "Howl" as a poetic work, leaving the legal arguments to others.

I consider "Howl" to be the most significant single long poem to be published in this country since World War II, perhaps since Eliot's "Four Quartets." In some sense it is a gestalt, an archetypal configuration of the mass culture which produced it. If it is also a condemnation of our official culture, if it is an unseemly voice of dissent, perhaps this is really why officials object to it. In condemning it, however, they are condemning their own American world. For it is not the poet but what he observes which is revealed as obscene. The great obscene wastes of "Howl" are the sad wastes of the mechanized world, lost among atom bombs and insane nationalisms, billboards and TV antennae. Ginsberg chooses to walk on the wild side of this world, along with Nelson Algren, Henry Miller, Kenneth Patchen, Kenneth Rexroth, not to mention some great American dead, mostly in the tradition of philosophical anarchism.

Ginsberg wrote his own best defense of "Howl" in another poem called "America." Here he asks: "America, when will we end the human war?" and "America, how can I write a holy litany in your silly mood?" Speaking of the "best minds" of his generation, Ginsberg writes in "Howl":
What sphinx of cement and aluminum bashed open their skulls and ate up their brains and imagination?
Moloch! Solitude! Filth! Ugliness! Ashcans and unobtainable dollars!
Children screaming under the stairways! Boys sobbing in the armies!
Old men weeping in the parks!
A world, in short, you wouldn't want your children to come across. I pity the Harvard prof in the "Partisan Review" who wasn't sure whether "Howl" was an imperative or a noun. It's an imperative. Considering the state of the world (not to mention the state of modern poetry) it was high time to howl. Thus was Goya obscene in depicting his Disasters of War, thus Whitman an exhibitionist, exhibiting man in his own strange skin.

Henry Rago, editor of "Poetry" (Chicago), will soon publish a defense of "Howl" which reads in part:
There is absolutely no question in my mind or in that of any other poet or critic with whom I have discussed the book that it is a work of the legitimacy and validity contemplated by existing American law . . . I would be unworthy of the tradition of this magazine . . . if I did not speak for the right of this book to free circulation, and against this affront not only to Allen Ginsberg and his publishers but to the possibilities of art and poetry in America.
The "Nation's" poetry editor has written that "censure of such works is ill-considered and justifiable neither morally nor legally." William Carlos Williams, who wrote the Introduction to "Howl,"

> **Kenneth Patchen wrote that "the really obscene four-letter words are in common use: 'hate,' 'kill,' 'maim,' 'bomb,' etc., while other four-letter words such as 'life' and 'poem' and 'love' are considered subversive and obscene . . ."**

said: "I'm amazed that 'Howl' has been denied release. Don't they know that release to the air and sun is the only thing in our lives to which the young can look to keep them virtuous?" Kenneth Patchen wrote that "the really obscene four-letter words are in common use: 'hate,' 'kill,' 'maim,' 'bomb,' etc., while other four-letter words such as 'life' and 'poem' and 'love' are considered subversive and obscene, especially if there is 'the remotest reference to that unclean and only fit to be starved and stoned and blinded and burned alive beast, our Fellowman!" Kenneth Rexroth, on his KPFA program, has regularly castigated the Customs for such seizures, noting that charges of obscenity in "Howl" are "a product of a particularly upside-down system of values."

Finally, in a letter signed by Robert Duncan and Professor Ruth Witt-Diamant, the San Francisco (State College) Poetry Center has made a statement which reads in part:

"'Howl' is a significant work in American poetry, deriving both spirit and form from Walt Whitman's 'Leaves of Grass,' from Jewish religious writing . . . it is rhapsodic, highly idealistic and inspired in cause and purpose. Like other inspired poets, Ginsberg strives to include all of life, especially the elements of suffering and dismay from which the voice of desire rises. Only by misunderstanding might these tortured outcryings for sexual and spiritual understanding be taken as salacious. The poet gives us painful details; he moves towards a statement of experience that is challenging and finally noble."

This World: Between the Lines
By William Hogan, SAN FRANCISCO CHRONICLE
May 19, 1957

HANRAHAN'S LAW, SAN FRANCISCO CHRONICLE, 1957

Making a Clown Of San Francisco

AS A CITY with some pretense to culture, enlightenment, liberality and sophistication, San Francisco has been sent sprawling into an unseemly and ludicrous posture.

The Police Department and the Public Library Commission, working independently but with equal witlessness, have contrived to give the community an appearance of profoundest imbecility.

The Police Department has not only set itself up as a censor of literature, but has enunciated a remarkable [illegible] of booksellers who are averse to jail. Police arrested a clerk at the City Lights Bookshop (and obtained a warrant for his employer) for having sold two books which the U.S. Government released from confiscation by an overzealous and notably prissy Customs Collector. Then the Department solemnly proclaimed that henceforth the legality of books will be measured with a kindergarten or grammar-school yardstick.

"We have purchased one of each of those books," said Police Captain William A. Hanrahan in reporting the arrest. "They are not fit for children to read."

Here is a new and startling doctrine and one which, if followed to the letter, would clear many of the world's classics from local bookstores, not excepting the Bible wherein is many a chapter and verse not recommended for perusal by tiny tots.

The Police Department's rampageous excursion into censorship may be explained by ignorance — not only of literature, but also of the laws and court decisions pertaining to censors. No such pleading can be advanced for the Library Board, which is clearly guilty not only of a perversion of its functions, but also of an almost hysterical attempt to duck responsibility.

For a year, the fearful board has kept under lock and key an assortment of Chinese books and pamphlets — ranging

111

from fairy tales through art folios to the political pronouncements of Mao Tse-tung — while frantically petitioning the FBI, the U.S. Attorney General, and the State Un-American Activities Committee to tell it if this reading matter is "subversive."

We submit that this is a finding that any adult, reasonably intelligent Library Board could and should make for itself. We further submit that even if the publications were "subversive" to the nth degree, a dutiful Library Board would be in there fighting for its constitutional right to stock and circulate them. For a library ought in all good conscience to be a repository for all writings, a collection of all books wherein the wisdom, and also the unwisdom, of all mankind can be glimpsed for the formation of judgments that are informed and intelligent.

If the Police Department and the Library Board prevail, San Francisco's judgments are henceforth to be based entirely on Mother Goose, The Sleeping Beauty, and Senator Hugh Burns' official correspondence.

Making of a Clown of San Francisco
SAN FRANCISCO CHRONICLE
June 6, 1957

Bookman's Notebook

Orwell's 'Big Brother' Is Watching Over Us

William Hogan

"ANYTHING not suitable for publication in newspapers shouldn't be published at all," the head of the police juvenile bureau was quoted as saying after two of his men raided a San Francisco bookstore the other day. They arrested a clerk on a charge of selling obscene literature. After it was over, the juvenile bureau chief explained that the books in question are "not fit for children to read."

John O'Hara put it simply not long ago when the Detroit police banned the paperback edition of his prize-winning novel, "Ten North Frederick," as unfit for children to read. O'Hara declared that he was not writing for children, and that few other serious adult authors were writing for children. The courts agreed.

The San Francisco case involved the now-famous "Howl and Other Poems," by Allen Ginsberg, earlier seized by the Collector of Customs when a shipment of books passed through the port en route from its English printers. It was subsequently cleared when a U.S. Attorney declined to file condemnation proceedings.

The second item that figured in Monday's municipal action was the Berkeley magazine, "The Miscellaneous Man," a quarterly that exists on a limited (almost microscopic) readership, none of which includes children, simply because much of the experimental rhetoric in it is unintelligible to them.

The point is that the cops are raiding the bookstores and presumably, with this precedent set, the literary patrol can march into any store in town and arrest the personnel at will. Not for selling "Howl and Other Poems," but for selling anything members of this Orwellian "Big Brother" agency doesn't like.

> "The point is that the cops are raiding the bookstores and presumably, with this precedent set, the literary patrol can march into any store in town and arrest the personnel at will."

The law in cases like this was laid down in 1933 in the case against James Joyce's "Ulysses." It was ruled then that a book could not be judged by its words, one by one, but must be read in its entirety — again presumably neither by children nor by a totalitarian Big Brother watching over us.

Dozens of people who called or wrote to me following this police action seem to agree with my personal view that the raiding of bookstores on such a slim pretext is dangerous, to say nothing of a stupid, precedent. I think an enlightened American community is in bad trouble if it permits this example of thought control to continue.

I hold no particular brief for "Howl and Other Poems," or for "The Miscellaneous Man." But I do go along with the President's letter to the American Library Association convention (June, 1953) which read: "As it is an ancient truth that freedom cannot be legislated into existence, so it is no less obvious that freedom cannot be censored into existence."

Orwell's Big Brother is Watching Over Us
A Bookman's Notebook by William Hogan
SAN FRANCISCO CHRONICLE
June 6, 1957

PAGE 2   SAN FRANCISCO CHRONICLE, Friday, June 7, 1957   FHE

Bookshop Owner Surrenders

Lawrence Ferlinghetti returned to the city yesterday and surrendered to police immediately on charges of selling "obscene" books in his Columbus Avenue shop.

As controversy over the case grew, Mayor George Christopher threw up his hands - in two different directions - at his press conference yesterday.

"I'm certainly opposed to censorship," he told reporters, but he added, "There is a very practical problem of law enforcement involving obscenity."

"Where is the line of demarcation? Is everything and anything supposed to go? Lewd shows are desired by some people but does that mean they're all right?" . . .

Ferlinghetti surrendered yesterday upon his return from a trip to Big Sur and his bail of $500 was likewise posted by the Civil Liberties group."

Bookshop Owner Surrenders
SAN FRANCISCO CHRONICLE
June 7, 1957

BOOKSELLERS: BOOKMEN ASK MAYOR TO BAN COP CENSORS

Twenty-one of San Francisco's leading booksellers petitioned Mayor George Christopher yesterday to "use all the power of your office" to end police censorship of books. "This sort of censorship has no place in a democratic society" and "is harmful to San Francisco's reputation as a center of culture and enlightenment."

. . . The bookstores they represent are: Bonanza Inn Book Shop, Fields Book Store, Old Book Store, Lawyers Book Exchange, French Book Store, Kepler's Book Shop, McDonald's Book Shop, Folio Book Shop, Ames Book Shop, Constance Spencer, Mageo David Book Shop, Kider's Books, Lord and Jordan, Argonaut Book Shop, Newbegin's Book Shop, Brentano's Book Shop, Macy's Book Department, Books, Inc., Town Book and Card Co., San Francisco News Co., and J.W. Stacey, Inc.

Booksellers: Bookmen Ask Mayor to Ban Cop Censors
SAN FRANCISCO CHRONICLE
August 16, 1957

"SAN FRANCISCO," said one exuberant visitor, "is a place where you turn the corner, and the world changes."

"San Francisco," said another, "is a warm Philadelphia with a New York accent."

"San Francisco," said a third, "is where you don't see much except a lot of water and rock. I'm in Alcatraz."

"San Francisco," said a gentleman at the Top of the Mark, "is where even the slums look good."

"San Francisco," said a cynic, "is getting too much like L.A. It's where neon goes when it dies."

"San Francisco," said Sue Lorenz, the United stewardess on the flight

out, "is a place to hang your hat for a day and a half until the trip back East. But what a hatrack!"

"San Francisco," said Flight Captain Reynolds of the same craft, "is the only damn place in the world to live."

YOU MIGHT CALL the lower part of Telegraph Hill—and its adjoining North Beach district—the Greenwich Village of San Francisco. A Saturday evening among the Bohemians there— real and pseudo—might find you squeezed on the floor of an eight-by-fourteen living room with just enough room to balance a warmish bourbon-and-water on your knees (for the ice is bound to have run low). You'd be sure to see a couple of girls with black sweaters, black skirts, black knee socks, and bright outlooks—and at

least three beards poking up over an equal number of tweed jackets. The talk will range from Picasso to Dali to Bartok to Dylan Thomas to Allen Ginsberg's poem "Howl," which has been rocking both the city and the country along with the now-famous trial. It is a case of provincial stupidity on the part of a customs inspector, a rectangular mayor, and a prosecuting attorney who should know better.

THE TRIAL ITSELF has been branded by some as a deliberate political gambit to save the face of Customs Official Chester McFee. McFee made the strategic error of holding up the copies of the poem "Howl," being shipped from England (where it was originally published with a few other Ginsberg poems) to bookseller and poet Lawrence Ferlinghetti, who was planning to publish it in this country. McFee forwarded the poem to Washington on the grounds that the material therein was obscene. But Washington failed to find it such, and refused to bar it on the grounds of obscenity. The local politicians refused to let it go at that, and arrested Ferlinghetti and his assistant, Shigeyoshi Murao, who now face a possible $500 fine and six months in jail on the charge of knowingly offering an obscene book for sale. McFee's error lies in the fact that the trial has boomeranged completely at this point, and the poem is receiving many times the attention it would have received. It is obviously a very serious effort and must be judged, according to Federal law, as a whole— not censored on the grounds of individual words in it. The local prosecution cannot hope to win in the face of the already-made Federal decision.

continued >

"But he [Ferlinghetti] feels with others that the battle for literary freedom will be won, and the case for honest literature will be strengthened."

FERLINGHETTI can be considered a part of the nebulous group which has become known as exponents of what is being called the San Francisco Renaissance (see book review on page 13) . . . the New Generation of Revolt . . . the Beat Generation . . . or various other combinations of phrases. In an effort to track down more of what this is all about we called first on its most articulate spokesman, Kenneth Rexroth. We found him at his Scott Street apartment in high spirits, surrounded by tons of books and a charming baby daughter's birthday party.

"The thing that makes San Francisco what it is from the creative

artist's viewpoint is that it's a far cry from the gossiping marketplace in New York. Writers can think about life and meet it on its own terms in an atmosphere of tolerance and enthusiasm. The Ginsberg trial is a freak anomaly—the city people have been cordial to creative imagination ever since the days of the Gold Rush. There is no cultural provincialism among the San Francisco group. They mainly come from other parts of the Shop (sic) at the corner of Grant and Green Streets, but we arrived too late. This coffee house has the flavor of Greenwich Village . . . where you can get a corned beef sandwich, an apple strudel, beer, and all the cerebral conversation you want, and still get change back from a dollar. We traced him to his apartment, half way up

Telegraph Hill, where the view of the Bay was equalled only by the striking originality of his abstract paintings.

Ferlinghetti and his wife Kirby are alert, intelligent, gracious people. They are treating the trial with a light touch, but underneath it they feel that it is, in a degree, like the Arkansas case. When the Federal Law is applied the local law must give way. His first reaction on being arrested was the notion: This is how San Francisco officially recognizes what has been heralded nationally as a Renaissance in modern poetry. But he feels with others that the battle for literary freedom will be won, and the case for honest literature will be strengthened.

Actually, Ferlinghetti himself was not in town when the warrants were served. Kirby was calmly sweeping out the City Lights Pocket Bookshop, as the store is known, when two plainclothesmen arrived with the warrants.

"They were terribly nice, really," she said. "I would have sworn they were just out of Yale. They said it was all in the line of duty, ma'am, and I guess I got a little emotional about the whole thing and told them there were a lot more obscene things in books you can buy every day at any bookshop. I think they might have been just a little embarrassed about the whole thing."

As this is being written the trial has not been decided. Whatever the outcome, the attitude of a few local politicians should in no way reflect on the attitude of San Francisco as a whole.

It's a city fired with imagination and energy and vitality.

It will far outrun the almost Gilbert and Sullivan aspect of the present comedy of errors.

—JOHN G. FULLER.

SAN FRANCISCO CHRONICLE, Saturday, Aug. 17, 1957   FHE ★★

Battle of the Books Is On

'Howl' Trial Starts ---A Sellout Crowd

Egypt Clai Syria Down U. S. Plane

Continued from Page 1

skirmishing the case of the people versus Ferlinghetti and Murao came to trial before Judge Horn. Both men waived a jury.

To the intense disappointment of a large crowd of Ferlinghetti's customers and friends, poetry lovers, intelligentsia, professional writers

LONDON, Aug. 16
Two Egyptian news cies reported today Syrian military a forced down a United plane on Syrian soil day. The U. S. immed denied it.
At the same time a diplomat in Rome, disi

Critics Say 'Howl' Is Art As Prosecutor Seeks Dirt

KENNETH REXROTH
"A prophetic work"

WALTER VAN T. CLARK
"Thoroughly honest"

MARK SCHORER
"Significant comment"

A book called "Howl and Other Poems" was hailed as a "significant comment on human experience" and likened to the Bible, Dante's "Divine Comedy" and the works of Ezra Pound by some of America's leading writers and critics yesterday . . .

The trial was before Municipal Judge Clayton Horn, without a jury, and Judge Horn himself insisted that he alone would judge the poetry's salaciousness — judging it as an entire work, and not merely on the basis of individual words.

For this penultimate session of the trial the courtroom was jammed with spectators. There were probably more beards and baggy jackets, more copies of the "Partisan Review" than the Hall of Justice has seen in its history.

Critics Say 'Howl' Is Art
As Prosecutor Seeks Dirt
By David Perlman
SAN FRANCISCO CHRONICLE
September 6, 1957

'Howl' Not Obscene, Court Rules

San Francisco Chronicle **FINAL**
THE VOICE OF THE WEST

WEATHER FORECAST
Bay Area: Early clouds today and tonight. High Friday, 67 in 62. Low, 49 to 51. Westerly winds 12 to 25 miles an hour.
Full Report, Page 13

99th YEAR No. 277   CCCCAAA   FRIDAY, OCTOBER 4, 1957   10 CENTS   GArfield 1-1112

Racing Shutdown

State Money Crisis Threatened By Track Strike

SACRAMENTO Oct. 2—The strike which has closed Tanforan and which may halt horse racing at California's remaining tracks could result in a State deficit this year State Finance Director John M. Peirce said today.

The cancellation of Tanforan's fall meeting and daily mutuel wagering, Sax with other racing revenue at other tracks threatened, Peirce said construction programs at colleges and fairgrounds may have to be postponed.

"This imposing structure the defense labour as the 45-day meeting has been cut...

'Howl' Not Obscene, Judge Rules

By David Perlman
"Howl and Other Poems," the booklet whose violent verse aroused the Police Department and the city's literary Bohemia last varying vice ...

Judge Clayton W. Horn ruled that the booklet was not lewd or pornographic and could not be censored.

He freed Lawrence Ferlinghetti, bookseller, publisher and a poet himself, from a misdemeanor accusation that could have meant a $500 fine and six months in jail.

He also freed Shigeyoshi Murao, clerk at Ferlinghetti's City Lights Pocket Book shop. In a 39-page decision studded...

Violence by Proxy

Hat in the Ring

Knowland Makes Formal Entry in Governor Race

By Earl C. Behrens, Political Editor
SACRAMENTO Oct. 2—U. S. Senator William F. Knowland formally announced his candidacy for Governor today.

"I shall be a candidate for Governor in 1958," Knowland said at a statewide read at a press conference as he slowly wrote here. It was his official declaration that he would contest with Governor Goodwin J. Knight at the June primary. Knight already has announced he will run for re-election.

"I now make my decision to run for the high office," Knowland declared, "without purpose other than, if nominated can elected to devote myself faithfully to the ser...

Hoffa To Put Brewster Out of Jobs

At the start of the "Howl" case there was reason to be uneasy about the outcome. Judge Clayton Horn of the municipal court had just achieved certain notoriety by requiring a group of lady shoplifters to write critical essays on De Mille's "Ten Commandments" and by basing his legal judgment on the quality of their essays; the punishment seemed unusual if not actually cruel, and Horn won the irreverent title of "literary judge . . ."

But as the trial drew on, it seemed reasonably certain that Horn would decide in favor of the defendants: he

Judge Rules 'Howl' Not Obscene; 'Heal the Breach'

expressed fear of the curtailment of the freedoms of speech and press, and he conducted the proceedings with intellectual agility and a nice sense of fairness.

Judge Rules 'Howl' Not Obscene; 'Heal the Breach'
By Dr. Mark Linenthal
SAN FRANCISCO NEWS
October 1957

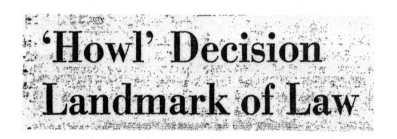

'Howl' Decision Landmark of Law

MUNICIPAL JUDGE CLAYTON HORN believes that his opinion in the "Howl" case—rejecting charges of obscenity against a collection of poems by Allen Ginsberg and thus acquitting the bookseller who was arrested for its sale—"might be helpful in California in the future."

In that belief we heartily concur. We find the decision sound and clear, foursquare with the Constitution and with the letter and spirit of various courts that have heretofore found the outcries of censorship lacking virtue. It upholds the right and suggests the necessity of an author to portray accurately the language of his characters. It finds that any effort to impose "vapid, innocuous euphemism" upon an author is in violation of the First and Fourteenth Amendments. It declares that a work is not to be judged on a few "unpalatable" words lifted from context, but as a whole — and then, from its effect not upon childish minds but upon the "average adult in the community."

Again, Judge Horn observes, a work may be deemed obscene only if it tends to deprave or corrupt readers by exciting lascivious thoughts or inciting to immoral actions — and there is no obscenity in a work which has "redeeming social importance."

These are admirable rules for the guidance of courts. Judge Horn's decision likewise offers an excellent rule for the public's adherence in matters of this kind. It says: "The people owe a duty to themselves and to each other to preserve and protect their constitutional freedoms from any encroachment by government . . . ."

To this he appends a quotation from Justice Douglas which bears repetition whenever censors rise up in their curious wrath to give the people unwanted and unneeded protection.

Said Justice Douglas:

"I have the same confidence in the ability of our people

122

> . . . a work is not to be judged on a few "unpalatable" words lifted from context, but as a whole—and then, from its effect not upon childish minds but upon the "average adult in the community."

JUDGE CLAYTON HORN

CONTINUED from previous page

to reject noxious literature as I have in their capacity to sort out the true from the false in theology, economics, politics, or any other field."

For a sharp and staggering blow to the chops of prurience and censorship, we congratulate Judge Clayton Horn.

'Howl' Decision; Landmark of Law
SAN FRANCISCO CHRONICLE
October 7, 1957

123

THE TRIAL

IN THE MUNICIPAL COURT OF THE CITY AND COUNTY OF
SAN FRANCISCO

STATE OF CALIFORNIA

HONORABLE CLAYTON W. HORN, JUDGE

PEOPLE OF THE
STATE OF CALIFORNIA

Plaintiff

vs.

SHIGEYOSHI MURAO No. B27083 311.3 of the Penal Code

LAWRENCE FERLINGHETTI No. B27585 311.3 of the Penal Code

Defendants

For the People

Thomas C. Lynch, District Attorney
Ralph McIntosh, Deputy District Attorney

For the Defendant

J. W. Ehrlich
Lawrence Speiser, ACLU
Albert Bendich, ACLU

Witness for the Prosecution

Russell Woods, Police Officer, City and County of San Francisco
David Kirk, Professor of English, University of San Francisco
Gail Potter, Teacher

Witnesses for the Defense

Mark Schorer, Professor of English, and Chairman of Graduate Studies in English, University of California. [Author of *The Wars of Love* and *The World We Imagine*]

Luther Nichols, Book Editor, *San Francisco Examiner.*

Walter Van Tilburg Clark, Professor of Language Arts, San Francisco State College. [Author of *The Oxbow Incident* and *The City of Trembling Leaves*]

Leo Lowenthal, Professor of Speech, Professor of Sociology [Frankfurt School], University of California. [Author of *Literature, Popular Culture, and Society*]

Kenneth Rexroth, Poet, editor, and book reviewer for *The New York Times, The Nation, Herald Tribune, KPFA,* and the *San Francisco Chronicle.* [Author of *Sacramental Acts* and *Communalism*]

Mark Linenthal, Asst. Professor of Language Arts, San Francisco State College. [Author of *Growing Light*]

Herbert Blau, Assoc. Professor in Humanities and Language Arts, San Francisco State College. [Dramatist, founder of KRAKEN, author of *The Impossible Theater* and *To All Appearances: Ideology and Performance.*]

Arthur Foff, Assoc. Professor of Language Arts, San Francisco State College.

Vincent McHugh, Poet, novelist, and translator. [Author of *I Am Thinking of My Darling*]

EXCERPTS FROM THE TRIAL TRANSCRIPT

September 1957

The Court: Gentlemen, you may proceed.

RUSSELL WOODS a witness called on behalf of the people, being first duly sworn, testified as follows:

Direct Examination by Mr. McIntosh

Mr. McIntosh: Q. State your name.
The Witness: A. Russell Woods.
Q. You are a police officer in the City and County of San Francisco?
A. Yes, sir.
Q. Calling your attention to May 21st, 1957, did you have occasion to go to the premises located at 261 Columbus Avenue, here in San Francisco?
A. Yes, sir.
Q. Whom did you go there with, Officer?
A. Officer Thomas Pagee.
Q. And what type of premises are those?
A. That's the City Lights Bookshop, a bookstore.
Q. Who did you see there?
A. I saw the clerk, Shigeyoshi Murao.
Q. And did you do anything there?
A. Yes, sir, I did.
Q. What?
A. I purchased a copy of a booklet entitled, *Howl and Other Poems.*
Q. All right. Is this the book that you purchased there [*indicating*]?
A. Yes, sir.
Mr. McIntosh: Just for the moment, Your Honor, may it just be identified?
The Court: People's One for Identification.
Q. Did you have any conversation with Mr. Murao?
A. No, I did not, other than asking him for a copy of *Howl*, which he gave to me and received my money—seventy-five cents.
Q. Was he the only one on the premises at the time?

A. Yes.

Q. And you obtained a warrant for Mr. Ferlinghetti's arrest?

A. Yes, sir.

Q. You determined that he was the owner of the City Lights Bookshop, is that right?

A. Yes, sir.

Q. Did you read this book of *Howl*, after you purchased it?

A. Yes, sir.

Mr. McIntosh: I see. I'll ask that the book be offered in evidence at this time.

The Court: All right. The book is admitted and may be marked People's One in evidence.

Mr. McIntosh: Now, you may cross-examine.

Mr. Ehrlich: May we have permission to reserve cross-examination of the witness until such time as your Honor has read this book? There are certain motions and objections we desire to make after your Honor has read the book.

It will be of no value to commence cross-examination today or to put in a defense, assuming that we should determine to do so, unless and until your Honor has read the book. Then we can call your attention to various parts. I have in mind that the matter may terminate on the presentation of this book.

The Court: Do you intend to make your motions before you go into the cross-examination of this witness, or just what do you plan?

Mr. Ehrlich: It is our present intention to make our motions before the cross-examination. Some of the motions must be necessarily made at that time; others can be made after we cross-examine.

The Court: In other words, as I understand it, some of your motions will be directed toward the contents of this book?

Mr. Ehrlich: Some of them will.

The Court: All right. What's your position, Mr. McIntosh?

Mr. McIntosh: Well, Mr. Ehrlich and I have discussed this matter and I have no objection. You have the book before you. Naturally, you will have to read it to determine whether or not it is obscene and/or indecent. And then, of course, we could continue on after you have read it just like we stopped at this moment, and he could make his cross-examination and make his motions if they are proper at that time.

The Court: I certainly would have a better understanding of what is before me after I read the book. I have not read it or seen it until today and I would be in a better position to understand the nature of the motions and the nature of the cross-examination, if any. The matter will be continued until August the 22nd at 2:00 P.M. for further hearing.

The Court: Are you ready, Gentlemen?

Mr. McIntosh: The people are ready, your Honor, but I understand the defense is waiting for their eminent counsel Jake Ehrlich.

· What I wanted to read into the record, your Honor, is not very much, but it is pertinent to our case. I want to show on the first page inside of *Howl* it says: "The Pocket Poets Series, Number Four, City Lights Pocketbook Shop, San Francisco." And on the second page it reads: "The Pocket Poets Series, Published by the City Lights Pocketbook Shop, 261 Columbus Avenue, San Francisco, Calif., and distributed nationally by the Paper Editions Corporation, manufactured in the United States of America." However, on the following page, way down at the bottom, is: "All these books are published in heaven." And I don't quite understand that, but let the record show anyway, your Honor, it's published by the City Lights Pocketbook Shop.

People's case, your Honor.

Mr. Ehrlich: Your Honor, the defendant now moves the Court for judgment that the publication is, one, not obscene, and two, that the defendants be found not guilty. We are prepared to argue for such judgment and, if your Honor desires it, to submit a written memorandum covering the various points involved.

★★★

I assume your Honor has now read the book. The question then arises whether as the result of your reading you have been able to form judgment as to whether this book is or is not obscene. In addition your Honor must not only determine what is the law as it is applicable to this issue, but you are to determine whether this book is an obscene book. If your Honor determines that the book is not obscene under the law, then, of course, that's the end of the issue.

There is yet another step, assuming for the sake of this argument only, that your Honor after reading this book has come to the conclusion that it is obscene. Then we are confronted with the second part of the description of the crime—whether the sale was wilfully and lewdly made.

There is nothing in the record showing any discussion or conduct on the part of the defendant other than selling the book. Now, let's see what is on the cover—"The Pocket Poets Series, *Howl and Other Poems*, Allen

Ginsberg, introduction by William Carlos Williams, Number Four." Let us stop with the cover. Is there anything about this book that indicates that there is something in it that will destroy the moral tenor of the community or do anything which would lead to a moral breakdown of the people of this City, to say nothing of Police Officer Woods?

The question is whether the community will be affected by it. So, your evaluation of the contents of this book must be made in the light of the community feeling about matters of this kind. I have looked at Mr. McIntosh's copy. He has underscored some words. I believe your Honor will agree with me that individual words in and of themselves do not make obscene books, and if it becomes a question of what the words mean, particularly some, I am ready, willing and able to define them. Some people think that certain four-letter words in and of themselves destroy mankind from a moral standpoint. This, of course, is not the law. There was a time, your Honor, when words which today are frowned upon, were in common usage, were not considered improper and were used daily by decent people.

We are confronted with the manner in which this book is to be evaluated by the court. As I understand the law, the court must construe the book as a whole. I presume that I could take the classic *Leaves of Grass* and by cutting it to pieces find a word here or there or an idea that some people may not like. But, in *Leaves of Grass*, there is the intent of the poet to convey a certain idea, not lewd and lascivious or licentious or common, but a story, laying out a certain format concerning life itself.

Your Honor probably recalls that it hasn't been too many years ago when the word "syphilis" was considered improper for use in so-called proper society, and it was not until we found an instant cure for this disease that we commenced openly discussing this terrible affliction for mankind. We delete words when we believe people are offended and not because of the words per se.

★★★

There is nothing in the record to indicate that *Howl* was purchased for its content. Nor is there any evidence before this court that any representation was made concerning the contents of the book, nor is there any evidence before the Court that in making the sale the purpose of the sale was the selling of a salacious, lewd or indecent book.

★★★

Specific intent cannot be inferred; it must be proved. There is not one word in the record going to the intent of this defendant in the sale of this book. Again, I am saying nothing about the contents. As a matter of law, the prosecution has failed to establish a case.

★★★

I conclude with the question whether, after reading this book, your Honor has come to the conclusion, one, that it is or is not obscene, and if obscene, what further proof there must be by the prosecution. If your Honor comes to the conclusion that this book is not obscene, that's the end of the case. Anticipating a reply from my opponent, I submit the matter. Of course, if it is necessary to reply, I shall have that opportunity, your Honor.

The Court: Mr. McIntosh?

Mr. McIntosh: Well, this trial is very unusual in its effect, your Honor, that before the defendant's case is in, before the matter is submitted to you, we are coming to the matter of arguing our case.

★★★

The Court: May I interrupt you? You are flying in the face of the First Amendment, freedom of the press and speech. The Supreme Court in the *Roth* case held that the exception to freedom of speech under the First Amendment was obscenity, and it limited it to obscenity. It didn't include anything else; it didn't even refer to anything else like indecency or anything of that sort. In other words, they stopped at the line of obscenity.

Mr. McIntosh: The point was not raised in that court, your Honor. They used the word but didn't follow and say anything about indecency.

The Court: Well, they very definitely made it clear. Many of the judges felt that even the word "obscene"—or obscene writing should be protected by the First Amendment. And your *Roth* case was actually a five-to-four decision. So, I think I can stop you right there as far as "indecent" is concerned. This Court feels that it will follow the *Roth* decision as the basis of what may or may not be the subject of an exclusion or exception to the First Amendment, and these books are either obscene or not obscene. I am not going to quibble about the word "indecent" or even consider that it is some thing lesser than obscene. It either has to be obscene or not.

★★★

Mr. McIntosh: Well, I am not going into this argument to point out from the pages of *Howl* the lewd passages at the moment, your Honor, because the defense has not presented their case and I think it is inappropriate to argue that point until the defense is in and the case is substantially before

131

your Honor for decision, and I contend that we have, by inference, shown that Ferlinghetti has knowledge of the character of this work, and I say your Honor might, in reading some of the cases, might have a feeling that these words in there are lewd, and if he puts on a defense that he doesn't know that there are such words as are in there, or that these words are not lewd, of course, I don't believe that would be pertinent to the case because, after all, the book stands and falls by whatever your Honor's decision is as to the obscene character of the writings there.

The Court: Now, coming back to the defense motions, which are in effect a motion to dismiss on the ground of the insufficiency of the evidence, the motions will be denied. So, it will be incumbent upon the defense either to submit the case without testimony and argue it, or to present testimony.

Mr. Ehrlich: Our thinking is, your Honor, that as a matter of law, you must first determine whether the book is obscene or not before we have the burden of introducing testimony. What testimony would your Honor receive in this type of a situation? Can the defense introduce evidence of reviewers, critics, literary people, and those who have made a life work of literature? Is it necessary to put into the record the thinking of men, who are instructors in this subject, that they believe after reading—and I quote from "Howl"—"saw the best minds of my generation destroyed by madness, starving hysterical naked"? What can they add, your Honor, to the testimony in this record by telling you that this is a reflection of the thinking of the writer as he sees this world? Will they say that the grammar is not exactly what it should be, or will they say that the construction of the poem is not what they think it should be, or will they say they see absolutely nothing immoral or improper in the poem or in the book, or are we going to get to the point where we're going to ask for definitions of words? I must assume that your Honor in construing this book is going to construe it as a book and not on what appears on page 3 or two words on page 27 and a couple of words on some other page.

***

The Court: Well, I would confine the admission of any testimony, if it were to be admitted at all, to literary critics and experts in that field. As far as sociologists and psychiatrists are concerned, and you can produce a number on both sides to come up here and testify both ways, and from the number of cases and different decisions throughout the United States, it is obvious that you are never going to get unanimous consent on anything that is involved in this case. That's the reason it is such a difficult question. That's the reason why the freedom of the press should be so stringently protected, so that no one segment of the country can censor to the injury of the rest, what they can read, see and hear and so forth. That is why this case is such an important one, why I am giving it such a lot of time and consideration.

★★★

Mr. McIntosh: You can see how far this thing could get out of hand, both sides bringing down all kinds of expert witnesses and telling your Honor how you should decide when your Honor has your own rules there. I think your Honor can fairly and conscientiously interpret the rules as set down, trying to take an objective view of it through the whole community and decide it yourself.

The Court: For the guidance of counsel, I feel that although certain testimony would be admissible, as I have related, that I would not permit the direct question to be asked of such a witness, "Do you consider this book obscene?" because that is something that the Court has to determine. I feel that a legitimate purpose would be served by submitting the book reviews or critics' reviews, even if you wanted to produce a critic or literary expert and propound questions to him such as whether or not—rather, regarding the theme of the book, plot—whether or not the use of certain words are consonant with the theme expressed, and things of that type. But I feel at this moment, unless I am persuaded to the contrary, that I would not allow such a witness to answer the direct question, feeling that this should be reserved for the Court with the guidance of such people, if any.

★★★

Mr. Ehrlich: The defense calls Mr. Schorer.

MARK SCHORER called as a witness on behalf of the defense, being first duly sworn, testified as follows:

Direct Examination by Mr. Ehrlich

Q. Your name, place of residence and occupation, please.

A. Mark Schorer, 68 Tamalpais Road, Berkeley, California. I am a teacher and a writer.

Q. Where do you teach?

A. At the University of California. I am professor of English and chairman of graduate studies in English.

Q. Tell us, Professor, whether you have done any writing, and if so, of what nature?

A. I have published three novels, about seventy-five short stories, thirty-two of them collected in one volume, more pieces of literary criticism than I know the number of, in practically every periodical one might name.

Q. Did your writing include articles of criticism of other men's work?

A. Yes.

Q. Do you mind naming them for the record, please?

A. No. The first was called *A House Too Old*, second, *The Hermit Place*, third, *The Wars of Love*.

Q. In addition to those three novels, you say you have written a great many articles for magazines?

A. Yes.

Q. Can you presently recall a few of the magazines in which these articles appeared?

A. Well, I am a regular reviewer for the *New York Times Book Review*; I have published in the so-called literary quarterlies, *Kenyon Review*, *Hudson Review*, *Sewanee Review*, *Partisan Review*, *The Reporter*—you want only criticism now?

Q. I am speaking only of criticism.

A. Yes. Well, that's a good sample; most recently in the *Evergreen Review*.

Q. Incidentally, does the *Evergreen Review* deal with poetry particularly?

A. Poetry and prose. I was dealing with D. H. Lawrence.

Q. Can you give us anything else concerning your background and learning which I haven't elicited by these questions?

A. I should have said that I have written or collaborated on half a dozen text books for college use, that I am a literary adviser as to publications of the Modern Language Association, a scholarly journal, that I frequently read books for university presses and advise as to publication, the Harvard University Press and Princeton University particularly, [and am] a paid consultant of the Army in choosing text books for its educational program.

★★★

Q. Your work on the *New York Times Book Review* is given over primarily to criticism?

A. Yes.

Q. Have you in mind presently any particular works which you were called upon to review for the *New York Times*?

★★★

A. I prefer to speak of one of my most recent critical publications.

Q. Very well. What is your most recent?

A. An examination of three texts of D. H. Lawrence's novel, *Lady Chatterley's Lover* in the *Evergreen Review*, an attempt to collate those texts, and among other things I considered the problem of the alleged impropriety of this work.

Q. Did your criticism of *Lady Chatterley's Lover* take into consideration any of the previous criticism by Anthony Comstock in New York?

A. No. I do not regard that as a serious critique.

Q. You ignored him altogether?

A. Yes.

Q. Are you presently engaged in the writing of any work or article which is of national consequence?

A. I am writing a biography of Sinclair Lewis, whose papers were bequeathed to Yale University. I have been given exclusive access by the executors of his estate. The book will be published in New York and in London.

Q. Have you received any specific honors as the result of the work which you have been doing?

A. Yes. I have had the Guggenheim Fellowship three times; I had a Fulbright award to Italy to pursue my works on D. H. Lawrence and Sinclair Lewis; and I was, last summer, invited to lecture in the University of Tokyo in Japan on another fellowship. I think those are the major honors.

Q. In addition to presently teaching at the University of California, where else have you taught?

A. I have taught on regular academic appointments, at the University of Wisconsin, Dartmouth College, Harvard University, and the University of California. I have also given more incidental courses of lectures in, I suppose, thirty or thirty-five universities in the United States and also in the University of Pisa in Italy and the University of Oslo in Norway and the University of Tokyo in Japan.

Q. I call your attention to the prosecution's Exhibit One in Evidence. Please tell me whether you have had occasion to read this work?

A. Yes, I have read this work.

Q. Do you have an opinion as to the literary value of Exhibit One, to which we refer as *Howl and Other Poems*, by Allen Ginsberg?

A. I think that "Howl," like any work of literature, attempts and intends to make a significant comment on or interpretation of human experience as the author knows it. And to that end he has devised what we would call an esthetic structure to sort of organize his material to demonstrate his theme. The theme is announced in the opening sentence. I don't know it; may I use my own copy?

The Court: Do you want the exhibit to refresh your memory?

A. Yes. The theme of the poem is announced very clearly in the opening line, "I saw the best minds of my generation destroyed by madness, starving hysterical naked." Then the following lines that make up the first part attempt to create the impression of a kind of nightmare world in which people representing "the best minds of my generation," in the author's view, are wandering like damned souls in hell. That is done through a kind of series of what one might call surrealistic images, a kind of state of hallucinations. Then in the second section the mood of the poem changes and it becomes an indictment of those elements in modern society that, in the author's view, are destructive of the best qualities in human nature and of the best minds. Those elements are, I would say, predominantly materialism, conformity and mechanization leading toward war. And then the last part is a personal address to a friend, real or fictional, of the poet or the person who is speaking in the poet's voice—those are not always the same thing— who is mad and in a madhouse, and is the specific representative of what the author regards as general condition, and with that final statement the poem ends.

This is, of course, only the first of the poems, that is, the title poem, but I believe it's the one under chief consideration. So that you have there an organized form to which the poet has devoted himself and through the use of—in order to make an indictment, a social criticism, if I may say so—of certain elements in modern life that he cannot approve. To that end he uses the rhythms of ordinary speech and also the diction of ordinary speech, language of ordinary speech, the language of vulgarity. I think I must stop with that. The language of the street, which is absolutely essential to the esthetic purpose of the work.

Q. So that the use of a particular word, which some think offensive, is necessary to paint the picture which the author tries to portray?

A. Definitely.

Mr. McIntosh: I would object to that as being leading and suggestive.

The Court: I think there is no harm in the question. The objection will be overruled.

Q. After reading "Howl," can you say that the author in his attempt to depict the conditions which he is condemning has by the use of specific words or otherwise accomplished the purpose which he set out to accomplish?

A. May I rephrase it? Do you mean to ask me whether I think he succeeds in what he wants to do?

Q. Yes.

A. Value judgments are relative. I think he succeeds, yes.

Q. In your opinion are there any phrases or terms used which detract or take away either from the purpose which he is trying to accomplish or destroy the medium which he uses?

A. No. I would say that within his intention, which is a serious intention, the elements that go into the linguistic organization of the poem are all essential.

Mr. Ehrlich: You may take the witness.

Cross-Examination by Mr. McIntosh

Q. Have you written any poetry, sir?

A. Not since I was a college boy. I have taught poetry, however, for twenty-five years.

★★★

Q. Well, would you call a book—a poem that is written one day with a serious purpose but must be cast aside, we'll say, in two months—of literary value?

A. One can't predict literary history. What will happen to that poem in twenty years, who knows?

Q. You are not answering the question, sir.

Mr. Ehrlich: I submit he has answered it.

The Court: I think the witness has answered the question.

Mr. McIntosh: Q. Well, what I'm getting at—I don't believe it is too obtuse. Would you say that a book, we'll say, was written seriously at one moment but had no particular appeal to anybody, would you say that it had any literary value even though it is written with seriousness?

A. Very great writers, as history has later revealed, had no audience in their own time. The only way I can answer that—

Q. I don't want to go into any double-talk with you. I am asking you whether a book written seriously, where its language is not interesting, we'll say, and perhaps nobody even looked at it, would you call it of any literary value?

The Court: I don't think that question is fair to the witness. I will, Mr. McIntosh, show you where that question is unfair. Suppose I decided—I felt that I was a pretty good author and I wrote a book and I was serious about it and my writing was atrocious, no one ever saw the book. How can you ask the witness whether or not that's any good?

Mr. McIntosh: Well, would you consider it of literary value? That is all I want to find out.

The Court: I know, but that question is not only unfair, but it is not founded on any autoptic profert that the witness can seize upon.

Mr. McIntosh: Q. Well, would you say that "Howl" has any literary merit?

A. Yes.

Q. I presume it was brought to you by counsel or one of his emissaries to read?

A. I bought it first at the U.C. Book Corner in Berkeley.

Q. And I presume you understand the whole thing, is that right?

A. I hope so. It's not always easy to know that one understands exactly what a contemporary poet is saying, but I think I do.

Q. Well, let's go into some of this. You have the book there. Will you open to page 9?

A. Yes.

Q. Well, about the third line down, you understand what "angelheaded hipsters burning for the ancient heavenly connection to the starry dynamo in the machinery of night" means?

A. Sir, you can't translate poetry into prose; that's why it is poetry.

Q. What are "angelheaded hipsters"?

A. That's a figurative statement: of "angelheaded"—I would say characters of some kind of celestial beauty like an angel; "hipsters" is part of the vernacular today. I'm not sure I can translate it into any literal way, though.

Q. In other words, you don't have to understand the words to—

A. You don't understand the individual words taken out of their context. You understand the whole impression that is being created and in this first part particularly, where I have already used the word surrealist to describe it. You can no more translate that back into logical prose English than you can say what a surrealistic painting means in words, because it's not prose. Poetry is a heightened form of language through the use of figurative language and rhythm, sometimes rhyme.

Q. Each word by itself certainly means something, doesn't it?

A. No. The words mean only in their context, I would say, and I can't possibly translate, nor I am sure, can anyone in the room, translate the opening part of this poem into rational prose.

Q. That's just what I wanted to find out.

A. It cannot be done, nor can it be done with any poetry. A sonnet of Shakespeare's cannot be translated into rational prose without becoming an entirely different thing.

Q. Well, are there any of these paragraphs which you can translate for us so I can understand it?

The Court: By "translate," do you mean translation into prose?

Mr. McIntosh: Well, so I can understand what the author is getting at.

The Court: Well, the witness just said that you couldn't translate it into prose. Do you mean interpretation or translation.

Mr. McIntosh: Translation—"Who got busted in their pubic beards returning through Laredo with a belt of marijuana for New York." What does that paragraph mean?

★★★

The Witness: I can only put it in my own language, which is not that of the poet, so there is going to be a different thing. I would take the line to mean something like this: Who in their wanderings across the United States all the way from Laredo to New York, probably hopped up, were assaulted—that is not a good word—were injured in their sexual beings. Not very—it is a very pompous paraphrase I am afraid.

Q. Skip down a couple of lines there: "With dreams, with drugs, with waking nightmares, alcohol and cock and endless balls." What significance does that have to you?

A. Well, there are uprooted people wandering around the United States, dreaming, drugged—that's clear isn't it? Even their waking hours like nightmares, loaded with liquor and enjoying, I take it, a variety of indiscriminate sexual experience.

Q. Do you understand some of these pages where there are just little dots in there?

A. I think I know the words that were intended.

Q. Let's take page 13.

A. Yes.

Q. Fifth line up: "Who let themselves be—" one, two, three, four, five, six dots—"in the—" three dots—"by saintly motorcyclists, and screamed with joy." What does that mean?

Mr. Ehrlich: I don't know how anybody can answer that; there are no words there. I am serious in this objection, your Honor. The objection is that there are no words printed there. Whatever construction Mr. McIntosh may put on it is the construction that he personally puts on it. He is asking the witness to tell him what those dots mean. It is calling for speculation.

Mr. McIntosh: I am asking what the whole thing means.

The Court: No. It calls for speculation on the part of this witness. The objection will be sustained.

Mr. McIntosh: I didn't ask him to supply, I don't believe, Judge; I didn't mean that.

The Court: Perhaps I misunderstood your question. You asked him what those words were supposed to be or what is meant by those dots and dashes.

Mr. McIntosh: I would like to know what is meant by that paragraph.

Mr. Ehrlich: May I make this point, Your Honor? It is the book as a whole, which is to be evaluated for either its literary or any other value, not each line or each word.

The Court: That's correct, but counsel has a right to cross-examine to ascertain whether or not the statement of the witness is based on the document as a whole, and besides this witness testified that there were certain words used in there, commonly used by the man on the street, which were a necessary part of the interpretation or picture portrayed by the author, and counsel for the prosecution has a right to go into that phase of it to ascertain why he so thinks, or whether or not he has some other thoughts on the particular phase.

Mr. Ehrlich: Does your Honor carry in mind the fact that vacant spaces can be filled by people in any way they want?

The Court: As to the vacant spaces, I have already indicated that I would not allow this witness to speculate as to what the author meant by leaving those vacant spaces. But I believe Mr. McIntosh's question now goes to the entire sentence. I think it would make it clearer for the witness if you read the particular sentence you have in mind and ask the witness for his interpretation, or whatever you want to take, as a whole without supplying anything that is missing in the spaces. Would you reframe your question?

Mr. McIntosh: Q. Well, in reading this "Howl," you have to know what certain words mean, don't you?

A. Yes.

Q. All right. Now then, let's take this next sentence: "Who blew and were blown by those human seraphim, the sailors, caresses of Atlantic and Caribbean love." Now, of course, you know what "blew" and "blown" mean, I hope . . .

A. Yes.

Q. They are words of the street, are they not?

A. I believe so.

Q. Now, are those words necessary to this "Howl?"

A. Those words are words that are intended to represent—let me start over. The essence of this poem is the impression of a world in which all sexuality is confused and corrupted. These words indicate a corrupt sexual act. Therefore, they are part of the essence of the picture which the author is trying to give us of modern life as a state of hell.

Q. In other words, they are necessary then?

A. They are illustrations of the general conditions that he's trying to impress us with.

Q. Getting over to page 22, starting with "Dreams!"

A. Yes.

Q. "Adorations! illuminations! religions! the whole boatload of sensitive bullshit!" Couldn't that have been worded some other way? Do they have to put words like that in there?

Mr. Ehrlich: I object to the question, your Honor, as to whether the author could have used another term or not. This witness can't testify to that.

The Court: I think it is obvious that the author could have used another term; whether or not it would have served the same purpose is another thing; that's up to the author. The objection is sustained.

Mr. McIntosh: Q. I didn't quite follow your explanation to page 27, "Footnote to Howl." Do you call that the second phase?

A. I didn't speak about "Footnote to Howl." I regard that as a separate poem. It is not one of the three parts that make up the first poem. It's a comment on, I take it, the attitude expressed in "Howl" proper, and I think what it says—if you would like my understanding of it—is that in spite of all of the depravity that "Howl" has shown, all of the despair, all of the defeat, life is essentially holy and should be so lived. In other words, the footnote gives us this state in contradistinction to the state that the poem proper has tried to present.

Q. Well, are some of these words in there necessary to the literary value of the piece of poetry? For example, going down to the second line in the "Footnote to Howl?"

A. I think he is saying every part of human life is holy, and he's not the first one who said it. William Blake, a great poet, said it in the eighteenth century. "All that lives is holy" was his way of saying it, his way of saying the same thing. No matter what part you want to mention is just as holy as any other part because it's human, and this, I say, is very much the essence of this poet's view of life.

Q. This poet's?

A. Ginsberg.

Q. Do you know him?

A. No, only as I infer it from this book.

Q. Did you read the one in the back called "America?"

A. Yes.

Q. What's the essence of that piece of poetry?

A. I think what the poem says is that the "I," the speaker feels that he has given a piece of himself to America and has been given nothing in return, and the poem laments certain people who have suffered at the hands of—well, specifically, the United States government, men like Tom Mooney, the Spanish Loyalists, Sacco & Vanzetti, the Scottsboro boys and so on.

Q. Is that in there?

A. It is in the book. In other words, that is the speaker associating himself with those figures in American history whom he regards as having been martyred. He feels that way about himself.

Q. Well, "America" is a little bit easier to understand than "Howl," isn't it?

A. I think it's a little more direct, yes.

Q. More direct. There is a little small piece of poetry in there like "An Asphodel." You read those too?

A. Yes.

Q. You think they are in a similar vein?

A. They are very different. Those are what one would call lyric poems and the earlier ones are hortatory poems.

Q. What?

A. Poems of diatribe and indictment, the mood is very different, hortatory.

Mr. McIntosh: That's all.

Mr. Ehrlich: Your Honor, we have other witnesses here, but this might be a good time to determine once and for all whether we are going to pick individual words and start debates on their meanings or the necessity of their use or their value to the work, whether it adds to or detracts from, whether it creates a literary value or destroys it. Mr. McIntosh has dedicated his entire cross-examination to that phase. Your Honor probably observed that the defense studiously avoided going into the construction of these poems piece by piece. We took it as a general over-all publication in line with your Honor's ruling at the last hearing.

★★★

The Court: Well, I don't think that I have deviated from the language which you have just read, Mr. Ehrlich. I think that on cross-examination the prosecution is entitled to ask certain questions of a witness who testifies to the literary merit of a work. For example, I certainly think the prosecution has a right to ask, "Do you consider certain parts or words of this necessary to the theme expressed?" or along those lines. I think that's legitimate cross-examination and doesn't detract from general outlines of evidence that I set forth and which you read from the transcript.

Perhaps we can resolve it this way: I think the rules that you are referring to are probably two, the first one being that the book is to be construed as a whole; there is no controversy about that. I don't think even the prosecution will dispute that rule. Number two, whether or not the use of certain words which may in their separate context be considered vulgar or coarse or filthy or disgusting or whatever it might be, whether they are necessary or a part of the theme of the book or whether they, together with passages that may encompass them, are just put in there for no purpose at all except to excite erotic or lustful desires. I think that generally is what the decisions hold with regard to constructions.

Mr. Ehrlich: I think that is a fair statement of the law, your Honor. There is no difference of opinion, but I do feel that determining whether Ginsberg was justified in using some particular word is not a question to be determined by this Court or to be determined upon the evidence of any witness. The question isn't whether Ginsberg was justified in his use; the question is the purpose for which it is used and whether it produced a certain idea. As I understood Professor Schorer, he said that it produced a certain idea, that he was using the words of today or the words of the street; so we have no difference of opinion, your Honor, if we stay with that line of examination. But, if we go into examination of what some particular words mean and whether or not they are necessary, then we are not reviewing the book, we are reviewing whether Ginsberg in his mind was justified in the use of some particular word. Now, how can any witness answer that?

★★★

LUTHER NICHOLS called as a witness on behalf of the defense, being first duly sworn, testified as follows:

Direct Examination by Mr. Ehrlich

Q. Your name is Luther Nichols?

A. It is.

Q. You reside where?

A. 2845 Woolsey Street in Berkeley.

Q. What is your business, occupation or profession?

A. I am a book reviewer for the *San Francisco Examiner*.

Q. Meaning the *San Francisco Examiner* newspaper?

A. Yes.

Q. Do you conduct or are you interested in any other forms of book review?

A. Yes. I have done other reviews, one for the *New York Times*. I have done television reviewing, an entirely different form, for television station KQED, a thirteen-program series for the Northern California Booksellers Association.

Q. Have you done any nationwide radio book reviews?

A. I have appeared twice on "Monitor," which is a nationwide network Sunday radio show.

Q. Have you done any particular work in reviewing books, which have been from time to time at issue, such as Exhibit One for the prosecution here?

A. None have come along during my tenure as a book reviewer.

Q. How long have you been in the work of book reviewing?

A. Nearly three years.

Q. I take it that the book review that appears on the page next to the editorial page in the *Examiner*, is your daily review column?

A. It is.

Q. I call your attention to the Prosecution's Exhibit One, entitled *Howl and Other Poems*, by Allen Ginsberg, and ask you if you have seen that before and have you read it.

A. Yes, I have.

Q. As a result of your experience in book reviewing, have you formed an opinion as to the literary value of Exhibit One?

A. I have.

Q. What is your opinion?

A. My opinion is that Mr. Ginsberg is expressing his personal view of a segment of life that he has experienced. It is a vagabond one; it's colored by exposure to jazz, to Columbia, a university, to a liberal and Bohemian education, to a great deal of traveling on the road, to a certain amount of what we call bumming around. He has seen in that experience things that do not agree with him, that have perhaps embittered him. He has also seen things at a social level concerned with the atom bomb, and the materialism of our time. In sum, I think it's a howl of pain. Figuratively speaking, his toes have been stepped on. He's poetically putting his cry of pain and protest into this book *Howl*.

Q. Do you think this book has definite literary value?

A. I do.

Q. And as to the format in which Mr. Ginsberg has done this work, both as to the context and as to construction, do you believe that his method adds to its literary value?

A. I do. As a matter of fact, I think in a way he is employing the jazz phraseology here and, may I say, I think he is also employing the words he heard in his life on the road and in his various experiences.

Mr. Ehrlich: You may take the witness.

Cross-Examination by Mr. McIntosh

Q. Have you done any writing yourself, sir? I mean outside of book reviews.

A. No, I haven't.

Q. And have you run across reviews of poetry, books of poetry very often?

A. Yes, I do.

Q. Of this type?

A. Not exactly of this type. I think one of the values of the poem is that it is somewhat unique; it is somewhat different, let's say.

Q. You are familiar with the San Francisco Renaissance, are you?

A. Yes.

Q. Have you read books in that vein, or from that group?

A. I have read very recently Jack Kerouac's book *On the Road*, which is a prose representation, I think, of this same segment of the American population.

Q. Do you understand most of the words in this book?

A. I think I understand their significance and the general context of it.

Q. I see. Taking on page 13 — the 14th line: "who howled on their knees in the subway and were dragged off the roof waving genitals and manuscripts." Now, do you understand what that paragraph is trying to say, as a part of the howl, I mean, this howl against civilization?

A. Not explicitly. I would say he's attempting to show the lack of inhibition of the persons he's talking of, the members of his group, you might say.

Q. Well, group of what?

A. Of the younger liberals. The post–World War II generation; those who returned, went into college or went into work immediately after World War II were perhaps somewhat displaced by the chaos of war and didn't immediately settle down.

Q. Well, do you understand the following sentence? I don't have to read it; you can read it.

The Court: Well, you better read it for the record.

Mr. McIntosh: All right.

Q. "who let themselves be——" bunch of dots——"in the——" three dots——"by saintly motorcyclists, and screamed with joy."

Mr. Ehrlich: Well, your Honor, we are getting right back to——

The Court: I think, Mr. McIntosh, that we have to go back to the basis that the book and its contents are to be construed as a whole. In addition to that, the sentence you just read, as you read it, has nothing in it that smacks or savors of eroticism or vulgar language. Now, it may be unusual language but there's nothing in there that contains either of those elements and certainly I can hold that as a matter of law. Now, if you have any particular words that you think are capable of inducing lustful thoughts or depraving anyone or inciting them to commit depraved acts as a result of reading those particular passages or words, or if you think there are some in there that are vulgar to the point of being pornographic, you may direct the witness to them along the lines that we have previously discussed, as to whether or not they are relevant to the theme and to the vehicle itself. But the question that you have just put will not be allowed because you could go through this book line by line and it would be a waste of time and not relevant to the question that's before the Court, to wit: Is the vehicle or book as a whole obscene?

Mr. McIntosh: Well, I am asking him about that sentence, your Honor, in this vein: There is a lot of dots in there; they must mean something to somebody.

The Court: No. I told you before that no witness will be allowed to speculate on what the author might have put in there. So, the Court will sustain the objection to that question.

Mr. McIntosh: All right.

Q. Now, the next paragraph: "who blew and were blown by those human seraphim, the sailors, caresses of Atlantic and Caribbean love." Now, you understand, of course, what "blew" and "blown" mean?

A. Well, I think they are words that have several meanings.

Q. What meaning do you attribute to the words in this paragraph?

A. I think you can attribute all of those meanings to the words in this context. I think it can at one level mean that they were vagabonds, that they were blown about by natural, literal winds. On the other hand, it perhaps does have a sexual connotation.

Q. In reference to oral copulation, right?

A. Yes, possibly.

Q. Now then, do you find that those words are necessary to the context to make it a work of literary value?

Mr. Ehrlich: I thought we settled that, your Honor.

The Court: Yes. Mr. McIntosh, if you will recall, I said that I would not allow the use of the word "necessary." You may ask the question, "Are they relevant?"

Mr. McIntosh: Q. Are they relevant to make this work of literary value?

A. Yes, I would say so.

Q. Well, if you took those words out of there would that spoil the portrayal?

Mr. Ehrlich: That's doing indirectly what your Honor won't permit him to do directly.

Mr. McIntosh: This man is an expert. He has to speculate.

The Court: No, no. Mr. McIntosh, I'm afraid I can't go along with you on that. Here again we get into the realm of speculation whether the author might have used other or different words, which might adequately have gone along with them. But, nevertheless, he chose these words and whether he could have used others or whether the deletions would destroy the vehicle, you are getting into the realm of speculation there. Objection sustained.

★★★

Q. Going down a little further, down to the seventeenth line from the top "who sweetened the snatches of a million girls trembling in the sunset, and were red eyed in the morning but prepared to sweeten the snatch of the sunrise, flashing buttocks under barns and naked in the lake."

The Court: What's your question?

Mr. McIntosh: Q. Now, is that word "snatches" in there, is that relevant to Mr. Ginsberg's literary endeavor?

A. Yes, I think it is.

Q. Of course, it goes along with the whole paragraph?

A. Yes. I think he's trying to convey an idea of fertility there, among other things, and this is his choice of language to convey that idea.

Q. All right. Next one: "who went out whoring through Colorado in myriad stolen night-cars—" and I don't understand that next—then an "N," period, and a "C" period, comma—"secret hero of these poems, cocksman and Adonis of Denver—joy to the memory of his innumerable lays of girls in empty lots and diner backyards, moviehouses, rickety rows on mountaintops in caves or with gaunt waitresses in familiar roadside lonely petticoat upliftings & especially secret gas station—" what's that next word?

The Court: Pardon me?

Mr. McIntosh: How do you pronounce that?

Mr. Ehrlich: Solipsisms.

Mr. McIntosh: ". . . solipsisms of johns, & hometown alleys too." It is a little hard to read because there are no commas in the spots where you expect them to be.

The Court: I believe the word "solipsisms" is misspelled in the book.

Mr. Ehrlich: Yes, it is. There is an extra "i" in it.

Mr. McIntosh: Q. Now, are these words relevant to the literary value of Mr. Ginsberg's poetry: "cocksman," about the "lays of girls in empty lots"?

A. Well, as I said before, Mr. Ginsberg is writing of his experiences, which have been on a hobo level at times. He's employing the language that is actually in reality used by hobos, by people of his experiences, hitchhikers, and I think in recounting some of these experiences, mentioning them all in this one stanza, if you want to call it that, the words are valid and necessary if he's to be honest to this purpose. I think to use euphemisms in describing this would be considered dishonest by Mr. Ginsberg.

Q. Now, take page 22. When I say, "lines," I mean stanzas, or whatever you call them. Go down about three, starts in with "Dreams!"

A. Yes.

Q. "Dreams! adorations! illuminations! religions! the whole boatload of sensitive bullshit!" Now, is that term, "bullshit," is that relevant to the literary value of Mr. Ginsberg's work?

A. I would say so, yes. Mr. Ginsberg is angry here. Obviously he is using the term that one might use in anger, again in preference to euphemism.

Q. By the way, Mr. Nichols, how do you define a book that has literary value?

A. There are many tests of literary value. The chief one historically is whether it survives its time, whether it is regarded by a consensus of educated qualified people as ultimately having literary value, as being worth reading for the educated person, as being a contribution to society and to the general education of readers.

Q. Well, then, merely because it's written seriously would you say that that alone would give it literary value?

A. Well, not necessarily.

Q. All right. Now, would you say then that this book *Howl* is worth reading for the educated person?

A. Yes, if he wants to hear a cry from a person who represents a certain part of American life, a certain experience of that life.

Q. Well, would he read it for entertainment value?

A. The word "entertainment" has a large and rather vague meaning. To some I would say it would be entertaining.

Q. Well, to what type of person would you feel that this poem would be entertaining?

A. Well, I would say to one who is familiar with the language and its experiences that Mr. Ginsberg is recording. He is expressing, perhaps, some experience of all of them and it would be entertaining to see in words, to see in his thoughts, an expression of some of the experiences they have had, some of the feelings they've had.

Q. Well, you also said, I believe, literary value sometimes is a book which will survive any test of time. Do you think that Mr. Ginsberg's work will survive the test of time?

A. I have no way of knowing.

Q. I ask you, do you think so?

Mr. Ehrlich: He has no way of knowing, no more than some people thought *Leaves of Grass* was going to survive.

Mr. McIntosh: I'm asking for his opinion, to give us an opinion on that book. He said literary value depends upon surviving the test of time. I want to know if it will.

Mr. Ehrlich: If Luther Nichols can answer that, the Good Lord can use a helper and he ought to be there. How can he tell? I object to the question as calling for a conclusion, not for a man's opinion.

Mr. McIntosh: I am asking for his opinion as an expert.

The Court: He has stated that he has no way of knowing. Now, you may ask him if he has anything to add to that but apparently that's his answer.

Mr. McIntosh: Well, I might call your Honor's attention to the fact that he said it's a work of literary value in response to Mr. Ehrlich's direct question. Now, he said one of the definitions of literary value is whether it lasts, whether it survives the test of time. He says it is a work of literary value. I'm asking him if in his opinion does he think Mr. Ginsberg's work will survive the test of time.

The Court: That does call for the opinion and conclusion and I think it goes beyond an allowable opinion and conclusion.

Mr. McIntosh: Well, your Honor, it's just a reverse play, you might call it.

The Court: Let me ask him—can you answer the question?

The Witness: It calls for a prediction. I don't think my prediction would be any more valid than anybody else's. Here I think the best possibility now in *Howl's* survival is for its value as a bit of literary history. I think this case will draw attention to it. It, perhaps, will have a wider readership than it might otherwise have had, and may go down in history as a stepping-stone along the way to greater or lesser liberality in the permitting of poems of its type expression.

Mr. McIntosh: That depends on the way his Honor rules.

The Court: In any event, you have your answer.

Mr. McIntosh: Q. Inasmuch as you apparently cannot say with any exactitude, or that it will survive the test of time, yet you say it has literary value. I believe some other test was—you said if it was worth reading by the educated; I think your answer was, yes, to certain types.

Mr. Ehrlich: Object to that question on the ground it is not stating the answer of the witness.

The Court: Well, you read several things there, Mr. McIntosh. I don't know whether you were summing up and asking a compound question or whether you are breaking this down into the component parts. What are you doing?

Mr. McIntosh: Well, first I am restating what he has more or less stated, that in reference to the term of literary value he said it is a book which survives the test of time.

The Court: I don't think you accurately stated the witness' response to the question of survival.

Mr. McIntosh: If I misstate you, I am sorry; I tried to write it down fairly fast here.

The Court: Just so that there will be no question in the record, you did not correctly state the answer of the witness with regard to survival.

Mr. McIntosh: Let's start in again.

The Court: Now, you better start again and get it straight.

Mr. McIntosh: Q. What is your definition of a book that has literary value?

The Court: Now, he has already gone into that.

Mr. McIntosh: That's what I say; that's what I stated.

The Court: You made a misstatement.

Mr. McIntosh: May I ask him then?

The Court: You made a misstatement of the fact and that is what I was merely calling your attention to.

Mr. McIntosh: Q. Did you not state, Mr. Nichols,—I am sorry; we could have read it back but it takes quite a little time for the reporter to find the notes. Did you not state that one of the tests of a book to have literary value, one of the tests among many would be the test of surviving time?

A. Yes, in part, yes.

Q. We have books that have gone down in history; we have them yet, the books themselves. We all read them. They look pretty dry sometimes, but they are all—they have survived the test of time and we expect to read them in school, is that right?

A. (*Witness nods affirmatively*)

Q. And I believe you gave some other definition of a book that has literary value, is that right?

A. Yes, that's right.

Q. Wasn't one of them that it was something worth reading to the—I believe you said—educated? I'm not positive on that last word, but worth reading to someone, is that it?

The Court: I'm not quite sure where you are going. Are you trying to bring out the answers to these same questions again or are you summing up or what? I'm trying to avoid repetitions here.

Mr. McIntosh: So was I, your Honor, but one of my questions—there was an objection made to it. Your Honor thought that I was not following through.

The Court: Well, so that we are not at cross-purposes here, you are going down the line here covering the same ground that you have previously covered.

★★★

Mr. McIntosh: Q. Now, taking this "Footnote to Howl." Read that, page 27, sir. Now, this first paragraph has fifteen "holy's" in there, "Holy! Holy! Holy!"

"The world is holy! The soul is holy! The skin is holy! The nose is holy! The tongue and cock and hand and asshole holy!" Now, are those last words there, are they relevant to the literary value of Mr. Ginsberg's work?

A. It seems to me they are relevant in that they are part of a contrast he is trying to show between the things that are conventionally accepted as holy and the things that he, in a Whitmanesque sense, [thinks] are holy in that they are all part of mankind and part of the world. He's showing that everything is holy within a sense, the sense that he is trying to convey here.

Q. Well, there is another part he says is holy, too; going down a little bit, one, two, three, four, five, six, seven lines down: "Holy my mother in the insane asylum! Holy the cocks of the grandfathers of Kansas!" Now, he uses that word again. Is that necessary to the relevancy of the literary value of Mr.—

The Court: Mr. McIntosh, will you delete the word "necessary" from your question? Reframe it.

Mr. McIntosh: Almost have to write it down. Is it relevant to the literary value of Mr. Ginsberg's work?

A. I would say it's relevant to his purpose.

Q. To his purpose?

A. Yes. Which I have just stated, which is to convey the totality of holiness in his interpretation.

Q. Going back to page 14, when I said I didn't know exactly what he meant in the fifth paragraph from the top of the page, when I cited the capital letter "N," period "C" period. Is that an abbreviation of a state or what does it mean, do you know?

A. I'm not sure just what he does mean.

Q. It has no particular significance to you, does it?

A. No.

Q. Did you read that "Transcription of Organ Music"?

A. Yes, I did.

Q. Is that a work of literary value?

The Court: I take it using the word "value," that is synonymous with "merit."

Mr. Ehrlich: They are interchangeable.

Mr. McIntosh: Mr. Ehrlich used the word. I'm following through on it.

The Court: I just wanted to get your thinking on it.

Mr. McIntosh: Yes, literary merit.

The Witness: Yes, I would say it is of some literary merit.

★★★

Q. By the way, have you ever written any book reviews on this book?

A. Not specifically. We did mention the book in an article that was done in the paper on the general problem of censorship of *Howl.*

Q. Nothing written by yourself?

A. No, I haven't specifically reviewed this book.

Q. I mean, but did you write this other article that you are talking about?

A. Yes.

Q. Did you also read "America?"

A. Yes.

Q. In "America," do you see a word in there, four-letter word, do you?

A. Yes.

Q. Is that relevant to the literary value?

The Court: For the record, Mr. McIntosh, what word are you referring to?

Mr. McIntosh: I will read down to the line:

"America I've given you all and now I'm nothing.

America two dollars and twentyseven cents January 17, 1956.

I can't stand my own mind.

America when will we end the human war?

Go fuck yourself with your atom bomb.

I don't feel good don't bother me."

Now, the word in there, that four-letter word, is that relevant to the literary merit of Mr. Ginsberg's work?

A. Well, Mr. Ginsberg is trying to—

Q. Will you answer my question?

Mr. Ehrlich: Let him answer it then.

The Witness: I am trying to answer. Mr. Ginsberg is trying to say as powerfully as he can or trying to express as powerfully as he can his indignation at certain things he sees taking place in the world today. He is obviously— perhaps one of our biggest problems is the atom bomb. He's tired of it. He's sick to the point of saying this. He doesn't want to temper it by saying it any less softly. He's angry, and when you are angry sometimes you do use words of this sort. I would say yes, it's relevant; it's in keeping with the wrath he feels, with the language that he has used throughout most of these poems. And, yes, I would say it was relevant to the literary value of the work.

Mr. McIntosh: That's all.

The Court: Call your next witness.

WALTER VAN TILBURG CLARK called as a witness on behalf of the defendants, being first duly sworn, testified as follows:

Direct Examination by Mr. Speiser

Q. Would you give your name and address?

A. My name is Walter Van Tilburg Clark; my address is 43 Molino Avenue, Mill Valley.

Q. Where are you presently employed?

A. I am presently employed as a Professor of Language Arts at San Francisco State College.

Q. And where had you previously been employed?

A. I had taught previously in English and specifically in creative writing at Stanford, University of Iowa, University of Montana, University of Nevada, and on shorter terms, including summer conferences, lecture trips, a Ford Foundation Tour, things of that sort, at Reed College, University of Oregon, University of Washington, Mills College, the University of Arkansas, the University of Missouri, the University of Wyoming, the University of Utah. There are some others.

Q. How long have you been a professor in English and Language Arts?

A. I have been a professor in creative writing specifically and in college level English for—probably twelve or fourteen years.

Q. Are you a professional writer?

A. I am.

Q. And can you name some of the books or other publications that you have authored?

A. Three books, *The Ox Bow Incident*, *City of Trembling Lights*, and *The Track of the Cat*, and a collection of short stories and one short novel, *Watchful Gods*, and a very early volume of verse that I would rather not name.

Q. Have any of your publications received any awards?

A. Yes, in 1945 or '46—the first award in the O'Henry Short Story Contest for one of the short stories. Aside from that, a number of pieces have been reprinted in anthologies. They have been overall translated into twenty-one languages.

Q. Have any of your books been dramatized in any form?

A. Yes, both *The Ox Bow Incident* and *The Track of the Cat* have had experimental stage versions presented and movies made from them.

Q. Major productions?

A. The movies were major productions; the others were made by experimental theaters.

Q. Have you had an opportunity to read *Howl and Other Poems* by Allen Ginsberg?

A. I have.

Q. Have you formed any opinion as to the literary merit of the publication?

A. I have.

Q. And would you give the opinion that you formed based on the experience that you have had, both as a professional writer and as an instructor and professor of English and creative writing?

A. They seem to me, all of the poems in the volume, to be the work of a thoroughly honest poet, who is also a highly competent technician. I have no reason to question in my own mind the feelings, Mr. Ginsberg's sincerity, in anything that he has said or the seriousness of his purpose in saying it.

Q. In forming your opinion as to the literary merit of the publication, have you considered some of the phrases and words about which Mr. McIntosh questioned other witnesses prior to your taking the stand?

A. Yes, when I knew that I might appear and have to offer an opinion, I examined the poem not only in a general way, but specifically for the purpose of determining my reaction to what I believe might be expressions or passages in question. I found none anywhere in any of the poems that seemed to me irrelevant to Mr. Ginsberg's purpose, and it seemed to me also that there is even esthetically a sound defense to be made for each use of what might be considered a questionable term in the way of the tone desired for the whole volume, particularly for the title poem, the tension, the sense of destruction, the sense — even if we wish that — of depravity that he wished to produce. These are victims, these are a lost generation that he is attempting to produce in that poem, and to give us the sense of the violence, the violence of activity, of the attitudes, of the feelings which destroyed them under the conditions he sets forth, I think he could not have done otherwise than use the language which might have been proper or current for them and bore directly the weight and mode of their feeling.

Mr. Speiser: Thank you. Your witness.

Cross-Examination by Mr. McIntosh

Q. What is your definition of literary merit, anyway?

A. It's very hard to define. I don't know if this is getting outside of my purview, but I don't know exactly why we have to define literary merit in this particular case.

The Court: Mr. Clark, we appreciate your coming here, but you're here as a witness, not to lecture the prosecution. We will have the question read. If you can't answer the question you may say so, but we're not interested in anything but your answer to the question. Read the question, Mr. Reporter.

(Record read.)

The Court: If you can answer the question, you may do so, if you can't answer it, you may say so.

The Witness: Your Honor, I can't answer it without going into repetitions of what has been said before by other witnesses.

The Court: Well, that is all right. Don't refer to what they said, but even if it is necessary for you to repeat what others have said, you may do so.

The Witness: Very well. The only final test, it seems to me, of literary merit, is the power to endure. Obviously such a test cannot be applied to a new or recent work, and one cannot, I think, offer soundly an opinion on the probability of endurance save on a much wider acquaintance with the work or works of a writer than I have of Mr. Ginsberg's or perhaps even with a greater mass of production than Mr. Ginsberg's. I would in the instance of some contemporary writers be quite willing to offer an opinion on the probability of status in time, as with William Faulkner, with a great, great number of novels and short stories to his credit. Aside from this test of durability, I think the test of literary merit must be, to my mind, first, the sincerity of the writer. I would be willing, I think, even to add the seriousness of purpose of the writer, if we do not by that leave out the fact that a writer can have a fundamental serious purpose and make a humorous approach to it. I would add also there are certain specific ways in which craftsmanship at least of a piece of work, if not in any sense the art, which to my mind involves more, may be tested.

Mr. McIntosh: Q. Well, in writing a piece of poetry or writing a book, part of the literary merit is that of fitting words together properly, is that right, sir?

A. Right.

Q. And you feel that Mr. Ginsberg has made the proper choice of words in this book to make it one of literary merit?

Mr. Ehrlich: Objected to on the ground that it is without the issues and therefore immaterial.

The Court: Sustained.

Mr. McIntosh: Q. Well, then, Mr. Ginsberg's work is one which you would recommend to others to read, is that right, having literary merit?

The Witness: That would depend upon the reader. To people of adult intelligence and perception, I would not hesitate to recommend *Howl and Other Poems.*

Mr. McIntosh: Q. Do you classify yourself as a liberal?

The Court: Now wait a minute.

Mr. Ehrlich: The objection is that it is irrelevant and immaterial, doesn't tend to prove or disprove anything in this case. The word "liberal" is too vague and uncertain.

The Court: Sustained. "Liberal" is too vague and uncertain; it might mean anything.

Mr. McIntosh: Q. Are you familiar with the San Francisco Renaissance?

A. No, I am not.

Mr. McIntosh: No further questions.

The defense calls Mr. Lowenthal.

LEO LOWENTHAL called as a witness on behalf of the defendants, being first duly sworn, testified as follows:

Direct Examination by Mr. Ehrlich

Q. Your name, address and profession please.

A. I am Leo Lowenthal, my residence is 1214 Contra Costa Drive, El Cerrito, and I teach and write.

Q. Where do you teach?

A. At the University of California.

Q. What are you teaching at the University of California?

A. I am Professor of Speech and Professor of Sociology, teaching courses in literature in society and popular culture.

Q. Have you taught elsewhere?

A. Yes. Before joining the University of California I was for one year a fellow for advanced study at Stanford, and preceding that, 1945, Research Director for the Voice of America, United States Department of State; preceding that I was employed by Columbia University and lecturing at Columbia University; before 1933 I was connected with the University of Frankfurt in Germany.

Q. Well, weren't you also at one time connected with the Bureau of Overseas Intelligence of the Office of War Information?

A. Yes, during the war.

Q. From 1941 to 1945 you were a consultant in the Office of War Information?

A. Yes.

Q. Have you written any works?

A. Yes, I have written several books and monographs during the last thirty years.

Q. Could you give us a few of them?

A. Yes. This year I published a book called *Literature and the Image of Man*, which studies literary criticism of serious works. Furthermore, I published this year, together with Marjorie Fisk, my wife, a monograph on the problems of eighteenth-century English literature called *Debate over Art and Popular Culture in Eighteenth Century England*. Furthermore, I have published during the last few years a number of studies on popular literature in America and the whole problem of censorship of literature, which have been printed and reprinted in various magazines and books. Before that I have done other studies in the field of literature and in the field of communications.

Shigeyoshi Murao, defense attorney Jake Ehrlich, and Lawrence Ferlinghetti at the *Howl* trial, 1957. City Lights Archive

Lawrence Speiser, ACLU attorney and Lawrence Ferlinghetti confer about court proceedings at the Hall of Justice, 1957. *San Francisco Call Bulletin* photo by Robbins. Courtesy, San Francisco History Center, San Francisco Public Library.

Lawrence Ferlinghetti and sculptor Beniamino Bufano during a court recess, 1957.
City Lights Archive

ACLU attorney Albert Bendich and Lenny Bruce, political satirist/comedian. After the vindication of *Howl*, Bendich defended Bruce, with Judge Clayton Horn again presiding. Photo courtesy of Albert Bendich.

Q. Have you had occasion to read and study the prosecution's Exhibit called *Howl and Other Poems* by Allen Ginsberg?

A. Yes, Sir.

Q. As the result of your education, your experience, your work in this field, and your teaching of this subject, have you formed any opinion as to the literary merit of *Howl?*

Mr. McIntosh: Your Honor, I would like to object to this witness' testimony. I don't believe he is particularly qualified, as a teacher of sociology. Although he has written books, I don't think that would qualify him to criticize or look at other people's writings, unless he is going to actually be in that type of work.

The Court: I'm not considering his background in sociology, just looking at the other elements that have been adduced here.

Mr. Ehrlich: We didn't go into that subject because your Honor indicated you didn't want that.

The Court: That's right. Do you want to question the witness on *voir dire* as to his qualifications?

Mr. McIntosh: Yes, just for a moment.

The Court: All right.

Voir Dire Examination by Mr. McIntosh

Mr. McIntosh: Q. What degrees do you have?

A. I have a Ph.D., and I have another higher degree in literature and history.

Q. You have made what is a hobby of studying literature?

A. It's not a hobby. I have studied literature and comparative literature and have taught it in German and American universities.

Q. Frankfurt?

A. Yes. My special field is the relationship of literature to society and I am a student of comparative literature.

Q. I see. When you worked with the Bureau of War Information, that had nothing to do with literature?

A. No, very indirectly.

Q. And I assume, though, in writing some of these books you had to read a lot of other books to give a criticism of them, is that right?

A. When I write my books on literature I read particularly the works of writers, of the artists, not other books on them.

Mr. McIntosh: I see. That's all, your Honor.

The Court: All right. For the record, I take it you have withdrawn your objection, then?

Mr. McIntosh: Yes, your Honor.

Mr. Ehrlich: Q. Professor, you haven't just made a hobby of this subject; this has been your life's work?

A. That's correct.

Q. Did you say that you had read the book *Howl and Other Poems* by Allen Ginsberg?

A. I did.

Q. As a result of reading it and predicated on your learning and your experience and your writing and your teaching, have you formed any opinion as to the literary merit of this work?

A. I have.

Q. What is your opinion?

A. Well, my opinion is that this is a genuine work of literature, which is very characteristic for a period of unrest and tension as the one we have been living through the last decade. I was reminded, by reading this poem, particularly "Howl," which I think is here at issue, of many other literary works as they have been written after times of great upheavals, particularly after World War I, and I found this work very much in line with similar literary works. With regard to the specific merits of the poem, "Howl," I would say that it is structured very well. As I see it, it consists of three parts, the first of which is the craving of the poet for self-identification, where he roams all over the field and tries to find allies in similar search for self-identification. He then indicts in the second part the villain, so to say, which does not permit him to find it, the Moloch of society, of the world as it is today. And in the third part he indicates the potentiality of fulfillment by friendship and love, although it ends on a sad and melancholic note actually indicating that he is in search of fulfillment he cannot find.

Q. In your opinion, Professor, has Mr. Ginsberg in this work used any method which would tend to corrupt people in the sense that we refer to corrupt motives?

A. I cannot discover a trace.

Cross-Examination by Mr. McIntosh

Q. When did you read this book?

A. About a week ago.

Q. And by whom was it called to your attention?

A. I read about it in the newspapers and some of my colleagues brought it to my attention.

Q. I see. And would you recommend it for reading to the average person?

A. I don't know. If I may ask you, what do you mean by the average person? I cannot answer the question.

Q. Well, that's what we have to determine here. Well, what type of person would you recommend it to?

Mr. Ehrlich: I object to that on the ground—

Mr. McIntosh: All right.

The Court: I think Mr. McIntosh, although similar questions were allowed of the previous witness, that you are stepping on the toes, you might say, of the Court's position in making the determination in this case. The rule is how a book as a whole will affect an average person in the community, taking into consideration the period and time involved.

Mr. McIntosh: I see what you mean.

The Court: To ask this witness the question that you are pursuing would depend upon the decision that the court would have to make.

Mr. McIntosh: I understand that, your Honor. I didn't mean it that way, though.

That's all.

Mr. Ehrlich: Step down. Thank you, Professor.

KENNETH REXROTH called as a witness on behalf of the defendant, being first duly sworn, testified as follows:

Direct Examination by Mr. Bendich

Q. You are Kenneth Rexroth?

A. That's right.

Q. Where do you reside, and what is your occupation?

A. I am a writer and reside at 250 Scott Street, San Francisco.

Q. Could you name some of your writings?

A. The most recent one is called *In Defense of the Earth;* before that I wrote *The Signature of All Things; The Dragon and the Unicorn; The Phoenix and the Horse;* I think that's enough. I have done books of— three books of translation in print, *A Hundred Poems from the Chinese, A Hundred Poems from the Japanese, Thirty Poems from Spanish.* I have edited several books, a collection of D. H. Lawrence, and have been editor and editorial adviser for the publishing house of New Directions for a good many years.

Q. In the course of your literary career have you had occasion to engage in the writing of other material than poetry?

A. Well, one of the principal sources of my income is the writing of criticism. I write for the *New York Times*, *The Nation*, *Herald Tribune*, and the *San Francisco Chronicle*. I have done this almost all of my life.

Q. What is the nature of the writing which you do for the *New York Times?*

A. Mostly reviews of poetry.

Q. What is the nature of the writing you do for *The Nation?*

A. Very little of that is poetry. It's work of science and scholarship and *belles lettres* of various sorts.

Q. Will you tell the Court whether there is anything in your professional background indicating your capacity as an expert witness in this matter?

A. I'm an American poet of recognized competence, and poetry critic of recognized competence. I have had a couple of Guggenheim Awards and other things and I am, I guess, by now, in most poetry anthologies.

Q. Have you had occasion to engage in critical work in any medium other than the written medium?

A. If you mean do I conduct a radio program on KPFA, yes.

Q. And what, Mr. Rexroth, is the nature of the KPFA radio program?

A. It's a book review program.

Q. I see. Now, Mr. Rexroth, have you had occasion to read *Howl and Other Poems* by Allen Ginsberg?

A. I have.

Q. And in the light of your professional background, how would you identify the nature, the theme of "Howl"?

A. Well, the simplest term for such writing is prophetic; it is easier to call it that than anything else because we have a large body of prophetic writing to refer to. These are the prophets of the Bible, which it greatly resembles in purpose and in language and in subject matter.

Q. How would you describe the theme?

A. Well, the theme is the denunciation of evil and a pointing out of the consequences and a call to repent and a pointing out of the way out, so to speak. That is prophetic literature. "Woe! Woe! Woe! The City of Jerusalem! The Syrian is about to come down or has already, and you are to do such and such a thing and you must repent and do thus and so." And the poem, "Howl," the four parts of the poem do this very specifically. They take up these various specifics *seriatim*, one after the other.

Q. Do you care to elaborate on that?

A. Well, I would be simply going over the statements made by Doctor Lowenthal. I mean, the first part is a picture of general alienation of one man from another throughout society and particularly throughout the society of youth which has been demoralized by actually two major wars, by the threat of imminent death and by the commercialism, and not just the commercialism, but the particularly predatory elements of the commercialism in modern society. And, of course, the terminology is almost entirely Biblical. Moloch, of course, is a symbol for Hebrew prophets of commercialism and they considered it bestiality of the Philistines. And the third part is the picture of the consequences, the utter demoralization of an individual. Incidentally, I might say the individual, Carl Solomon, is a poet; he actually exists, and at one time was considered to have considerably more talent than Allen Ginsberg himself. And "Footnote to Howl," of course, again is Biblical in reference, the reference is to the Benedicite, which says over and over again, "Blessed is the fire, Blessed is the light, Blessed are the trees, and Blessed is this and Blessed is that," and he is saying, "Everything that is human is Holy to me," and that the possibility of salvation in this terrible situation which he reveals is through love and through the love of everything Holy in man. So I would say, that this just about covers the field of typically prophetic poetry.

Q. Have you had an opportunity to form an opinion as to the literary merit of the work?

A. I have.

Q. Would you state what your opinion is in that regard?

A. Well, it is, of course, impossible to tell what will survive the test of history and what will not and, of course, it's even impossible to tell if history is ever going to judge right. There are many works of great merit that are extremely obscure, known only to scholars, but I would say a work like this, that is a contemporary work and in the field of contemporary poetry, that its merit is extraordinarily high, that it is probably the most—certainly in my opinion—is probably the most remarkable single poem, published by a young man since the second war.

Q. Would you care to specify further your understanding of the criteria of literary merit?

A. Well, again that has been covered by all the other witnesses and I agree with them. I mean, for a work to have literary merit it must have sincerity and seriousness of purpose and should also, I believe, probably have a certain wholeness, which I think that this has. I don't think "Howl" is just a cry of wrath of the hipsters because I think that it has something more, that it is an affirmation of the possibility of being a whole man and I think all great literature, even contemporary literature, must have that. Then, it must have technical competence, and for a young man I would say the technical competence and handling of rhythms and accents and so forth, of living speech, and in the organization of material, I would say the technical competence is great. So that all of these factors which enable us to make a contemporary judgment I think is satisfied by the book in abundance.

Mr. Bendich: Your witness, Mr. McIntosh.

Cross-Examination by Mr. McIntosh

Q. How long ago did you read this book, sir?

A. I read it in manuscript.

Mr. McIntosh: That is all.

★★★

DAVID KIRK called as a witness on behalf of the people, being first duly sworn, testified as follows:

Direct Examination by Mr. McIntosh

Q. Will you state your name, sir?

A. David Kirk.

Q. And where do you live?

A. 1021 Menlo Oaks Drive, Menlo Park.

Q. What is your business or occupation at the present?

A. I am an Assistant Professor of English at the University of San Francisco.

Q. How long have you been so employed?

A. I am in my eighth year.

Q. And previous to that time did you have some connection with Stanford?

A. I was an assistant instructor at Stanford, yes.

Q. For how long?

A. About two and a half years.

Q. And are you presently taking some work there at Stanford?

A. Yes, I'm finishing my Ph.D. degree at Stanford.

Q. And have you also written, published poetry at times?

A. On occasion in the past I have published some poetry, yes.

Q. Now, at my request you have looked at People's Number One in Evidence, the edition called *Howl and Other Poems* by Allen Ginsberg?

A. I have.

Q. And have you formed an opinion, sir, as to whether or not that publication has any literary value?

A. I formed an opinion. It's my opinion that if it has any literary value, it is negligible.

Q. Negligible. Can you explain that to us, Mr. Kirk, how you arrived at that opinion?

A. There are many bases for criticism, of course, subjective and objective. I endeavored to arrive at my opinion on an objective basis. For example, a great literary work, or even fairly great literary work, would obviously be exceedingly successful in form, but this poem is really just a weak imitation of a form that was used eighty to ninety years ago by Walt Whitman. Imitation.

Q. Do you recall the title of that poem?

A. *Leaves of Grass* would be the name of the poem. Literary value could also reside in theme, and what little literary value there is in "Howl" it seems to me does come in theme. The statement of the idea of the poem was relatively clear, but it has little validity, and, therefore, the theme has a negative value, no value at all.

The third basis of objective criticism would be the—well, what for lack of a better term, I would call opportunity. The poet or the writer and his time and his problems—pardon me—the problems of the time, should have some kind of significant interaction. This poem is apparently dedicated to a long-dead movement—Dadaism—and some late followers of Dadaism. And, therefore, the opportunity is long past for any significant literary contribution of this poem. Those are my objective bases.

Mr. McIntosh: All right. You may cross-examine.

Cross-Examination by Mr. Ehrlich

Q. You have done some writing?

A. In a small way, yes.

Q. And you have done some studying of literature generally, I take it?

A. Yes, the last ten years of my life have been spent in that.

Q. In what field did you do this studying?

A. My specialty is the English novel. I have concentrated, however, on all English literature from 1660 to date, and do teach courses in such works.

Q. What subject did you instruct?

A. Well, I taught freshman English and engineering English and narration during that period.

Q. You set out three bases which you used as guides in your evaluation of poetic works, is that right?

A. Yes, my objective bases.

Q. Do you apply those three guides to your evaluation of every poetic work?

A. Yes, that is my consistent objective aim.

Q. Have you had occasion to review poetry for the general public?

A. Oh, for publication, no.

Q. These three guides which you have set up, do you use them in instructing your classes?

A. That is correct.

Q. Are your three guides accepted by men who are critics of poetry? Are they accepted as rules to be followed or are those just your bases?

A. Doubtless they are accepted by some critics of poetry because they are fairly standard rules.

Q. I see. Some accept it and some do not.

A. That's right. There is another general basis, the subjective basis of criticism. They would not accept such bases.

Q. Did I understand you to say that Ginsberg used the Walt Whitman style?

A. The form, the form of the book *Leaves of Grass.*

Q. That Ginsberg used the same format or form—is that what you are saying?

A. That's right.

Q. And because of Ginsberg's using that format, it is your opinion that the poem "Howl" has no literary value or merit, is that right?

A. On the basis of form, that is correct, because great literature always creates its own form for each significant occasion.

Q. By that you do not mean that Walt Whitman's *Leaves of Grass* doesn't quite qualify?

A. That is great literature; the form was created by Walt Whitman.

Q. And it is great literature?

A. Right.

Q. And that form is a great form?

A. That's right.

Q. All right.

A. For Walt Whitman and on that occasion.

Q. And at the same time you say that because Ginsberg copied that format, "Howl" has no value or merit, is that correct, sir?

169

A. That is correct. An imitation never does have the value of the original.

Q. Have you ever imitated anything, Mr. Kirk?

A. In forming what little style I have, of course I have. Every student in trying to form his own style obviously begins on a basis of imitation, not of just one writer, but of many writers.

Q. Well, then, in your opinion, Mr. Kirk, it is good to imitate, isn't it?

A. As a student exercise, yes, but it does not create literature.

Q. Who did Walt Whitman copy?

A. To my knowledge, no one.

Q. You don't know, isn't that your answer, you don't know?

A. That's right.

Q. I understand your next signpost to be that the idea of "Howl" is clear, but has little validity. Do I quote you correctly?

A. That is the general conclusion, yes, in theme; the idea of "Howl" is clear in theme.

Q. In theme. Well now, you'll have to explain that a little bit to me, if you will. The idea is good, we agree on that, do we?

A. No, we do not. The idea is clear.

Q. The idea is clear. I didn't understand you. Now, what is the idea of Ginsberg in "Howl"? What idea does he have there?

A. Well, he celebrates the unfortunate life of—I can't remember the man's name—Solomon—the unfortunate life of the man, Solomon, who is a drifter of Dadaist persuasion.

Q. Drift what?

A. Drifter of Dadaist persuasion.

Q. He portrays that?

A. That's correct.

Q. And does that portrayal have any validity?

A. Not as literature, no.

Q. Now, let's take one step at a time. Is there any validity as he is telling the story as he sees it?

A. A representation of Solomon's life. I take it on faith that it must be a valid, true picture.

Q. And then when Ginsberg goes a little bit further and he condemns this existence, which has soured and engulfed Solomon, that is a valid description of what Ginsberg feels, is that right, sir?

A. I am sorry, but I didn't identify any condemnation.

Q. You didn't?

A. No, I found only sympathy.

Q. Well, let's put it your way. This sympathy which Ginsberg shows for Solomon, would you say that that is honestly portrayed as Ginsberg saw it?

A. As an individual writer, yes.

Q. What impression do you have of the end of the third portion of "Howl"? What is your understanding of it?

A. My understanding there would be based on a reference to the value, the value statement of the third portion, wherein the poet expresses the usual Dadaist line that everything is created for man's despair and everything must be forgotten and destroyed, and that Solomon's life apparently has had this kind of rhythm. Therefore, there is some validity of theme, you see, in that area.

Q. Then there is validity of theme there?

A. As a Dadaist statement, yes.

Q. Well, I don't care what qualifications you put on it, but there is some validity to Ginsberg's theme, isn't there, whether you personally approve of it, or not?

A. Well, I am afraid that I have got my tongue tripped up here—this clarity—I should have said "clarity" instead of "validity."

Q. But you have been using the term validity all of the time you have been on the stand. By the way, Mr. Kirk, have you read the Holy Bible?

A. I have.

Q. You and I don't know who wrote Job, do we?

A. I am sure I didn't.

Q. Or do you know?

Mr. McIntosh: I will object to that, your Honor. He is going far afield.

The Court: What is the purpose of the question?

Mr. Ehrlich: The witness testified that Ginsberg said everything was created for the destruction of man. I want to make some comparisons to ascertain whether the witness knows the subject or whether he is just testifying. If he has read Job, as he says he has, let's compare it. This man is an expert.

The Court: He's testified as to three bases or to three premises on which he made a determination.

Mr. Ehrlich: Yes, but he said in answering one of my questions that the third portion of "Howl" merely is a condemnation of the world as it treated man exemplified by Solomon. Is that correct, sir?

A. The third portion of the book is that area in which the Dadaist theme of the unworthiness of life, of the necessity of forgetting all past history, of the necessity for starting over life again and wiping out everything in the past is celebrated.

Q. Now tell me, did you read Job?

A. I have.

Q. Isn't Job crying the very same cry as Ginsberg's "Howl"?

A. Not at all . . .

Mr. McIntosh: I object and ask the answer be stricken, your Honor.

The Court: Motion granted.

Mr. Ehrlich: Q. Well, isn't it a fact that other writers have condemned life and its application to mankind as well as Ginsberg?

A. I suppose. I don't know of any individual example at this moment.

Q. May I suggest Job to you, Mr. Kirk?

A. Yes.

Q. And would you agree with me, sir, that Job does condemn life?

A. Not to the same end that the Dadaist does, no.

Q. Well, let's leave the Dadaist out. Let's just stick with Job and "Howl" for a moment. Doesn't Job condemn the position of man's fortune on earth?

Mr. McIntosh: I will object to any comparison with the Bible, your Honor, as to what Job said.

The Court: No. The witness stated that he didn't know of any particular example of any writer in the same vein and he stated that he has read Job and that Job, I presume, counsel is going to show that Job does cover the same theme in somewhat the same way. I don't know whether—

Mr. Ehrlich: That is right.

The Court: I think that is what he is driving at. So I will overrule the objection. Mr. Kirk, so that you won't be confused, that requires a "yes" or "no" answer, and you may explain your answer after you have answered it. In other words, you are not confined to a "yes" or a "no" answer.

The Witness: Job does condemn man's condition, then, yes, but he does not go on then as the Dadaist goes on to desire to wipe out all memory of the past, to wipe out all human memory of everything that the human race has ever done so that there can be a fresh start made as the Dadaist does.

Mr. Ehrlich: Q. And that's one of the reasons why you think "Howl" has no validity, because it wants to wipe out everything and start over, is that it?

A. Well, no. That was the only small validity that I found in "Howl" because that gives it some literary merit, some message of some sort.

Q. Mr. Kirk, I am quoting from the Holy Bible and I must assume that these are the words of Job:

"When shall I arrive, and the night begone? And I am full of tossings to and fro unto the dawning of the day.

"My flesh is clothed with worms and clods of dust; my skin is broken, and become loathsome.

"My days are swifter than a weaver's shuttle, and are spent without hope.

"Therefore I will not refrain my mouth; I will speak in the anguish of my spirit; I will complain in the bitterness of my soul.

"When I say, my bed shall not comfort me, my couch shall ease my complaint;

"Then thou scarest me with dreams, and terrifiest me through visions:

"So that my soul chooseth strangling, and death rather than my life.

"I loathe it; I would not live always, let me alone; for my days are vanity.

"I have sinned; what shall I do unto thee, O thou preserver of man? Why hast thou set me as a mark against thee, so that I am a burden to myself?

"And why dost thou not pardon my transgression, and take away my iniquity? For now shall I sleep in the dust; and thou shalt seek me in the morning, but I shall not be."

Q. In theme, where is Job different from Ginsberg's third portion of "Howl"?

A. There seems no resemblance at all, just a vast difference.

Q. In your mind there is no resemblance, but I am talking about the words.

A. In the words, there is no resemblance.

Q. None?

A. No resemblance, neither in style nor in theme nor in opportunity.

Q. In other words, you think, Mr. Kirk, that all thinking of all men must go through the same funnel, is that it?

A. I do not understand.

Q. Isn't Job condemning the futility of life as Ginsberg condemns the futility of life?

A. Not at all. Job may be condemning the suffering of his own life, futility of his own life, but he is not condemning anything that's being talked about in "Howl."

Q. Well, what is Ginsberg doing with Solomon? Isn't he doing the same thing only speaking in the third person?

A. I found no air of condemnation in the poem at all.

The Court: I think the word you used was "sympathy," wasn't it?

The Witness: I did find sympathy, yes.

Mr. Ehrlich: Q. Are you teaching poetry now?

A. Yes.

Q. Where?

A. At the University of San Francisco.

Q. Isn't Job the same type of condemnation that Ginsberg seeks to make in "Howl"?

A. I—

The Court: Pardon me, Mr. Kirk. May I interrupt you, Mr. Ehrlich? You are going to be at cross-purposes here because the witness has several times stated that "Howl" is not condemnation. Am I correct in that?

The Witness: Yes.

The Court: So that you are using a word there that has not been used by this witness. In other words, your premise is wrong as a basis of the question.

Mr. Ehrlich: Yes, your Honor. Either this testimony means that Ginsberg has condemned life or that Ginsberg has not condemned life. He said a few moments ago, as I understood it, that Ginsberg was preaching the futility of all life, that we ought to wipe it all out and apparently start all over.

Q. Did I understand that correctly, sir?

A. That's not clearly stated in the poem, but he identifies sympathy with the Dadaist theme, he identifies his sympathy with their aim, that is, the Dadaist aim.

Q. And what is the Dadaist aim? Let's get that into the record?

A. Well, as a literary movement about 1918 to 1921, this group of French writers decided that the world was in such a mess that the only hope for the world was to destroy all memory of everything that men had ever accomplished through history, that each individual should destroy all memory of everything that ever happened to him, that language and communications should be destroyed, and then on that basis perhaps a fresh start toward a better world might be made. That is a generalization of the Dadaist theme.

Q. In your opinion, that is what Ginsberg has tried to do, is that right, sir?

A. As he portrays the life of Solomon, who is identified as a Dadaist, and shows sympathy with Solomon, who is identified as a Dadaist, he seems to indicate that he has a friendship toward that idea, yes.

Q. And you don't believe in that philosophy, do you?

A. Not at all. It has been dead since about 1922 or '23 when the followers moved into the area of surrealism almost unanimously.

Q. That does not necessarily mean that a person who does think that is wrong, does it?

A. No, but that does not create literature.

Q. Well, what creates literature, Mr. Kirk?

A. I'd have to return to my three bases for an objective criticism.

Q. Those are three you gave?

A. Form, theme and opportunity.

Q. Well, let's get to the third one, then. Your third point is opportunity, sir?

A. That is correct.

Q. And when you say "opportunity" you mean what, with relation to the subject matter here?

A. Well, as I first said, the word "opportunity" I inserted for the want of a better word. It means the correlation of the poet and his ideas with his time and with all times. Great pieces of literature appear with a definite message and application to the problems of the particular time in which they appear, and if they are great pieces of literature they continue to have this validity and they continue to have a message. There is opportunity.

Q. Well, do you think that Ginsberg, in his travels had the opportunity to observe life and to write about it?

A. A small segment, yes.

Q. And this is the segment he is writing about, is that not true?

A. One thing—

Q. Answer that, sir, "yes" or "no," please.

A. I am confused.

Q. This is the segment he is writing about, isn't that right, sir?

A. I can't answer that either "yes" or "no."

Q. You say that in his travels he wrote about a small segment of the community.

A. Here is where the confusion comes in: I believe the travels are Solomon's, isn't that right?

Q. What is that, please?

A. I believe the travels are Solomon's, not Ginsberg's. That is the basis of my confusion.

Q. Well, Ginsberg is writing it about Solomon; it's his own observations. You have read that, haven't you?

A. Yes.

Q. All right. You know Ginsberg wrote about it, don't you?

A. Know that he wrote the poem, yes.

Q. And you know in Solomon he is depicting his own travels?

A. No, I do not know that.

Q. All right. He is depicting the travels of someone else?

A. That seems to me—

Q. And watches them? He's watching the travels of this man Solomon and he is describing them, isn't that right?

A. That is what appears to be there, yes.

Q. Yes. Now, he had the opportunity to do so, isn't that right?

A. What is the antecedent to "he"?

Q. Ginsberg.

A. Ginsberg—I don't know.

Q. Then, not knowing, you are unable to form an opinion as to whether he did or did not have the opportunity to write this?

A. I am unable to know whether he has an acquaintance with Solomon. That is the thing beyond my experience, beyond my knowledge.

Q. Well, let me ask you Mr. Kirk—whether you know Ginsberg or Solomon or whether Ginsberg knew Solomon or not—we're talking about this work and about the impression you get of this work, and your answer now is that you don't know whether Ginsberg knows Solomon.

A. That is correct.

Q. Do you evaluate a work by knowing whether the writer knew the person he is talking about?

A. Absolutely.

Q. In *Vanity Fair* was Becky Sharp a personal friend of the author?

A. I don't think so, no.

Q. Well, would you say that *Vanity Fair* is one of the great outstanding works of literature?

A. That is correct.

Q. And you don't know—

A. I am certain Becky Sharp never lived as an individual, if that's what you are driving at.

Q. Are you certain that Solomon lived?

A. No.

Q. Then you don't know, do you?

A. Not at all.

Q. So that your former answer that you couldn't answer my question as to whether Ginsberg was properly describing Solomon's life is that you do not know whether Ginsberg knew Solomon and therefore you couldn't tell whether he was properly describing it?

A. I didn't say that I did not know Solomon; I said that I did not know if he knew Solomon.

Q. Let's go back to Becky Sharp and *Vanity Fair*. Did Becky Sharp know the author?

A. That is a frivolous question.

Q. Is that a frivolous question?

A. Yes.

Mr. McIntosh: Already asked and answered, too.

Mr. Ehrlich: The answer, I think, to every question is frivolous when he can't answer it.

Mr. McIntosh: I will object to these scurrilous remarks.

Mr. Ehrlich: If it is scurrilous it's not intended to be offensive to Mr. Kirk, but he can't answer the question.

The Court: All right, gentlemen. Next question.

Mr. Ehrlich: Q. Well, a lot of books have been written over the years depicting life as the writer saw it. That's generally true, isn't it, sir?

A. I am under that impression.

Q. Yes. Now, you have heard of Erasmus, haven't you?

A. I have.

Q. And Erasmus was quite a writer, wasn't he?

A. I have little acquaintance with Erasmus. My study begins with 1660.

Q. 1660. You wouldn't dare go back a day before 1660, would you?

Mr. McIntosh: Object to that, your Honor.

The Court: The objection is sustained. Mr. Ehrlich, the witness is entitled to courtesy on the stand. The Court admonishes you to treat him with courtesy and refrain from badgering the witness.

Mr. Ehrlich: Q. Well, let me tell you about Erasmus, then. Maybe you did read about it and have forgotten it. He wrote a great deal —

Mr. McIntosh: I'll object to that type of question, your Honor, telling him a story and then going to ask him a question on it.

Mr. Ehrlich: Let me tell him about Erasmus. He doesn't know anything about Erasmus, just heard about it. As I understand, he wasn't completely acquainted with —

The Court: Let me hear the question.

Mr. Ehrlich: Q. Eramus did a great deal of writing, and one of the things he wrote which has come down to us through the years is a little work titled *In Praise of Folly.* Do you recall ever reading that?

A. I have never read it.

Q. Well, have you read Voltaire?

A. I read one work, *Candide.*

Q. What is your opinion of *Candide?*

A. As literature? It is great literature.

Q. When you say "great literature," you mean what?

A. I'd have to return to the three bases again for objective criticism, form, theme, opportunity.

Q. He copied Walt Whitman's style, is that right?

A. Not Voltaire, no.

Q. Whose style did Voltaire copy?

A. I do not know enough about French stylists and French forms to answer that. I have read the work only in translation.

Q. So there is some qualification to style copying to which you originally referred?

A. I don't see there is. No.

Mr. McIntosh: Oh—

Mr. Ehrlich: Please.

The Court: Well, Counsel has a right to make an objection.

Mr. Ehrlich: If he objects.

Mr. McIntosh: I would like to. I didn't want to box with him; he's disturbing me. I get my mouth open and out fly fists.

Mr. Ehrlich: Q. Well now, going back to Voltaire, and the only thing you read written by Voltaire—by the way, you know how much he wrote, don't you?

A. I have a general idea.

Q. Safe to say that he wrote hundreds and hundreds of things, didn't he?

A. Without a doubt.

Q. Now, getting back to *Candide*, would you say that Voltaire had the idea of *Candide* as a clear-cut idea?

A. That's not my recollection of it, no. It took some little reflection to get at an approximation of the idea.

Q. Well, did you feel that there was any validity in the nature and character of his work?

A. That's the memory I have of *Candide*, yes.

Q. Well, if you had difficulty in understanding what Voltaire's idea was, how can you come to the conclusion—or give us your reason for coming to the conclusion that it had validity?

A. Upon the basis of reflection.

Q. What was your reflection?

A. Well, I am afraid it's been ten or twelve years since I read this. The pattern of reflection would be difficult to recall. My identification as a valid theme would not come immediately upon reading *Candide*, only upon reflection.

Q. How long have you reflected on *Howl*?

A. Let's see. What is the date?

The Court: Today is the 19th of September.

The Witness: 19th. I believe two weeks.

Mr. Ehrlich: Q. Two weeks?

A. Two weeks would be the limit of my opportunity. However, I made up my mind after five minutes.

Q. Two weeks was the limit of your opportunity. And you reflected for a long, long time on Voltaire's *Candide*, is that right?

A. Exactly. A great work of literature frequently conveys all kinds of challenges.

Q. Well, do you believe that if you reflected for another ten years on "Howl" that you might change your opinion?

A. I am quite certain I would not.

Q. You are quite certain today that you will not change your mind in the next ten years, is that right, sir?

A. That is correct.

Mr. Ehrlich: That is all.

GAIL POTTER called as a witness on behalf of the people, being first duly sworn, testified as follows:

Direct Examination by Mr. McIntosh

Q. May I have your name, please?

A. Gail Potter.

Q. And where do you reside?

A. 21 Bella Vista Way, San Francisco.

Q. I see. And what is your occupation?

A. My occupation is teaching.

Q. I see. Now, I believe you have a degree from Stanford, is that right?

A. I have a degree from Stanford. The fact is I have attended nine universities in Europe and America.

Q. Will you list them and tell us what degrees you have in some way, if you can remember them all?

A. Would you like to know—some of the places I didn't work for degrees.

Q. I see.

A. I was at State Normal School, I graduated from a professional school of music and drama, two years, graduated from the State University of Nebraska, I graduated from Stanford, I went to school at Wisconsin University, New York University, University of Southern California, London University, and in Salzburg, Austria.

Q. I see. Now, you made advanced studies at a lot of these universities?

A. Some of them were advanced studies.

Q. I see. And have you done any writing yourself?

A. Yes, I have done considerable. I was on an NBC station ten years while I was teaching, Community Service Director, and I was Educational Coordinator; I have rewritten *Faust*—took three years to do that, but I did it; I rewrote *Everyman*.

Now, that isn't as funny as you might think.

The Court: Pardon me, Madam. Ladies and gentlemen, we are not playing games; this is a trial that involves serious issues. Now kindly accord the witness the courtesy that you would want to be accorded. I know occasionally you can't help this laughter, but please try to maintain decorum in the courtroom; otherwise, I will have to clear it.

The Witness: May I say something else about that?

The Court: You just answer the questions of the District Attorney. He will ask you if he wants any more information.

The Witness: All right.

Mr. McIntosh: Q. Well, I think you wanted to tell us about some of the books you have rewritten?

A. Forty *Fausts*—I wrote from the forty *Fausts*, so it isn't laughable unless you have read only one, which most of you probably have—excuse me. Then I also have written thirty-five feature articles for the last two or three years, and all of the time I was on this radio station I wrote "Drama in the News" once a week in cooperation with *Time Magazine; Life Magazine* sent galley proofs to criticize; and also I had Romance and Music Series, taking the great musicians and writing dramas on their lives, and I was on the station ten years besides my university work. I wrote "Know Your City," the series of articles for one city, for which I was paid, of course, and then I wrote a pageant for one of the big affairs in Florida.

Q. Now, you have done some teaching, also?

A. I have taught fifteen years in universities.

Q. Various colleges, is that right?

A. Yes, at three different colleges.

Q. Which ones?

A. I taught at Golden Gate College when it was a city college—I taught there for three years; Dominican College, two years; and the College of Southern Florida for ten years.

Q. I see. Now then, at my request did you have an opportunity to take a look at *Howl*, People's Number One in evidence?

A. Yes, I did; I have had the opportunity.

Q. All right. And did you form an opinion as to whether or not the book called *Howl and Other Poems* has any literary merit?

A. I think it has no literary merit.

Q. Go ahead.

A. I think you cannot separate literary style and literary content.

Q. I see. Now, could you give us some idea of how you arrived at your opinion?

A. To have literary style you must have form, diction, fluidity, clarity. Now, I am speaking only of style, and in content, every great piece of literature, anything that can really be classified as literature is of some moral greatness, and I think this fails to the nth degree.

Q. I see. Can you think of any other reasons?

A. Yes, use of language. Now, in regard to the figures of speech which he uses, he fails in rhetoric, of course, for one thing, because his figures of speech are crude and you feel like you are going through the gutter when you have to read that stuff. I didn't linger on it too long, I assure you.

Mr. McIntosh: You may cross-examine.

Mr. Ehrlich: Step down.

The Witness: There is something else you want?

Mr. Ehrlich: Step down.

Mr. McIntosh: Mr. Ehrlich doesn't want to cross-examine.

The Witness: Are you through with me?

Mr. Ehrlich: Step down.

The Witness: Oh, thank you; thank you, Mr. Ehrlich.

Mr. Ehrlich: Thank you, Miss Potter.

Mr. McIntosh: The People rest, your Honor.

The Court: Any sur-rebuttal?

Mr. Ehrlich: None, your Honor.

The Court: All right. Both sides have rested. I will hear from the prosecution.

Mr. McIntosh: All right, your Honor.

We only brought two rebuttal witnesses here today merely for the purpose of showing that sometimes the experts do not agree. Now, you know very well throughout this trial I have taken the position that the opinion of experts as to literary merit of this particular book, *Howl*, is irrelevant. However, the Court has allowed experts to testify and I believe for the purpose of aiding your Honor in coming to a proper decision. However, I would like to point this out: Our courts, of course, have held that certain types of books, for example, medical books, even though they may contain words which may be obscene by themselves, if they are proper to the text, illustrating something in the medical books, that they are not obscene; the books are not obscene per se. In other words, they are written for the medical profession alone, and as long as they were written for the medical profession, if they are not written for the general public, why, then, the courts have generally agreed that they are not in the purview of obscenity statutes of practically all the states.

Now, here we have a book. *Howl* contains words, if by themselves, that is, taken just by themselves, your Honor, I believe they are words, are definitely obscene. And we have had different literary experts testify that the books have literary merit, that the words are necessary to that so-called merit. I believe Mark Schorer testified to that effect, and some of the others, and even Mark Schorer stated that the book necessarily must use a language of vulgarity, that is to say, to illustrate the theme of *Howl*. But it's funny in our law; we are allowed to use expert witnesses to testify as to literary merit, but we are not allowed to bring in, we will say, the average man to testify that when he reads the book he doesn't understand it, doesn't know what it's all about; perhaps it's over his head.

But is that book written for him, your Honor, the average man, or is it written for the literary expert, or, I would say, the expert on modern poetry? That is what the book has been termed, I believe, by defense witnesses, particularly Mark Schorer. Is this book pointed for that particular type of person, those who understand modern poetry in what they call the San Francisco Renaissance? Well, certainly a book, your Honor, is written to be sold on the stands to the average person, the general person who is here to buy it, not just particularly pointed to the literary expert, because it's not like a medical book written for them alone; it's written for a person who walks in to buy it. And I think that when the book is written it should be considered as its effect upon the average person who is going to buy it, not the modern person.

Now, for example, Mark Schorer—I believe he was the one who said something about surrealistic paintings. He likened "Howl" to such things. Now, surrealistic paintings, I believe, were mentioned even by Mr. Kirk, of the Modern School, and you have seen these paintings at various museums; I know you have. And we have seen them, splotches of paint going this way, circular lines going this way, diagonals and all this sort of thing. And modern painters have described what they mean in knowing terms, sometimes a lot of double-talk about it, but, anyway, they have described them as hav-

182

ing some meaning. Sometimes they have been rather red-faced to find out that some of their prize winners have turned out to be the work, for example, [in] one case of a monkey doing finger-painting. In another case, where a boy threw a paintbrush at a canvas, a big splotch, and they entered that in a modern painting exhibition and it won a prize.

Well, there is the modern, surrealistic painter, the modern person, the person who reads modern poetry, who understands that. I don't believe the average citizen understands surrealistic paintings, nor does he understand modern painting or poetry. Take [*Howl*], for example: I have read it; I can't put on witnesses to testify that they have read it and don't know what it's all about. Frankly—I made the comment in open court here that I read it; I don't understand it very well. In fact, looking it all over, I think it is a lot of sensitive bullshit, using the language of Mr. Ginsberg. So then, if the sale of a book is not being limited to just the modern book reviewers and experts on modern poetry, but falls into the hands of the general public, that is, the average reader, this court should take that into consideration in determining whether or not *Howl* is obscene under Section 311.

The test as outlined in the *Roth* case—I would like to read that again, your Honor, because I think it shows the position of what you will have to do in deciding this case, to take the position of the average reader. I would like to read that again, your Honor, if I may. In the *Roth* case, on page 1509, going down a little ways, it says that:

"The test is not whether it would arouse sexual desires or sexually impure thoughts in those comprising a particular segment of the community, the young, the immature, or the highly prudish or would leave another segment, the scientific or highly educated or the so-called worldly-wise and sophisticated indifferent and unmoved.

"The test in each case is the effect of the book, picture or publication considered as a whole, not upon any particular class, but upon all those whom it is likely to reach. In other words, you determine its impact upon the average person in the community. The books, pictures and circulars must be judged as a whole, in their entire context, and you are not to consider detached or separate portions in reaching a conclusion. You judge the circulars, pictures and publications which have been put in evidence by present-day standards of the community. You may ask yourself does it offend the common conscience of the community by present-day standards.

"In this case, ladies and gentlemen of the jury, you and you alone are the exclusive judges of what the common conscience of the community is, and in determining that conscience, you are to consider the community as a whole, young and old, educated and uneducated, the religious and the irreligious—men, women and children."

Now, I think that sums up pretty well what the average man is, the average person that's going to buy this book, and it is not published just for the modern reader of poetry who understands modern poetry. I think that should be taken into consideration.

Now then, I believe your Honor has no quarrel with the statement in *Weplo,* and also in some of the cases cited therein, to the effect that the fact that a book has literary merit does not prevent it from being obscene if otherwise it has that character. I don't believe you have any quarrel with that.

Now, let's look at the obscene character of the book. I'm not going to repeat to you or read any of the passages; we have had enough of that here, I believe, to present you with the obscene words. But in determining the obscenity of this book, your Honor, I would like to ask you this: Does the fact that poetry is bound in a book give it any immunity from an obscenity statute? Because Section 311 certainly covers writings, papers, books, pictures, or prints. The mere fact it is bound in a volume doesn't give it any immunity whatsoever. And going back to some of this other modern poetry such as surrealism, would the picture, for example, of genitals under the guise of surrealistic painting give the painting immunity just by itself?

The Court: Well, aren't you being a little impractical there? In your surrealistic paintings you can't readily recognize any object.

Mr. McIntosh: I grant you that. That is what I am talking about.

The Court: So you couldn't recognize genitals; they wouldn't be portrayed as such.

Mr. McIntosh: In one of these books here—I don't know whether they have it here. No, they don't have all the dirty books. I can't think of the name of it now but anyway in one of the works there are pictures of various things which are very violently done, but anybody can see what they are talking about and see what they are portraying. That's what I'm getting at, your Honor. I will go along with you; I can look at one of those modern paintings and I can't tell what it's all about myself. I would like you to ask yourself, your Honor, in determining whether or not these books are obscene, would you like to see this sort of poetry printed in your local newspaper, that is to say, to be read by your family, that type of thing? or would you like to have this poetry read to you over the air on the radio as a diet? In other words, your Honor, how far are we going to license the use of filthy, vulgar, obscene and disgusting language? How far can we go? And I might say, you might note that the newspapers, the television, the radio, they don't use that type of words at all. Do you know the reason? Because that consumption is for the average reader. That's the one we are trying to protect here.

The Court: I would like to put a question to you, Mr. McIntosh. Can you point to — or rather, will you point to any particular part, passage or parts of *Howl* which you contend arouse prurient interest?

Mr. McIntosh: I don't know how far you can go with a word like "fuck," your Honor.

The Court: Perhaps we don't understand one another. The mere use of that word, you might say as a cussword or as an epithet, would not necessarily arouse prurient interest. In other words, you may use coarse or vulgar words, so-called coarse or vulgar words, without arousing prurient interest. Now, the cases all hold that regardless of whether there are coarse or vulgar epithets, they must be such as to arouse a prurient interest, according to Mr. Justice Brennan in the latest Supreme Court decision. So for the court's guidance, and for something that the defense should meet, I wish that you would call to my attention what parts you feel would tend to arouse impure thoughts, impure sexual thoughts or prurient interest.

Mr. McIntosh: I think, your Honor, perhaps you are confining me to one issue of what the definition of obscenity is. If you would look in Corpus Juris.

The Court: Don't cite Corpus Juris. That is mere textbook language. The test of obscenity, while it is never certain and can never be definite and varies from community to community and from the changing times, has at least been given some interpretation by the courts of this state, the courts of New York State, the courts of Massachusetts, the courts of Pennsylvania, and finally in the *Roth* case by the United States Supreme Court. Now, if I recall correctly, all of those cases state that the use of coarse or vulgar words, in the absence of their arousing prurient interests, is not obscenity.

Mr. McIntosh: Well, we have *Gore v. State*, 545 Southeastern 2nd 79, Georgia Appellate, it states this: "The word 'obscene,' as used in the statute making possession or exhibition of obscene pictures, etc., a felony, means not only language suggestive of sexual intercourse or tending to excite lewdness or to debauch the public morals, but means offensive to the senses, repulsive, disgusting, foul, filthy, offensive to modesty."

The Court: That is not the rule today, but just for the sake of argument, assuming that my premise is correct, without conceding anything on your part, can you point to any parts of *Howl* that you feel would excite prurient interest?

Mr. McIntosh: Well, of course, the definition of prurient is: disposed to lewdness.

The Court: Or exciting impure sexual thoughts.

Mr. McIntosh: Lascivious thoughts.

The Court: That would excite a person to lewd or lascivious thoughts, impure sexual thoughts.

Mr. McIntosh: Of course, the people's contention, your Honor, is that the obscenity goes further than that. Otherwise, it would not be against the law to write these words anywhere you felt like it.

The Court: Well, can you comply with my request?

Mr. McIntosh: How about page 14?

The Court: All right. If you'll read the passage that you are referring to.

Mr. McIntosh: All right. Down at the bottom: "Who sweetened the snatches of a million girls trembling in the sunset," and the next one, a little further, after "Adonis of Denver"—"Joy to the memory of his innumerable lays of girls in empty lots." Two at the moment, your Honor.

Page 33: "I remember when I first got laid, H.P.—" whoever that is— "graciously took my cherry, I sat on the docks of Provincetown, age 23, joyful, elevated in hope with the Father, the door to the womb was open to admit me if I wished to enter."

That's three at the moment, your Honor.

The Court: All right. Now, let me ask you this question: Have you read *Ulysses?*

Mr. McIntosh: I have not, your Honor. I might make this other observation, your Honor. If this were a jury trial, certainly the jury would not be able to compare books and I don't think we have any right to compare any of these books here to the one in issue.

The Court: I am afraid you are wrong, Mr. McIntosh. In the trial of *Hecate County* here in San Francisco, it's my recollection that there were other books submitted to the jury for comparison.

Mr. McIntosh: Never went up on appeal, your Honor.

The Court: I know it didn't go up on appeal. That's not the only trial. I can't put my finger on a citation now, but you'll find there are other cases where books were submitted to juries for comparison purposes.

Mr. McIntosh: Oh, I had a whole load of them in the last case I tried, your Honor. That was the case with the nudist books. They had everything but the Bible in there.

The Court: Well, there are a number of cases that hold that books may be submitted to the jury for comparison purposes. All right, I will hear from the defense.

Mr. Ehrlich: Your Honor, if it please you, on page 79 of the record, you said:

"We have to go back to the basis that the book and its contents are to be construed as a whole. In addition to that, the sentence you just read, as you read it, has nothing in it that smacks or savors of eroticism or vulgar language. Now, it may be unusual language but there's nothing in there that contains either of those elements and certainly I can hold that as a matter of law. Now, if you have any particular words that you think are capable of inducing lustful thoughts or depraving anyone or inciting them to commit depraved acts as the result of reading these particular passages or words, or if you think there are some in there that are vulgar to the point of being pornographic, you may direct the witness to them along the lines that we have previously discussed as to whether or not they are relative to the theme and to the vehicle itself. But the question that you have just put will not be allowed because you could go through this book line by line and it would be a waste of time and not relevant to the question that's before the court, to wit: Is the vehicle or book as a whole obscene?"

That is a correct and clear statement of the law. The United States Supreme Court has said that obscenity is construed to mean having a substantial tendency to corrupt by arousing lustful desires. I read from the Pennsylvania case of *Gordon v. Commonwealth*:

"It is because Joyce has been loyal to his technique and has not flunked its necessary implications, but has honestly attempted to tell fully what his characters think about, that he has been the subject of so many attacks and that his purpose has been so often misunderstood and misrepresented. For his attempt sincerely and honestly to realize his objective has required him incidentally to use certain words which are generally considered dirty words and has led at times to what many think is a too poignant preoccupation with sex in the thoughts of his character.

"The words which are criticized as dirty are old, Saxon words known to almost all men and, I venture, to many women, and are such words as would be naturally and habitually used, I believe, by the types of folk whose life, physical and mental, Joyce is seeking to describe. As I have stated, *Ulysses* is not an easy book to read. It is brilliant and dull, intelligible and obscure, by turns. In many places it seems to me to be disgusting, but although it contains, as I have mentioned above, many words, usually considered dirty, I have not found anything that I considered to be dirt for dirt's sake. Each word of the book contributes like a bit of Mosaic to the detail of the picture which Joyce is seeking to construct for his readers.

"If one does not wish to associate with such folk as Joyce describes, that is one's own choice. In order to avoid indirect contact with them, one may not wish to read *Ulysses;* that is quite understandable. But when such a great artist in words, as Joyce undoubtedly is, seeks to draw a true picture of the lower middle-class in a European city, ought it to be impossible for the American public legally to see that picture?"

And in affirming Judge Woolsey, Judge Hand said:

"That numerous long passages in *Ulysses* contain matter that is obscene under any fair definition of the word cannot be gainsaid; yet they are relevant to the purpose of depicting the thoughts of the characters and are introduced to give meaning to the whole, rather than to promote lust or portray filth for its own sake. The net effect even of portions most open to attack, such as the closing monologue of the wife of Leopold Bloom, is pitiful and tragic, rather than lustful. The book depicts the souls of men and women that are by turns bewildered and keenly apprehensive, sordid and aspiring, ugly and beautiful, hateful and loving. In the end one feels, more than anything else, pity and sorrow for the confusion, misery, and degradation of humanity. The book as a whole is not pornographic, and, while in not a few spots it is coarse, blasphemous, and obscene, it does not, in our opinion, tend to promote lust. The erotic passages are submerged in the book as a whole and have little resultant effect."

In our case much has been made by the prosecution concerning the four-letter word, and there's been hesitance on the part of the District Attorney to use the word. I, for one, see nothing wrong with the word since it is a word commonly used in the English language, and was used up to and past the time of Queen Elizabeth. It is a plain, common Anglo-Saxon word meaning "to plant." This word is known to all and it has been used in some beautiful poetry. I will read to Your Honor by way of illustration three stanzas from a poem by Christopher Marlowe, who lived between 1564 and

1593. If we believe what some have written, Shakespeare copied several of Christopher Marlowe's great dramas. Marlowe wrote:

"I love thee not for Sacred Chastity.
Who loves for that? Nor for thy sprightly wit:
I love thee not for thy sweet modesty,
Which makes thee in perfection's throne to sit.
I love thee not for thy enchanting eye,
Thy beauty, ravishing perfection:
I love thee not for that my soul doth dance,
And leap with pleasure when those lips of thine,
Give musical and graceful utterance,
To some (by thee made happy) Poet's line.
I love thee not for voice or slender small,
But wilt thee know wherefore? Fair sweet, for all.
'Faith Wench! I cannot court thy sprightly eyes
With the base viol placed between my thighs;
I cannot lisp, nor to some fiddle sing,
Nor run upon a high minikin.
I cannot whine in puling elegies.
Entombing cupid with sad obsequies:
I am not fashioned for these amorous times,
To court thy beauty with lascivious rhymes:
I cannot dally, caper, dance and sing,
Oiling my saint with supple sonneting:
I cannot cross my arms, or sigh, "Ah me,"
"Ah me forlorn!" Egregious foppery!
I cannot buss thy fill, play with thy hair,
Swearing by Jove, "Thou art most debonnaire!"
Not I, by cock! But I shall tell thee roundly,
Hark in thine ear, zounds I can fuck thee soundly."

That was written by one of England's greatest poets. There are those who, when they read, attribute everything wrong and improper to what they read because mentally they want it to be that way. You do not think common, lewd or lascivious thoughts just because you have read something in a book, unless it is your mental purpose to do so. Impure sexual thoughts or prurient interest is self-generated by a desiring mind which is disposed to lewdness and impure sexual thoughts.

The prosecution confuses this work with the question raised in *Roth v. United States*. In the *Roth* case there was a pornographic work advertised, sent through the mails, sold with advertising suggesting lewd sexual relationships. We do not have any such thing here. Would we, if he were alive today, arrest Christopher Marlowe for writing his poem because Mr. Kirk suggests it? The four letter word "fuck" is not used in our work to cater to prurient interest.

The Court: May I interrupt you there for a minute? I don't think you contend that that word is used in so-called polite society, do you?

Mr. Ehrlich: Well, I don't know what your Honor means by "polite society." Polite society? Are there degrees?

The Court: In other words, if you were invited to a party, would you use that word while discussing something with someone there, some ladies, for example?

Mr. Ehrlich: I do not think that the mere use of one word is going to destroy anyone's morals or cause them to embrace that which is base and unworthy of an intellect of decency.

The Court: No, I am not approaching it from that standpoint. I am approaching it from the standpoint that—let me ask you this question: Are you willing to concede that there are certain words in *Howl* that generally at this time, in this place—I don't mean this courtroom; I mean in the community—may be considered coarse and vulgar?

Mr. Ehrlich: Yes, I will concede that they may be so considered. I can't visualize the use of so-called discolored words, whether acceptable or unacceptable, unless they are relevant to the theme. Our problem is whether these words are relevant to the theme of the book and not where and when we should use these words. As has been aptly said, a word is not a crystal, transparent and unchanged. It is the skin of a living thought and may vary greatly in color and content according to the circumstances and the time in which it is used. Is the word relevant to what the author is saying, or did he use it just to be dirty and filthy? In *Howl*, is it relevant to what he is saying when Ginsberg cries out:

"America I've given you all and now I'm nothing.
America two dollars and twentyseven cents January 17, 1956
I can't stand my own mind.
America when will we end the human war?"

He then answers the threat, he says:

"Go fuck yourself with your atom bomb.
I don't feel good don't bother me."

What prurient interest is Ginsberg generating with that cry of pain? This man is at the end of the road. He is crying out in the wilderness. Nobody is listening. Your Honor can't feel that anguished cry nor can I. We cannot understand it. We have never lived his life. A man doesn't know the pain of a toothache unless he has a toothache. In love with your wife and devoted to her, you still cannot share or feel her toothache.

We do not know what Ginsberg's mind was saying at the moment he wrote these lines because we haven't experienced hunger; we haven't reached the bottom of the pit. And who can say what a man would say or do in any given set of circumstances.

Mr. McIntosh referred to the top of page 9 where Ginsberg is telling us in his "Howl for Carl Solomon" that:

"I saw the best minds of my generation destroyed by madness, starving
      hysterical naked,
Dragging themselves through the negro streets at dawn looking for an
      angry fix,"

And he continues describing what is going on. He keeps talking about what he sees. He sees endless subways from the Battery to the Bronx, benzedrine, noise of wheels, "Battered bleak of brain all drained of brilliance," "a lost battalion," "screaming vomiting whispering facts and memories and anecdotes," "whole intellects disgorged in total recall," "meat for the Synagogue cast on the pavement." He continues describing the man who studied philosophy, "studied St. John of the Cross," the Kabbalah "who jumped in limousines with the Chinaman of Oklahoma," "who lounged hungry and lonesome through Houston seeking jazz or sex or soup," seeking, seeking, seeking, always, broken down, crying, everything is wrong with him, they do everything Solomon is doing, everything he ought not to do, he associates with millions of girls, "red-eyed in the morning but prepared to sweeten the snatch of the sunrise, flashing buttocks under barns and naked in the lake," he goes on through Colorado, sees what he terms as the "Adonis of Denver," joy to the memory of his innumerable conquests. Instead of saying "innumerable conquests," he says "Lays of girls in empty lots and diner backyards, moviehouses, rickety rows on mountaintops." After reciting all this turmoil and all he had seen, he could have said that the secret hero of these poems, this cocksman, an Adonis of Denver, joy to memory of his innumerable conquests in the Waldorf Astoria, in dinner at Chasen's, and a drink or two before going to bed in the Stork Club. I presume he could have said that, but that isn't the type of people he was talking about. He was talking here about Solomon, this figurative man who marches through all this turmoil and degradation.

If the prosecution can say, that because Adonis laid girls in empty lots and movie houses and on mountaintops and in caves, makes this book an obscene book, then the law and the decisions are valueless. It isn't for us to choose the words. When Ginsberg tells his story, he tells it as he sees it, uses the words as he knows them, and portrays in his language that which he sees.

And another place referred to by Mr. McIntosh:

"The kitchen has no door, the hole there will admit me should I wish to enter the kitchen.

I remember when I first got laid, H. P. graciously took my cherry, I sat on the docks of Provincetown, age 23, joyful, elevated in the hope with the Father, The door to the womb was open to admit me if I wished to enter."

I can show your Honor passages in the Bible that describe what this man is thinking and much clearer than he has said it. What is wrong? What creates lewd and lascivious thoughts in the fact that the man has come to a realization of one of the natural urges of life, which is the opening of an entire new world to him, and he says it and says it reverently, "elevated in hope with the Father"? What in that, may I ask the prosecution, will destroy mankind? I find nothing that is salacious, filthy, dirty, lewd, lascivious or licentious.

There is no evidence of any obscenity. I can find no evidence here of any salacious appeal nor is there any evidence of anything which urges that the book be bought and read on account of it.

There is no evidence of the lewd intent required by the law. There is no evidence that defendant sold this book lewdly. The prosecution sought to make the point that the book was published by the City Lights Pocket Bookshop. That's what it says, but that isn't enough, your Honor. There must be something else. The mere fact that the man published it, the mere fact that he sold it is not enough. There must be something else. There must be some act on his part. Mr. Chief Justice Warren says that first a man is on trial. What was his conduct in relation to the book? Did he sell it for the purpose of creating lewd interests? Did he sell it in order to urge and awaken the prurient desires and purpose and interests of others? The only evidence before this Court is that a police officer bought this book.

★★★

The defendant could and did rely on the opinion of those who are qualified to weigh the literary merit of a writing or book.

Mr. McIntosh inquired whether the Court would like to have "Howl" read over the radio or on television. While it is not in the record, I inform the Court that it has been televised and broadcast on Station KPFA. It is a book that has been highly publicized as the result of this trial, and has been discussed in literary groups who were not interested in this new howl of human pain.

Your Honor, what shall I quote to convey the thought that great works and classics of literature are at first condemned by those who see destruction in everything they cannot understand and find pornographic skeletons in every closet?

I point out that Voltaire's *Candide* was originally condemned as obscene because it dealt with sex. But even the prosecution's star witness says that this work is a classic. Words dealing with and describing sex do not destroy literary merit.

Shall we cull the lines from Balzac's stories? Shall we forthwith ban his works, take the volumes from the library shelves and hide behind the barn to read? Seek filth and you will find it. Seek beauty of narration and you will find that too. But to find filth you must search for it with a wanton mind and a willing application.

Any book can be declared unsafe since a moron could pervert to some sexual fantasy to which his mind is open the listings in a seed catalogue. Not even the Bible would be exempt; Annie Besant once compiled a list of 150 passages in Scripture that might fairly be considered obscene—it is enough to cite the story of Lot and his daughters, Genesis 19: 30–38. Portions of Shakespeare would also be offensive and of Chaucer, to say nothing of Aristophanes, Juvenal, Ovid, Swift, Defoe, Fielding, Smollett, Rousseau, Maupassant, Voltaire, Balzac, Baudelaire, Rabelais, Swinburne, Shelley, Byron, Boccaccio, Marguerite de Naverre, Hardy, Shaw, Whitman, and a host more.

Mr. Kirk testified that copying does not produce literature. He must have overlooked the *Jew of Malta*, a tragic drama by Christopher Marlowe written about 1590 and anticipating Shakespeare's *The Merchant of Venice* in plot. Much of the plot of *The Merchant of Venice* first appeared in the *Gesta Romanorum* in the 14th Century.

Now, your Honor, who copied whom, and who created literature? Perhaps our Mr. Kirk should not have limited his field of education.

There are books that have the power to change men's minds, and call attention to situations which are visible but unseen. Whether *Howl* is or is not "obscene" is of small importance in our world faced as it is with the problem of physical survival, but the problem of what is legally permissible in the description of sexual acts and feelings in art and literature is of the greatest importance in a free society.

It is generally established that the intention of a book as a whole, rather than the language of any particular passage, is the criterion of judging obscenity. There is not now, nor has there ever been, a workable definition of obscenity. Every person will react to sex writings according to their own sexual tastes.

The so-called legal yardstick of "prurient" or "obscene" when applied to books is much like judging the color of a horse by how fast he can run. What is "prurient"? And to whom? "Prurient" it is said means "lewd," "lascivious" or some other synonym that defies precise definition. And the material so described is dangerous to some unspecified susceptible reader. It is interesting that the person applying such standards in censorship never feels that his own physical or moral health is in jeopardy. The desire to censor, however, is not limited to crackpots and bigots. There is in most of us a strong desire to make the world conform to our own ideas, and it takes all the force of our reason and our legal institutions to defy so human an urge. The courts have long wandered in a maze, and in their efforts to apply the concept of "contemporary community standards" have often appeared to be deciding matters of law by the watery drippings of public opinion.

No one wishes to give free license for the publication of obscene works. Yet the difficulties in deciding what is or is not obscene have forced many of us into extreme positions. The liberal sees the threat of censorship and would let everything pass to give freedom to what is good. Another man would risk the suppression of an occasional book to guard the community from what he considers the danger of obscene literature.

The battle of censorship will not be finally settled by your Honor's decision, but you will either add to liberal educated thinking or by your decision add fuel to the fire of ignorance.

I have seen the efforts of the prosecution to build up a case by counting four-letter words. I have seen the honest confusion of honest men trying to determine what is obscene with no real background of information to help them. I have seen the struggle with the semantic nonsense that is written into the law books as definitions of obscenity.

Let there be light. Let there be honesty. Let there be no running from non-existent destroyers of morals. Let there be honest understanding. In the end the four-letter words will not appear draped in glaring headlights, but will be submerged in the decentralization of small thinking in small minds. Your Honor, Dr. Samuel Johnson could have been speaking of our self-appointed censor when he describes Iago, the villain of Shakespeare's tragedy *Othello*, who deliberately strings together such a mass of circumstantial evidence in proof of Desdemona's love for Cassio, that the Moor kills her out of jealousy.

"The cool malignity of Iago, silent in his
resentment, subtle in his designs, and studious
at once of his interest and his vengeance,"

to which I add, his ignorance.

The Court: Gentlemen, is the matter submitted?
Mr. McIntosh: Yes, your Honor.
Mr. Ehrlich: It may stand submitted.
The Court: October 3rd, at 2 PM for decision.

from
THE DECISION
by Judge Clayton W. Horn

The freedoms of speech and press are inherent in a nation of free people. These freedoms must be protected if we are to remain free, both individually and as a nation. The protection for this freedom is found in the First and Fourteenth Amendments to the United States Constitution, and in the Constitution of California. . . .

I do not believe that *Howl* is without redeeming social importance. The first part of "Howl" presents a picture of a nightmare world; the second part is an indictment of those elements in modern society destructive of the best qualities of human nature; such elements are predominantly identified as materialism, conformity, and mechanization leading toward war. The third part presents a picture of an individual who is a specific representation of what the author conceives as a general condition.

The "Footnote to Howl" seems to be a declamation that everything in the world is holy, including parts of the body by name. It ends in a plea for holy living.

The poems "Supermarket," "Sunflower Sutra," "In the Baggage Room at Greyhound," "An Asphodel," "Song" and "Wild Orphan" require no discussion relative to obscenity. In "Transcription of Organ Music" the "I" in four lines remembers his first sex relation at age twenty-three but only the bare ultimate fact and that he enjoyed it. Even out of context it is written in language that is not obscene, and included in the whole it becomes a part of the individual's experience "real or imagined," but lyric rather than hortatory and violent, like "Howl."

The theme of "Howl" presents "unorthodox and controversial ideas." Coarse and vulgar language is used in treatment and sex acts are mentioned, but unless the book is entirely lacking in "social importance" it cannot be held obscene. This point does not seem to have been specifically presented or decided in any of the cases leading up to *Roth v. United States*.

No hard and fast rule can be fixed for the determination of what is obscene, because such determination depends on the locale, the time, the mind of the community and the prevailing mores. Even the word itself has had a chameleon-like history through the past, and as Mr. Justice Cardozo said: "A word is not a crystal, transparent and unchanged. It is the skin of living thought and may vary greatly in color and content according to the circumstances and the time in which it is used."

There are a number of words used in *Howl* that are presently considered coarse and vulgar in some circles of the community; in other circles such words are in everyday use. It would be unrealistic to deny these facts. The author of *Howl* has used those words because he believed that his portrayal required them as being in character. The People state that it is not necessary to use such words and that others would be more palatable to good taste. The answer is that life is not encased in one formula whereby everyone acts the same or conforms to a particular pattern. No two persons think alike; we were all made from the same mold but in different patterns. Would there be any freedom of press or speech if one must reduce his vocabulary to vapid innocuous euphemism? An author should be real in treating his subject and be allowed to express his thoughts and ideas in his own words.

Material is not obscene unless it arouses lustful thoughts of sex and tends to corrupt and deprave *l'homme moyen sensual* by inciting him to anti-social activity or tending to create a clear and present danger that he will be so incited as the result of exposure thereto.

If the material is disgusting, revolting or filthy, to use just a few adjectives, the antithesis of pleasurable sexual desires is born, and it cannot be obscene.

While the publishing and distribution of "smut" or "hard core pornography" is without any social importance and obscene by present-day standards, and should be punished for the good of the community, since there is no straight and unwavering line to act as a guide, censorship by Government should be held in tight reign. To act otherwise would destroy our freedoms of free speech and press. Even religion can be censored by the medium of taxation. The best method of censorship is by the people as self-guardians of public opinion and not by government.

From the foregoing, certain rules can be set up, but as has been noted, they are not inflexible and are subject to changing conditions, and above all each case must be judged individually.

1. If the material has the slightest redeeming social importance it is not obscene because it is protected by the First and Fourteenth Amendments of the United States Constitution, and the California Constitution.

2. If it does not have the slightest redeeming social importance it may be obscene.

3. The test of obscenity in California is that the material must have a tendency to deprave or corrupt readers by exciting lascivious thoughts or arousing lustful desire to the point that it presents a clear and present danger of inciting to anti-social or immoral action.

4. The book or material must be judged as a whole by its effect on the *average adult* in the community.

5. If the material is objectionable only because of coarse and vulgar language which is not erotic or aphrodisiac in character it is not obscene.

6. Scienter must be proved [that he/she had knowledge the act was illegal].

7. Book reviews may be received in evidence if properly authenticated.

8. Evidence of expert witnesses in the literary field is proper.

9. Comparison of the material with other similar material previously adjudicated is proper.

10. The people owe a duty to themselves and to each other to preserve and protect their Constitutional freedoms from any encroachment by government unless it appears that the allowable limits of such protection have been breached, and then to take only such action as will heal the breach.

11. I agree with Mr. Justice Douglas: I have the same confidence in the ability of our people to reject noxious literature as I have in their capacity to sort out the true from the false in theology, economics, politics, or any other field.

12. In considering material claimed to be obscene it is well to remember the motto: *"Honi soit qui mal y pense."* (Evil to him who evil thinks.)

Therefore, I conclude the book *Howl and Other Poems* does have some redeeming social importance, and I find the book is not obscene.

The defendant is found not guilty.

October 3, 1957

Lawrence Ferlinghetti at City Lights Bookstore in front of window display: "All books in this window have been censored or suppressed at some time in the past," 1957. © Harry Redl

HOW CAPTAIN HANRAHAN
MADE *HOWL* A BEST-SELLER
By David Perlman

San Francisco, an easy-going, tolerant, and highly literate community, was surprised not long ago to learn that two officers of the police department's Juvenile Bureau had made a purchase in a local bookstore and had promptly sworn out warrants for the proprietor and his clerk on charges that they "did willfully and lewdly publish and sell obscene and indecent writings."

The warrants were served, and the defendants duly arrested, fingerprinted, and freed on bail. They pleaded not guilty and the stage was set for the first test of California's obscenity law since the Supreme Court's ruling, last June, that the law itself is Constitutional.

The preparations for the trial produced a certain amount of concern in both legal and literary circles. Captain William Hanrahan, chief of the department's Juvenile Bureau, announced, "We will await the outcome of this case before we go ahead with other books." He did not reveal what books he had in mind, but he made it clear he had quite a list. He also disclosed that his men had been taking a look around the shelves of the city's bookstores—of which there are far more per capita than in any other metropolis outside New York.

A Judgment of Solomon

When Captain Hanrahan was asked what standards he used to judge a book, his reply was brief but vague: "When I say filthy I don't mean suggestive, I mean filthy words that are very vulgar." He was also asked whether he was planning to send his men out to confiscate the Bible. His denial was vehement. "Let me tell you, though," the captain added, "what King Solomon was doing with all those women wouldn't be tolerated in San Francisco!"

The City Lights Pocket Bookshop, where Captain Hanrahan's men had dragged their net for filth, is not an ordinary emporium of literature. Its owner, and the principal defendant in the case, is Lawrence Ferlinghetti, a poet himself, a painter, and a canny and relatively affluent citizen of a San Francisco district called North Beach, which is a largely Italian neighborhood near the waterfront, between Telegraph and Russian Hills. Ferlinghetti's store is right in the center of the district, where ravioli factories, Italian steamship agencies, *caffé espresso* bars, grocery stores redolent of salami and gorgonzola, and crowded blocks of old frame apartment buildings surround small islands of Bohemia.

The islands contain warrens of artistically decorated back-alley studios with north light and no heat, off-beat night clubs, and hangouts with such names as the Purple Onion, the Old Spaghetti Factory and Excelsior Coffee House, and the Coexistence Bagel Shop. There are a number of cellar joints where Ferlinghetti and poets like the renowned Kenneth Rexroth read their verse to the accompaniment of cool jazz. The jazz-and-poetry medium is currently the rage — and quite successful in commercial terms, too. Kenneth Patchen, another widely known poet, has drawn down as much as two hundred dollars a week reciting his poems to the paying customers at a more tony establishment called the Blackhawk which is situated well outside the undefined city limits of Bohemia.

Ferlinghetti's bookshop sells no hard covers, but it does stock all the quarterlies, all the soft-cover prestige lines of the major publishers, a lot of foreign imprints and periodicals, and just about every other sort of pocket book except the kind whose bosomy covers leer from the racks of drugstores and bus terminals.

His store also contains a lively bulletin board, on which appear notices of art exhibits, beer blasts, little-theater castings, ceramic sales, and odd jobs wanted. The City Lights is tiny and crowded, but it is open far into the night. Many residents in the quarter find it an ideal place for browsing, meeting friends, catching up on North Beach gossip, and even buying books. It is, in a way, the intellectual center of North Beach.

Ferlinghetti is also a publisher. He has issued, under the City Lights imprint, a "Pocket Poets" series, retailing for seventy-five cents each. The first three works offered were Ferlinghetti's own *Pictures of the Gone World*, Rexroth's *Thirty Spanish Poems of Love and Exile*, and Patchen's *Poems of Humor and Protest*. The fourth was a forty-four-page volume called *Howl and Other Poems* by Allen Ginsberg, a thirty-one-year-old member of what Jack Kerouac, author of *On the Road*, must be given credit for naming the "Beat Generation."

Ginsberg's title poem starts: "I saw the best minds of my generation destroyed by madness, starving hysterical naked." In what follows there is a great deal of anger, despair, four-letter words, and grotesque sexual imagery. There are also explicit promises of redemption from the gutter purgatory.

Oyez! Oyez!

This was the poem that aroused the San Francisco Police Department and was the actual defendant in the case of *People* vs. *Ferlinghetti*. Ginsberg himself was far away on a trip to Europe, and the owner of the bookstore never took the stand, nor was any evidence presented against him beyond the fact that he had published *Howl*. His clerk, Shigeyoshi Murao, was even less involved. The prosecutor conceded that there was no evidence to show the clerk even knew what was in the book, and it was quickly agreed that Murao should be acquitted. It was also agreed that the trial would be held without a jury.

The judge was Clayton W. Horn of the San Francisco Municipal Court, who functions primarily as one of the city's four police magistrates. Judge Horn, who regularly teaches Bible class at a Sunday school, was under something of a cloud when he mounted the bench for the *Howl* case. He had just been raked over by the local press for a decision in which he had sentenced five lady shoplifters to attend *The Ten Commandments* and write penitential essays on the supercolossal epic's moral lesson.

The chief defense counsel was J. W. Ehrlich, known for thirty years in San Francisco as "Jake The Master." Small, wiry, and intense, with dark, lugubrious eyes, Ehrlich is at fifty-seven the city's most famous criminal lawyer. He has defended such varied clients as Sally Rand, the fan dancer; Fritz Weidemann, the Nazi; Walter Wanger, the producer; and Caryl Chessman, the kidnaper and author of *Death Row*. Ehrlich has never been particularly interested in political cases, but when the American Civil Liberties Union asked him to take Ferlinghetti as a free client, "The Master" agreed.

Ehrlich's opponent was Ralph McIntosh, an elderly assistant district attorney who had studied law at night while working as a linotype operator on a newspaper. McIntosh has been an assistant district attorney for most of his career, and he has become something of a specialist in smut cases. Pornographic movies, nudist magazines, and Jane Russell's appearance in *The Outlaw* have all been targets of his zeal.

There were two other defense attorneys: Lawrence Speiser, who has handled many civil-rights cases up and down the West Coast; and Albert Bendich, a brisk young labor lawyer making his debut as staff counsel for the local American Civil Liberties Union. They let "The Master" run with the ball.

Mark Schorer on the Stand

The first major encounter of the trial came when Ehrlich carefully pitted McIntosh against the defense's principal witness, Mark Schorer. Schorer is professor of English and chairman of graduate studies at the University of California; he is one of America's leading critics, is a textbook consultant to the U.S. Army, has published three novels and seventy-five short stories, and has been awarded a Fulbright and three Guggenheim fellowships.

In his characteristically imperturbable drawl, Schorer testified on direct examination by Ehrlich: "I think that 'Howl,' like any work of literature, attempts and intends to make a significant comment on or interpretation of human experience as the author knows it."

He said the theme and structure "create the impression of a nightmare world in which the 'best minds of our generation' are wandering like damned souls in hell." Much of the content, Schorer said, is "a series of what one might call surrealistic images."

Judge Horn, having carefully read the evolving common law on the subject, ruled that while Schorer and other experts could not testify whether or not they thought the poem obscene, they could state whether they thought the controversial language contained in the poem was "relevant" to the intent and theme of the poet.

"Ginsberg uses the rhythms of ordinary speech and also the diction of ordinary speech," Schorer said. "I would say the poem uses necessarily the language of vulgarity."

Then came the cross-examination. For an hour McIntosh pecked at Schorer, stormed at him, and read him nearly every questionable line in the book. The prosecutor railed at the poem too, and it was sometimes difficult to tell which he objected to more, its dirt or its incomprehensibility.

"I presume you understand the whole thing, is that right?" McIntosh asked Schorer at one point, a dare in his voice.

Schorer smiled. "I hope so," he said. "It's not always easy to know that one understands exactly what a contemporary poet is saying, but I think I do."

McIntosh flourished the book triumphantly. "Do you understand," he demanded, "what 'angelheaded hipsters burning for the ancient heavenly connection to the starry dynamo in the machinery of night' means?"

"Sir, you can't translate poetry into prose," Schorer answered. "That's why it's poetry."

The audience, among whom were North Beach writers, downtown booksellers, and a few criminal-courts regulars, roared. The judge smiled tolerantly, but McIntosh would not give up.

"In other words," he asked, "you don't have to understand the words?"

"You don't understand the individual words taken out of their context," Schorer explained patiently. "You can no more translate it back into logical prose English than you can say what a surrealistic painting means in words because it's *not* prose."

This still didn't satisfy McIntosh, who kept reading the poem's opening lines and demanding a literal explanation. Finally Schorer said: "I can't possibly translate, nor, I am sure, can anyone in this room translate the opening part of this poem into rational prose."

For some reason, this testimony set McIntosh up immensely. "That's just what I wanted to find out," he declared with the air of one who has just clinched his case.

Having established the impossibility of translation, the prosecutor then read aloud one line of "Howl" after another, each with its quota of Anglo-Saxon words or vivid sexual images, and demanded more translations.

Schorer patiently declined to give them, and McIntosh finally turned to Judge Horn to complain: "Your Honor, frankly I have only got a batch of law degrees. I don't know anything about literature. But I would like to find out what this is all about. It's like this modern painting nowadays, surrealism or whatever they call it, where they have a monkey come in and do some finger painting."

The judge declined to instruct the witness to enlighten McIntosh on the poem's meaning, so the prosecutor tried another tack. He read a few more vivid phrases into the record and then asked Schorer: "Now couldn't that have been worded some other way? Do they have to put words like that in there?"

But Judge Horn disallowed the question, and offered a bit of literary criticism himself: "I think it is obvious," he said, "that the author could have used another term; whether or not it would have served the same purpose is another thing; that's up to the author."

By this time McIntosh was about ready to give up on Schorer. But he decided to have one final go at him. Turning to some of the poems that followed "Howl" in the volume, he asked Schorer to characterize them.

"Those are what one would call lyric poems," Schorer explained, "and the earlier ones are hortatory poems."

McIntosh pricked up his ears.

"Are what?" he demanded.

"Hortatory, Mr. McIntosh."

"That's all," said the prosecutor, and sat down. Schorer bowed gracefully towards McIntosh, and withdrew amid applause.

The defense placed nine expert witnesses on the stand in all, and with each one of them McIntosh went through the same maneuvers: bewilderment at the poem, contempt for the expert on the stand, and glee at the extraction of four-letter words. But no jury was present to see his act.

From Luther Nichols, book critic of the *San Francisco Examiner*, he learned that "Ginsberg's life is a vagabond one; it's colored by exposure to jazz, to Columbia University, to a liberal and Bohemian education, to a certain amount of bumming around. The words he has used are valid and necessary if he's to be honest with his purpose. I think to use euphemisms in describing this would be considered dishonest by Mr. Ginsberg."

From Walter Van Tilburg Clark, author of *The Ox Bow Incident*, came this statement: "They seem to, all of the poems in the volume, to be the work of a thoroughly honest poet, who is also a highly competent technician."

"Do you classify yourself as a liberal?" McIntosh asked Clark. But that was as far as he got. Judge Horn barred the question the instant it was uttered.

It was from Kenneth Rexroth—who described himself as a "recognized American poet of recognized competence, and a poetry critic of recognized competence"—that Ehrlich drew the highest qualitative judgment on "Howl." "Its merit is extraordinarily high," Rexroth said. "It is probably the most remarkable single poem published by a young man since the second war."

The Summing Up

McIntosh made an effort to discredit the poem by bringing in two expert witnesses of his own to testify in rebuttal.

One was David Kirk, assistant professor of English at the University of San Francisco, a Catholic school. Kirk condemned "Howl" as a "poem apparently dedicated to a long-dead movement called Dadaism" and as a "weak imitation of a form that was used eighty or ninety years ago by Walt Whitman."

The second was a blonde named Gail Potter who passed out little printed brochures announcing that she gives private lessons in speech and diction, and who offered a formidable array of qualifications as an expert. She had, she said, rewritten *Faust* from its forty original versions; she had written thirty-five feature articles; she had written a pageant for what she called "one of the big affairs in Florida"; and she had taught at a business college, a church school for girls, and the College of Southern Florida at Lakeland.

"You feel like you are going through the gutter when you have to read that stuff," Miss Potter said of "Howl." Then she shuddered in distaste and added: "I didn't linger on it too long, I assure you."

Jake Ehrlich bowed Miss Potter off the stand without a question, and that was the prosecution's case.

In the arguments of opposing counsel as the trial wound up, the debate ran true to form. McIntosh cried aloud that San Francisco was in dire danger:

"I would like you to ask yourself, Your Honor, in determining whether or not these books are obscene, would you like to see this sort of poetry printed in your local newspaper? Or would you like to have this poetry read to you over the radio as a diet? In other words, Your Honor, how far are we going to license the use of filthy, vulgar, obscene, and disgusting language? How far can we go?"

For Jake Ehrlich, "Howl" was honest poetry, written by an honest poet, and dirty only to the dirty-minded. As for its potential tendency to arouse lustful thoughts in readers, "The Master" dismissed that key question in a sentence. "You can't think common, rotten things just because you read something in a book unless it is your purpose to read common, rotten things and apply a common, rotten purpose to what you read."

Judge Horn took two weeks to deliberate before reaching a verdict. He took the trouble to read *Ulysses* and the famous court decisions that are part of its publishing history. He read other works that were once attacked as obscene. He read the law, both statute and common.

He found *Howl* not obscene and Ferlinghetti not guilty. His written opinion, although it comes from the state's lowest-ranking bench, must now stand as a major codification of obscenity law in California. "The freedoms of speech and press are inherent in a nation of free people," wrote this municipal-court judge. "These freedoms must be protected if we are to remain free, both individually and as a nation." As to the controversial phrasing, Judge Horn declared: "The people state that it is not necessary to use such words and that others would be more palatable to good taste. The answer is that life is not encased in one formula whereby everyone acts the same or conforms to a particular pattern. No two persons think alike. We are all made from the same mould, but in different patterns. Would there be any freedom of press or speech if one must reduce his vocabulary to vapid innocuous euphemism? An author should be real in treating his subject and be allowed to express his thoughts and ideas in his own words."

Nothing has been heard from Captain Hanrahan since, and *Howl* is now a best-seller throughout San Francisco.

San Francisco Reporter
December 12, 1957

Allen Ginsberg standing at the top of the steps in Alta Plaza. © Chester Kessler

Ginsberg "Howls" Again—
On the S.F. Poetry Controversy
Letter to the *San Francisco Chronicle*
by Allen Ginsberg

July 26, 1959

The most unnerving reply received to date in our recent poetry controversy (Activists versus Beat, and variations thereof), is the following document from Allen Ginsberg, author of the controversial "Howl" and other works. In effect, it is another "Howl" from Ginsberg. While we feel it is a curiosity piece rather than a profound social or literary criticism, it is nonetheless a revealing statement by the most publicized, and perhaps most talented, of the young poets practicing under the avowedly "Beat" banner.—W.N.

Recent history is the record of a vast conspiracy to impose one level of mechanical consciousness on mankind and exterminate all manifestations of that unique part of human sentience, identical in all men, which the individual shares with his Creator. The suppression of contemplative individuality is nearly complete.

The only immediate historical data that we can know and act on are those fed to our senses through systems of mass communication.

These media are exactly the place where the deepest and most personal sensitivities and confessions of reality are most prohibited, mocked, and suppressed.

At the same time there is a crack in the mass consciousness of America— sudden emergence of insight into a vast national subconscious netherworld filled with nerve gases, universal death bombs, malevolent bureaucracies, secret police systems, drugs that open the door to God, ships leaving Earth, unknown chemical terrors, evil dreams at hand.

Because systems of mass communication can communicate only officially acceptable levels of reality, no one can know the extent of the secret unconscious life. No one in America can know what will happen. No one is in real control. America is having a nervous breakdown.

Poetry is the record of individual insights into the secret soul of the individual, and, because all individuals are one in the eyes of their Creator, into the soul of the World. The world has a soul.

America is having a nervous breakdown. San Francisco is one of many places where a few individuals, poets, have had the luck and courage and fate to glimpse something new through the crack in mass consciousness; they have been exposed to some insight into their own nature, the nature of governments, and the nature of God.

Therefore, there has been great exaltation, despair, prophecy, strain, suicide, secrecy and public gaiety among the poets of the city.

Those of the general populace whose individual perception is sufficiently weak to be formed by stereotypes of mass communication disapprove and deny the insight. The police and newspapers have moved in, mad movie manufacturers from Hollywood are at this moment preparing bestial stereo-types of the scene.

The poets and those who share their activities, or exhibit some sign of dress, hair or demeanor of understanding, or hipness, are ridiculed. Those of us who have used certain benevolent drugs (marijuana) to alter our consciousness in order to gain insight are hunted down in the street by police. Peyote, an historic vision-producing agent, is prohibited on pain of arrest. Those who have used opiates and junk are threatened with perma-nent jail and death. To be junky in America is like having been a Jew in Nazi Germany.

A huge sadistic police bureaucracy has risen in every State, encouraged by the central government, to persecute the illuminati, to brainwash the public with official Lies about the drugs, and to terrify and destroy those addicts whose spiritual search has made them sick.

Deviants from the mass sexual stereotype, quietists, those who will not work for money, fib and make arms for hire, join Armies in murder and threat, those who wish to loaf, think, rest in visions, act beautifully on their own, speak truthfully in public, inspired by Democracy—what is their psychic fate now in America?

An America, the greater portion of whose Economy is yoked to mental and mechanical preparations for War?

Literature expressing these insights has been mocked, misinterpreted, and suppressed by a horde of middlemen whose fearful allegiance to the organ-ization of mass stereotype communication prevents them from sympathy (not only with their own inner nature but) with any manifestation of unconditioned individuality. I mean journalists, commercial publishers, book review fellows, multitudes of professors of literature, etc., etc. Poetry is hated. Whole schools of academic criticism have risen to prove that human consciousness of unconditioned spirit is a myth. A poetic renaissance glimpsed in San Francisco has been responded to with ugliness, anger, jealousy, vitriol, sullen protestations of superiority.

And violence. By police, by customs officials, by trustees of great universities. By anyone whose love of Power has led him to a position where he can push other people around over a difference of opinion—or Vision.

The stakes are too great—an America gone mad with materialism, a police state America, a sexless and soulless America prepared to battle the world in defense of a false image of its authority. Not the wild and beautiful America of comrades of Whitman, not the historic America of Blake and Thoreau where the spiritual Independence of each individual was an America, a Universe, more huge and awesome than all the abstract bureaucracies and authoritative officialdoms of the world combined.

Only those who have entered into the world of spirit know what a vast laugh there is in the illusory appearance of worldly authority. And all men at one time or other enter that Spirit, whether in life or death.

How many Hypocrites are there in America? How many trembling lambs, fearful of discovery? What Authority have we set up over ourselves, that we are not as we are? Who shall prohibit an art from being published in the world? What conspirators have power to determine our mode of consciousness, our sexual enjoyments, our different labors and our loves? What fiends determine our Wars?

When will we discover an America that will not deny its own God? Who takes up arms, money, police and a million hands to murder the consciousness of God? Who spits in the beautiful face of Poetry which sings of the glory of God and weeps in the dust of the world?

San Francisco Chronicle
July 26, 1959

Bob Donlin, Neal Cassady, Allen Ginsberg, Robert LaVigne, and Lawrence Ferlinghetti in front of City Lights Book Shop, 261 Columbus Avenue, 1956.
© Allen Ginsberg Trust

FIFTY YEARS OF CITY LIGHTS
by Albert M. Bendich

I am proud and happy to help celebrate the 50th anniversary of City Lights. It has been a wonderful source of support for peace, freedom, art, literature— in short, for the values of truth and beauty and the freedom and democracy they nourish and which they require for their own growth and development.

You may recall that Lawrence Ferlinghetti and Peter D. Martin started City Lights in 1953 as the first all paperback bookstore in the United States, carrying all the literary quarterlies and all the soft cover prestige books of the major publishers, as well as foreign imprints and periodicals. It became a sort of intellectual center. In addition, Ferlinghetti, a poet and painter himself, became a publisher, starting The Pocket Poets Series. The first work he issued under the City Lights imprint for the Series, each volume retailing for 75 cents, was his own *Pictures of the Gone World*. Kenneth Rexroth's *Thirty Spanish Poems of Love & Exile* was second. Kenneth Patchen's *Poems of Humor & Protest* was third. Number four in the Series was *Howl* by Allen Ginsberg, which appeared in the fall of 1956. Part of a second printing was stopped by Customs on March 25, 1957 (having been printed in England).

The collector of Customs, Chester MacPhee, confiscated 520 copies because, as he said, "The words and the sense of the writing is obscene. . . you wouldn't want your children to come across it." U.S. Customs law required a Federal Judge, upon application of the U.S. Attorney, to grant permission to destroy the books. But as Ferlinghetti wisely had sought the assistance of the ACLU *prior* to sending *Howl* to the printer in England, and had gotten its assurance of support in defending the book if it was seized, the ACLU notified MacPhee that it was prepared to defend *Howl*. The U.S. Attorney then decided not to proceed and MacPhee had to release the books. Then the San Francisco police arrested Ferlinghetti and Shig Murao, who worked at City Lights, for selling *Howl*.

Captain William Hanrahan, of the juvenile department, concluded that the book was not fit for children and, in June 1957, Ferlinghetti and Murao were booked, fingerprinted, and charged with the crime of obscenity. Murao said: "Imagine being arrested for selling poetry!" One newspaper headline said: "The Cops Don't Allow No Renaissance Here."

The trial reflected the tension between the values of democracy, embodying the fundamental requirements necessary for a society to be capable of self government, that its people be free to seek to learn as much as possible about truth, beauty, life, inasmuch as we the people and our ways of life are our own work in progress; and opposing them, the values of patriarchy, authoritarianism, of one sort or another, based on the proposition that the work of human development is complete, that the truth is known, that the authority in possession of this knowledge, whoever it may be, has the right and duty to rule the people because, monopolizing the truth, there can be no room for challenge, growth, development which can only lead to deviation from the right path and therefore can only be bad, evil, immoral, dangerous. Thus, censorship versus democracy.

The founding fathers and the people understood a great deal of the nature of this tension between democracy and authoritarianism; this understanding helped generate the revolution against George III and the divine right of kings and the adoption of our own Constitution and Bill of Rights. That is why the First Amendment required the separation of Church and State and prohibited government from infringing the freedom of speech, press and assembly.

Obscenity is a victimless crime; it deals with prohibited thoughts, not conduct subject to regulation and is related to such earlier crimes as blasphemy and heresy. One would therefore assume that it falls squarely with the protection of freedom of thought guaranteed by the First Amendment and therefore that it must be unconstitutional. But strangely, the issue of the constitutionality of obscenity laws had never been ruled on by the U.S. Supreme Court until it decided the *Roth* case in April, 1957.

The case resulted in five different opinions from the nine Justices. Only two, Justices Douglas and Black, dissenting, said the First Amendment was violated by the conviction of Roth for sending obscene material through the mail. As Justice Douglas wrote: "When we sustain these convictions, we make the legality of a publication turn on the purity of thought which a book or tract instills in the mind of the reader." He pointed to the fact that "punishment is inflicted for thoughts provoked, not for overt acts nor anti-social conduct. . ." And he concluded, "The test of obscenity the Court endorses today gives the censor free range over a vast domain. To allow the State to step in and punish mere speech or publication that the judge or jury thinks has an undesirable impact on thoughts but that is not shown to be a part of unlawful action is drastically to curtail the First Amendment."

What was undesirable about the thoughts provoked? What was undesirable was the stimulation of sexual desire. But, even assuming Roth's materials could have that effect, it would be absurd to single out those materials, or their like, from the overwhelming variety of sources of sexual stimulation. And finally, what sense can be made of the proposition that sexual desire is undesirable? Justice Douglas addressed this concern by quoting the results of a questionnaire he said had been sent to college and normal school women some thirty years earlier, asking the women what things they found most sexually stimulating. The results showed that "Of the 409 replies nine said 'music'; eighteen said 'pictures'; twenty-nine said 'dancing'; forty said 'drama'; ninety-five said 'books'; and 218 said 'man.'" I believe it was Judge Bok who once observed that a man reading such stimulating fare as the mechanics lien law might find a stray thought causing something to stand between him and his text.

But Justice Brennan, writing the Court's opinion, took a very different view. He wrote that the First Amendment had been designed to protect all ideas having even the slightest redeeming social importance, but that "implicit" in its history was that obscenity had no such redeeming importance and therefore was not within the protection of the First Amendment. How did he find this meaning to be implicit? He reasoned that obscenity was so commonly made a crime that it must have been "assumed" not to have been intended to fall within the First Amendment's protection.

"The test of obscenity," Justice Brennan declared, "is whether to the average person, applying contemporary community standards, the dominant theme of the material appeals to prurient interest." ("Prurient" is a word deriving from the Latin *purire* meaning "physical itch" and later meaning "impure itch" and "lewd ideas." "Lewd" is derived from the Old English "laewede," meaning "lay," as in "lay brother," not in holy orders and further, "unlearned, rude, artless, common, low, vulgar, ignorant, ill bred, bad, vile, evil, lascivious, unchaste." "Lascivious," also Latin derived, means "lustful," "licentious." "Licentious," from the Latin *licere*, means "permitted, excessive assumption of liberty, lax, immoral, lascivious, lewd." "Lust," a Teutonic derivative, originally meant "pleasure, delight, to long for. . .")

That was the state of obscenity law when the *Howl* trial started in September of 1957. What this meant to us was that we would have to prove that the book had some social importance in order to show that it was not obscene. What was sad about this process was the ignorance of the prosecution, reflecting the poverty of the state of general education.

The prosecutor was an assistant district attorney named Ralph McIntosh who had been active in protecting the people of San Francisco against lustful thoughts and prurient interest, having prosecuted porn movies, nudist magazines and Howard Hughes' Jane Russell movie, *The Outlaw.* He admitted that he did not understand *Howl*; but he understood that it contained dirty words. He actually said: "Your Honor, frankly I have only got a batch of law degrees. I don't know anything about literature. But I would like to find out what this is all about. It's like this modern painting nowadays, surrealism or whatever they call it, where they have a monkey come in and do some finger painting."

It was my task to present and argue the constitutional issues. My brief argued that the First Amendment protects literature from the application of obscenity formulae unless the literature is first found to be utterly without redeeming social importance. It quoted Justice Brennan's reference in his *Roth* opinion to language from an earlier Supreme Court free speech decision (*Thornhill v. Alabama*):

The freedom of speech and of the press . . . embraces at the least the liberty to discuss publicly and truthfully all matters of public concern . . . . all issues about which information is needed or appropriate to enable members of society to cope with the exigencies of their time.

Such speech, the brief argued, could not be constitutionally suppressed unless it presented a clear and present danger of a substantive evil which a legislature has a right to proscribe and punish.

A finding of social value, the brief said, would require the dismissal of the case, since by definition, the literature in question could not be obscene. The brief asked the Court to consider George Bernard Shaw's statement, in his introduction to *Mrs. Warren's Profession,* that "fine art is the subtlest, the most seductive, the most effective instrument of moral propaganda in the world, excepting only the example of personal conduct." And it urged that the Court, in applying the redeeming social value test must, in the first instance, decide whether, for example, a novel containing moral propaganda for integration of the Southern schools could be suppressed merely because a jury might find it also to be erotic. The brief quoted from another Supreme Court free speech decision (*Martin v. Struthers*): "The authors of the First Amendment knew that novel and unconventional ideas might disturb the complacent, but they chose to encourage a freedom which they believed essential if vigorous enlightenment was ever to triumph over slothful ignorance. This freedom embraces the right to distribute literature and necessarily the right to receive it."

The brief quoted Rexroth's testimony that Ginsberg, like the prophet Hosea, was embodying the regenerative power of love, that Ginsberg's message, like Hosea's, was that we can save ourselves from destruction by the nightmare world by focusing on the supreme values of love and reverence for everything human. The brief pointed out that the prosecution had not even attempted to question this basic proposition, whether the nature and content of "Howl" manifested any social value.

The brief further argued that even if the poem were found to have not the slightest redeeming social importance, the essence of the obscenity requirement was that the material in its dominant theme tend to excite lust, not disgust, and that as the prosecution conceded it did not understand the poem it could hardly identify its dominant theme, let alone deal with its tendency.

Finally, the brief argued that *Roth* set down minimum standards and that California had a higher standard, quoting Justice Harlan's concurring opinion in the *Alberts* case, a companion case to *Roth*, that "the [California] state legislature has made the judgment that printed words . . . can incite to antisocial or immoral action. The assumption seems to be that . . . certain types of literature will induce criminal or immoral sexual conduct." Therefore, the brief argued, the prosecution must prove that *Howl* would induce such conduct and that the defendant willfully and lewdly published that material with that specific intent. Chief Justice Warren, concurring in *Roth*, specifically said, "the conduct of the defendant is the central issue . . . the prohibited activity must be done willfully and lewdly." Therefore, it would not be enough for the book to be found obscene, for without the defendant's willful and lewd intent, the librarian of the British Museum could be found guilty if he allowed a reader to see an obscene book.

The Judge, Clayton Horn, found *Howl and Other Poems* to have social importance and acquitted Ferlinghetti, writing an opinion that virtually echoed the defense brief's points.

Four years later, the comedian Lenny Bruce was prosecuted in San Francisco for giving an allegedly obscene show. I represented Bruce in the case, a jury trial, with Judge Horn presiding. The case was tried along the lines of the *Howl* trial and the judge issued instructions to the jury that followed the formula in the *Howl* decision. The jury reluctantly acquitted Bruce, explaining that, given the Court's instructions on the law, they had no choice.

The irony of Bruce's grudging acquittal by the jury is that while Bruce, who understood the law and who said that in order to be guilty of obscenity his show would have to "get you horny"—which no one ever claimed his shows did do—was ultimately driven out of all performance venues by incessant prosecution for obscenity, while today the pornography business, whose products are designed admittedly for the purpose, among others, of stimulating sexual desire, is one of the most flourishing economic enterprises, reflecting the public's desire for the products.

Brennan's *Roth* opinion, though flawed, was a huge advance over what had been prevailing law, and it allowed us to defend *Howl* successfully.

Justice Brennan conceived the *Roth* obscenity test in 1957. By 1973, dissenting, he had come to the conclusion that all obscenity laws relating to consenting adults ought to be deemed unconstitutional as hopelessly overbroad and vague. In 1985, President Reagan directed the Attorney General, William French Smith, to set up a commission on pornography that became known as the Meese Commission. The question of the definition of obscenity or pornography came up during the Commission's initial discussion and illustrate the validity of Brennan's conclusion:

Vice Chairman, Harold "Tex" Lezar: "I don't get the purpose of defining pornography . . ."

Father Bruce Ritter: "If we were asked what was the subject matter of our survey, what would we say?"

Judge Edward Garcia: "Well, you wouldn't tell them one word . . ."

Father Bruce Ritter: "The problem we face, Tex, is that no one on the Commission can really say what we are talking about . . ."

Vice Chairman Harold "Tex" Lezar: "The definition we want is one that will allow us to include everything that other people are saying is pornographic. It's not a value judgment. This should cover everything that people who come before the Commission say 'This is pornography.' "

The Commission issued a letter on official Department of Justice letterhead implicitly incorporating the non-definition of pornography that was received by several national distributors of magazines and books, some cable TV program distributors, some of the country's largest convenience, variety store, drugstore, and department store chains.

The letter suggested that the recipients were suspected of selling pornography and that they should cease doing so if they wished not to be identified as pornographers in the Commission's Final Report. It could also be inferred that otherwise prosecutions might follow.

Robert Yoakum in the *Columbia Journalism Review* wrote that: "The Reagan administration had been looking for raw meat to satisfy the appetite of the religious right—people vexed at the administration because the Constitution had not yet been amended to permit school prayers, abolish abortion rights, outlaw pornography, and balance the budget.

"In a single stroke, Meese, Sears, or whoever, censored not smut but political reporting and commentary, and criticism of the Reagan administration and the religious right. *Playboy's* newsstand sales dropped 700,000. *Playboy* and *Penthouse* . . . reached hundreds of thousands of readers [more accurately millions— *Playboy's* circulation was 4 million and Penthouse's was 3 million before the attack] with political articles by some of our best writers.

"In what other magazines will people in those newly purified towns read, routinely, articles that criticize the religious right, Reagan's policies, government censorship, the politics of anti-abortionists, Pentagon and C.I.A. blunders, and Justice Department injustices.

". . . The U.S. is by no means the only country in which sexual and political censorship go hand in hand. Sex magazines are banned in the Soviet Union and all Eastern Block countries, in Iran and Iraq, in South Africa and Chile and China. . . .

"The specific lesson for journalists is that censors are censors. And a free press must stoutly oppose them whether they come garbed as commissars, clerics, or clowns."

After the death of Anthony Comstock in 1915, John Sumner took his place as the head of the Anti-Vice Society. He targeted *The Little Review* for printing chapters of James Joyce's *Ulysses*. Margaret Anderson and Jane Heap, the founders of the *Review*, were prosecuted for the crime of purveying obscenity and convicted. This was in the year 1920. From then until 1933, when Judge Woolsey ruled *Ulysses* not obscene, the book was not legally available in the United States.

When Margaret Anderson and Jane Heap were convicted, their lawyer said, "And now, for God's sake, don't publish any more obscene literature." Anderson said, "How am I to know when it's obscene?" He replied, "I'm sure I don't know, but don't do it."

Jane Heap said: "It was the poet, the artist, who discovered love, created the lover, made sex everything that it is beyond a function. It was the Mr. Sumners who have made it an obscenity."

She commented on her trial:

The heavy farce and sad futility of trying a creative work in a court of law appalled me. Was there ever a judge qualified to judge even the simplest psychic outburst? How then a work of art? What man not nincompoop has ever been heard by a jury of his peers? . . . The society for which Mr. Sumner is agent, I am told, was founded to protect the public from corruption. When asked *what public,* its defenders spring to the rock on which America was founded, the cream purr of sentimentality, and answer chivalrously: "Our young girls!" So the mind of the young girl rules this country? . . . If there is anything to be feared it is the mind of a young girl.

The defense of civil liberties will always require vigilance and courage and intelligence. In our quest for understanding, for knowledge, for truth, beauty and wisdom, we need our artists, our scientists, our best thinkers and philosophers to light the path. City Lights has been lighting the way for fifty years.
May it continue. . . .

This talk was delivered at City Lights Bookstore in November, 2003, to celebrate the 50th anniversary of City Lights.

THE CENSORSHIP BATTLE CONTINUES
by Bill Morgan

Not being a baseball fan, Allen Ginsberg probably never heard Yogi Berra say, "It ain't over 'til it's over," but when it came to *Howl's* censorship problems, no quote could be more appropriate. For thirty years following Judge Horn's historic decision, Ginsberg's poem enjoyed widespread publication in anthologies and textbooks and was broadcast on radio and television without complaint. Then, in the 1980s, Reverend Jerry Falwell founded a new political/religious minority known as the "Moral Majority." It immediately began to exert pressure on government to control what the group perceived as obscenity and indecency in art, music, and literature. Since obscenity had been too difficult to prove in court, they wisely decided that indecency was the better term for their grievances. Even though Judge Horn made it clear that there was no legal difference between obscenity and indecency, the new conservatives found that they could win support by applying the word to moral comments about local standards of what was acceptable in a community.

On April 16, 1987, bowing to pressure from political action groups like the Heritage Foundation, the Federal Communications Commission ruled that radio and television stations risked penalty if they broadcast indecent material. They defined indecency as "material that depicts or describes, in terms patently offensive as measured by contemporary community standards for the broadcast medium, sexual or excretory activities or organs." In their new guidelines, the commission ignored the standard established in the *Howl* case, whereby material needed to have only the "slightest redeeming social importance" to be sanctioned. The 1973 U.S. Supreme Court had clearly defined obscenity as "Something that, taken as a whole, appeals to the prurient interest; that depicts or describes in a patently offensive way sexual conduct, and that lacks serious artistic, political and scientific value." But the F.C.C.'s new rules left out that final test of redeeming social value.

The impetus for the new ruling was the increasingly raw language used by some hip-hop and rap songwriters as well as the growing popularity of "shock jock" disc jockeys. Once again, the battle was fought "to protect the children," but the ban on indecency could be applied to every type of programming, including poetry. On November 24, 1987, the F.C.C. backed off on total prohibition and ruled that "indecent" material could be broadcast only between midnight and 6 AM, a time when children were less likely to be in the audience. Instead of being a compromise, that ruling disturbed everyone, liberal and conservative alike.

It was the perfect opportunity for politicians to enter the fray and legislate morality, for what elected official would dare stand up in support of obscene and indecent material? North Carolina Senator Jesse Helms was more than happy to speak out against what he perceived as smut. Allen Ginsberg was outraged and composed an open letter. "This arts censorship rot gut originated in the beer-soaked bucks of Joseph Coors, was moonshined in Heritage Foundation think-tanks, and is peddled nationwide by notorious tobacco-cult Senator Jesse Helms. These alcohol-nicotine kingpins have the insolence to appoint themselves arbiters of Public Morality. Legal narcotics pushers wrapped in the flag, they threaten to give the needle to any politician opposing their takeover of culturally free turf in America," he wrote.

Broadcasters, put in an awkward position, had to guess whether a work was offensive to their particular communities. The reality of the situation was that stations became afraid to broadcast anything remotely sensitive because they could not risk the expense of a court battle. Allen's poem "Howl," which had been read frequently over the air since the trial, was once again banned. This ban was more insidious than the first because it was the self-censoring stations themselves who prohibited his poetry, for fear of losing their licenses. Allen found that he had no law to fight, no statute to overturn. His poem was not obscene, but still it could not be read.

On January 6, 1988, "Howl" was to be broadcast on several radio stations as part of a weeklong series on censorship called Open Ears/Open Minds. Five Pacifica stations chose not to air the reading because the F.C.C. was threatening prosecution for a program they had aired the previous year on the subject of homosexuality. Pacifica had already spent $100,000 in legal fees preparing that case, and they could not afford to take on another. "The government now has set out rules which have had an intimidating effect on broadcasters," Ginsberg declared.

Intimidation quickly became the new tactic of choice for the censors. The mere threat of a lawsuit was enough to silence many. Any legal action would be expensive, so it was easier for a station not to air controversial programs, rather than risk litigation. The broadcasters censored themselves and took no chances. Ginsberg took it personally, and held that it restricted his ability to practice his trade and earn a living. It was like fighting a phantom, though, as there was no specific law to challenge. In 1956, Lawrence Ferlinghetti, with the legal backing of the ACLU, took a financial risk by publishing "Howl," but now no one in the broadcast sector stepped forward to risk financial ruin by challenging the power of the F.C.C.

Several cases that the F.C.C. brought against radio and television stations for broadcasting "indecent" programs came to court in 1988. KZKC-TV in Kansas City aired an R-rated movie called "Private Lessons" at 8 PM and was accused of breaking the 6 AM to midnight ban. KSJO-FM in San Jose broadcast the "Perry Stone Show," which used humorous sexual double-entendre, and was fined $20,000. The F.C.C. fined several other stations for similar offenses and instilled fear in all liberal broadcasters. It seemed that the enforced self-rating by music producers and motion picture companies might be extended to book publishers, too, so that *Howl and Other Poems* along with many other great literary works might end up x-rated and relegated to the back room with pornography.

On July 26, 1988, Senator Helms introduced an amendment to end the F.C.C.'s policy that allowed adult material on the airways from midnight to 6 AM. "The American people are fed up with this trash that corrupts the minds of our children and erodes the values of our society," Helms said. He wanted no "safe harbor" for what he didn't like. To help make his case, he explained that some stations' signals were heard in other time zones so even though it might be after midnight in New York or Boston, it could be heard by people in the Midwest an hour earlier. Eventually the courts overturned this proposed complete prohibition and a 6 AM to 8 PM ban was implemented, which still stands today.

With the new restrictions in place, some lines of "Howl" could not be read on the air at all. Ginsberg felt that the prevailing marketplace of ideas was on radio, television, and the new information highway, so his poem was virtually back in the same position it had been in before the 1957 trial. The increasingly adept opposition triumphed in the end, requiring that all art must be "suitable for children." Ironic, since it had originally been the juvenile division of the San Francisco Police Department who had raided City Lights in 1956. The ideas that an artwork could support many interpretations, that audiences could make up their own minds, and that a society benefits from multiple points of view were judged too liberal.

In that climate of conservatism, it wasn't long before the National Endowment for the Arts became the next target of the censors. In the summer of 1990 it came to the attention of Representative Dick Armey of Texas that public monies had been spent to create a work of art by Andrés Serrano entitled "Piss Christ" in which a photograph of Jesus was immersed in a container of what appeared to be urine. At the same time an N.E.A.–

funded exhibition that included seven erotic photographs by Robert Mapplethorpe opened at the Cincinnati Contemporary Arts Center. Representative Dick Armey and others had a difficult time seeing the value of these artworks, and politicians threatened to cut spending on a host of programs and possibly eliminate the N.E.A. altogether. Senator Helms was quoted as saying, "If artists want to go in a men's room and write dirty words on the wall, let them furnish their own crayon. Let them furnish their own wall. But don't ask the taxpayers to support it." Ginsberg spoke on behalf of the N.E.A. at a rally in front of New York City Hall, and in interviews condemned the new wave of censorship.

During the 1990s the N.E.A. came under increasing attack from the Christian right for supporting art that fundamentalists considered blasphemous, degenerate, and obscene. As a result, by 1996, N.E.A. funding had plummeted and the possibility that the organization might be eliminated was a very real threat. The N.E.A. had gotten the message and shifted its emphasis to funding non-controversial projects and school programs.

By that time Newt Gingrich was the Speaker of the House, and debate began on the issue of whether the government should provide funding for public broadcasting with no strings attached. Many conservatives held that the government should have more editorial control of programming.

When Ginsberg died in 1997, these issues were not settled and there was no clear decision about whether "Howl" could be read on the air or not. Emotions flared again in 1999 when New York Mayor Rudy Giuliani threatened to evict the Brooklyn Museum of Art from its building for hosting an exhibition called "Sensation," which included Chris Ofili's dung-covered work "The Holy Virgin Mary." The show continued to run its course, and later a judge ruled that the city had violated the First Amendment, restoring $7.2 million in city subsidies to the museum.

And so it goes, ten years later, the question of "Howl's" alleged "indecency" is still unresolved. Perhaps the best spokesman was Ginsberg himself, who wrote in 1990: "Censorship of my poetry and the work of my peers is a direct violation of our freedom of expression. I am a citizen. I pay my taxes and I want the opinions, the political and social ideas and emotions of my art to be free from government censorship. I petition for my right to exercise liberty of speech guaranteed me by the Constitution. I reject the insolence of self-righteous moralistic fundraising politicians or politically ambitious priests in using my poetry as a political football for their quasi-religious agendas. I have my own agenda for emotional and intellectual and political liberty in the U.S.A. and behind the Iron Curtain. This is expressed in my poetry."